STAFF
DEVELOP
STRATEGIES
THAT WORK!

Stories and Strategies
from New Librarians

Edited by
Georgie L. Donovan
and Miguel A. Figueroa

Neal-Schuman Publishers, Inc.

New York   London

Published by Neal-Schuman Publishers, Inc.
100 William St., Suite 2004
New York, NY 10038

Printed and bound in the United States of America.

The paper used in this publication meets the minimum requirements of American National Standard for Information Sciences-Permanence of Paper for Printed Library Materials, ANSI Z39.48-1992.

Library of Congress Cataloging-in-Publication Data

Staff development strategies that work! : stories and strategies from new librarians / Georgie L. Donovan, Miguel A. Figueroa, editors.
    p. cm.
  Includes bibliographical references and index.
  ISBN 978-1-55570-644-9 (alk. paper)
  1. Library science—Vocational guidance—United States—Case studies. 2. Librarians—Employment—United States—Case studies. 3. Library employees—In-service training—United States—Case studies. 4. Career development—United States—Case studies. I. Donovan, Georgie L., 1974- II. Figueroa, Miguel A., 1980-

Z682.35.V62S73 2009
020.71'55—dc22

2008042236

Dedication

To three leaders, my friends and mentors, Janice Simmons-Welburn,
William Welburn, and M. Mueller

—Georgie

To my mentors and friends, Patricia Tarin and Patricia Glass Schuman,
without whom nothing in this career would have been possible

—Miguel

contents

list of illustrations

foreword

In recent years, we occasionally hear library administrators at the podium or in publications deplore the shortage of emerging leaders in the LIS field. This book deflates that myth. Here are the voices of the imminent new leaders. Their accomplishments make a strong case for the supervisor, the director, and the system to mentor, empower, and provide opportunities for new professionals to expand their knowledge, contribute to our professional organizations, and move into increasingly responsible positions.

Leaders, supervisors, and directors of libraries would do well to read and heed these stories. They are more than "It's all about me." They are the essence of what it takes to create a work environment for new library professionals that provides not only the tools and opportunities for individual development but also consistent support and acknowledgment of the worth of their efforts. Rosabeth Moss Kantor said, "Leaders are more powerful role models when they learn than when they teach." This book is a compendium of advice from a new generation of professionals who appreciate their opportunities while also seeing the need for change. It's not always convenient or easy to accept counsel, and even easier to dismiss opinions from those who lack depth of experience, but administrators who make the effort will learn much.

I feel a special interest, pride, and excitement in the publication of this book because both of the editors and five of the other contributors are former students. As noted earlier, they appreciate the special opportunities afforded them by such projects as the Spectrum Scholarships (ALA), the Knowledge River Institute at the University of Arizona (IMLS), and similar leadership initiatives. At Arizona, I observed from the first day they met Pat Tarin, Director of Knowledge River, and watched as they became library professionals and developed the self-confidence evident in these pages. For some, this is their first published effort. Others are accomplished editors and writers. All are making a significant contribution to our profession.

Every so often we read or hear about the reluctance of professional staff to move into leadership positions. *Staff Development Strategies That Work!* discredits that assumption. It also makes a strong case that current administrators have many options to use in the nourishment and growth of the leaders the library profession so urgently needs.

Brooke E. Sheldon
Santa Fe, New Mexico

preface

How do libraries transform new or early-career librarians into the leaders of the future? They invest in engaging, encouraging, and effective staff development. *Staff Development Strategies That Work! Stories and Strategies from New Librarians* presents a wealth of ideas from a unique perspective—the new librarians who have benefited from effective supervisors' practices.

In the pages that follow, 18 new librarians talk about what worked for them. Reading their stories reveals what was done to make them satisfied in their jobs; to build their leadership skills; to transform them into managers and supervisors; and to move them from novices to specialists in their respective areas. Each chapter has been written for a supervisor to read and consider. The lessons and practices are intended to be easily replicable and to involve little or no cost to the institution. This collection includes examples of well-designed and established programs administered by managers, simple attitudes or actions exerted by supervisors, and a few unique charges or responsibilities built into new librarians' job descriptions. Because the chapters were written by the librarian experiencing the strategy, they will include both the good and the bad lessons learned as well as some warnings.

As this collection is written for supervisors and managers to glean ideas, we have chosen to use the term "staff development," conceived as a regimen or program influenced by a manager or management team and prescribed for staff. We have avoided using the term "professional development," which we consider to be an individual's own plan for development or progression, or the term "career development," which would emphasize each unique individual's concept of how his or her career should advance. While staff, professional, and career development are related, we do recognize that they are slightly different. It is our hope that the ideas in this collection can be applied across broad ranks of staff to improve the general team.

Each of the new librarians writing in this collection was invited to contribute by the editors. These are new professionals—all within a decade of graduating from library school—who have made a strong impact in the few years they have been working. Many of us are friends, having worked together at various institutions or on association committees. Many have also achieved special distinction—Spectrum Scholars, *Library Journal* Movers and Shakers, American Library Association Emerging Leaders. Our sole criteria for inclusion were the ability and desire to share a successful strategy and personal story of staff development. The librarians included here represent a diversity of perspectives and experience but share an appreciation of the development efforts that they have experienced.

Throughout the chapters, you will see "Quick Tips" that digest much of the narrative lessons into easy-to-understand statements. These tips are intended to focus your reading and make the stories shared even more illustrative and revealing.

Perhaps the most noticeable and impressionable element of this book will be the numerous stories that have been collected. It is certainly by design. We have encouraged authors to tell their stories so that supervisors can understand the unique circumstances of new librarians. Now more than ever, our profession is filled with a diversity of people who have come to librarianship for different reasons and through different routes. The practices that have proven effective often reflect an understanding or have been created specifically out of these circumstances. By framing each section within a story, supervisors can draw connections between the new librarians writing these chapters and the new librarians staffing their own libraries.

Staff Development Strategies That Work! is a guidebook to the best experiences of new librarians—experiences that have helped to bring new professionals into an organization and move them into new levels of leadership.

Organization

This book is organized into two large parts—"In the Library" and "Out of the Library." Some contributors shared many ideas that were centered in the library and could easily be put into action at any time during the work year. Many other contributors focused on parts of our professional lives that happen outside of the library. These strategies may be unique to the professional calendar and may require more planning and coordination. Each of the chapter authors has worked to provide a new perspective on staff development. Some chapters discuss similar experiences but all provide a new piece of advice worthy of consideration.

Part I, "In the Library," features nine chapters that include recommendations for management styles, formalized staff development programs, and options for allowing new librarians to participate in the professional process. In Chapter 1, "Staff Development Opportunities at Work: Building Leadership Skills," Jennifer Rutner opens with an overview of her experiences at Columbia University Libraries. Her chapter includes initiatives laid out by her direct supervisor, those provided by the institution, and several initiatives of her own that might be encouraged by supervisors of new librarians. Chapter 2, "Guidelines for Knowing and Showing: From Good to Great Bosses," helps managers build trust among new hires, manage time and schedules, and develop personal, but professional, relationships. Author Mary Evangeliste describes several tools for helping bosses make the leap from good to great. Chapter 3, Kim Leeder's "The Power of Trust in Cultivating New Leaders," explores the role of psychology in training new leaders. Through an analysis of her experiences, she illustrates how library leaders who express trust in their younger colleagues can inspire and develop new librarians' leadership abilities.

Coaching is one of the buzzwords gaining momentum as the millennial generation moves into the workforce. In Chapter 4, "Coaching from the Ground Up:

Building Goal-Oriented Relationships," Scott Collard introduces this tool through a firsthand account of his own experience in a coaching program and focuses particularly on its value in working with new employees. Readers will learn about the basics of the coaching approach, some tips for how to create a coaching program, and some of the outcomes that might be expected. In Chapter 5, Antonia Olivas takes on the much talked about and very tricky prospect of mentoring. "Mentoring New Librarians: The Good, the Bad, and the Ugly" looks at how mentoring can play a role in staff development and various ways to build these relationships—by assignment, encouragement, or organic development. For those who have pondered a mentorship program, this firsthand account—of both pros and cons—is worth time and consideration.

Stephen Brooks charts his course from student worker to manager in Chapter 6, "From Paraprofessional to Department Head: Lessons in Cultivating a New Professional." Brooks draws on his experience as a staff member who became a department head to provide examples of effective staff development strategies. Chapter 7, "The Librarian as Researcher: Support for Research and Modeling a Research Mind-Set," by Cat Saleeby McDowell, reveals the strong impact a manager can have in developing researchers in the profession. McDowell's chapter shows how research can benefit not only the new professional's skills, but also the library as a whole. Toni Anaya shares her experiences in governance in Chapter 8, "Getting the Big Picture Through Participating in Library-Shared Governance." Anaya outlines the reasons for her selection and involvement, the discussions and topics she sat in on, and the impact her participation had on her leadership role in the library. Finally, in Chapter 9, Alanna Aiko Moore of the University of California, San Diego, discusses how her involvement on campus has made her a leader in her library. Her chapter, "Campus Connections: Building a Library and Campus Leader," explains how she cultivated relationships on campus and conducted outreach to different organizations and student centers. The creation of a supportive campus community helped her succeed on a personal level, grow as a professional, and position the library as a visible and viable partner in campus activities.

Part II, "Out of the Library," explores important aspects of staff development that occur outside of the library. These eight chapters explore formalized, external development programs, conference and association involvement, and community engagement. Mark A. Puente surveys the library landscape in Chapter 10, "Leadership Training Programs and Institutes: Models for Learning to Lead." Tamika Barnes McCollough and Iyanna Sims share their personal stories of diversity and development in Chapter 11, "Tilling Fresh Ground: Cultivating Minority Librarians for Library Leadership Through Programs and Initiatives." In Chapter 12, "Networking as Staff Development: Introductions, Invitations, and Associations," Miguel A. Figueroa explores the value of networking for development and offers managers a process for getting the ball rolling with new employees. While networking is certainly a process that can happen outside of the library, by taking an active role and devoting work time to the process, managers can create a valuable and rewarding experience for both their employees and their institutions. Ida Z. daRoza guides us A to Z through the experience of conferences for new librarians in Chapter 13. "Staff Development Through Association Conferences and Meetings; or, The Developing of a Latino Librarian," takes readers from selecting first associations and conferences, to exploring local opportunities, finding community in conferences, and reinvesting in associations.

Where daRoza leaves off, Georgie L. Donovan picks up in Chapter 14, "Professional Service on National Library Committees: Developing the Skills to Lead." Donovan talks about her experiences working with the Association of College & Research Libraries (ACRL) and the ways in which her library and supervisors encouraged and incorporated those efforts into her position. Joseph Nicholson moves out of the library world by looking at librarians' participation in non-library conferences. Chapter 15, "Non-Library Conferences for Development," draws on Nicholson's experience in the American Public Health Association (APHA), the benefits his involvement brings to his professional work and his library, and the ways in which he has made inroads as a librarian in a non-library world. Chapter 16, "Supporting Active Conference Participation by New Staff," shares Monecia Samuel's experiences as a conference presenter. She discusses the value of conference presentation to the development of a new librarian, and the relative freedom that can be experienced in submitting a conference proposal. Annabelle Nuñez, in Chapter 17, "Community Engagement and Advocacy: Skills and Knowledge to Expand Library Services," relates how her passion for her community was incorporated into her role as a librarian. Her unique contacts with local groups and organizations allowed her to take the lead on several library projects, and her ability to make connections has made her a go-to resource among her staff.

A last thought

When the editors were discussing the idea for *Staff Development Strategies That Work! Stories and Strategies from New Librarians*, one of the main goals was to turn the idea of staff development on its head. So often, ideas come only from the top down, from the established and experienced leaders who have built our libraries into great institutions. While their knowledge is incredibly valuable, and none of us could be where we are without them, we knew from personal experience that many new librarians have excellent ideas and lessons to share. It is our hope that these stories will present not only lessons learned from the best programs that were distributed from the top down, but also some bold new directions and ideas that will spring forth from the grassroots level. If reading these stories inspires you and your management team to take on a new challenge or initiate a new program, then perhaps it will also encourage you to sit down with your new librarians and hear their stories about what is working in your library, what they need, and what they want to contribute.

Part I

in the library

staff development opportunities at work: building leadership skills

Jennifer Rutner

A s a new librarian in a newly created position, I spend a good deal of time making to-do lists that often include projects, e-mails, phone calls, readings, or meetings. Some of the things that find their way onto these lists are professional development opportunities: "Register for ALA," "renew membership," "post to blog," "e-mail colleague," "draft poster session proposal." Throughout the first 18 months of my first job out of library school, I have been fortunate to have had many opportunities to begin to develop a presence in the greater library community—to build a network outside of my library and find ways to contribute to my field while learning how to contribute to my organization. My work outside the library has mirrored and built upon my work within the library. The skills I've been developing at my job are the same ones used in networking events, panel discussions, workshops, and blog posts. By involving myself actively in the work environment, I am building leadership skills through networking with potential collaborators among my colleagues, continuously finding ways to learn, engaging myself in innovative work, getting involved with committees, and becoming increasingly self-aware—all thanks to my manager's support and encouragement of my professional development.

Foster a supportive staff development environment

The Columbia University Libraries are committed to providing staff with development opportunities. The Professional Development Committee (PDC), currently chaired by Karen Green, Librarian for Ancient & Medieval History and Religion, allocates the development budget to professional staff. The PDC is made up of a rotating staff of librarians and works closely with the Libraries' Manager of

Training and Staff Development. It is charged with assisting the latter in developing policies and guidelines for the support of professional development in the Libraries. It administers and allocates the professional development budget and monitors its use as well as presents special awards for professional development support.

Chairing the PDC has exposed Green to the types of professional development her colleagues are engaged in, which she notes "can broaden your horizons and help inform your own career choices; it also enlightens you about the breadth of expertise within the organization." Green offers another motivation for getting involved with the PDC: "it's a great way to learn how the system works, and how to use it to your best advantage" (from an interview, November 8, 2007).

In 2007 alone, Columbia University Libraries allocated funding for 54 staff members to attend more than 40 conferences. "The Libraries really do make it possible for staff to take advantage of an unbelievable range of opportunities," notes Green. The constant influx of new experiences and ideas, gained through professional development, contributes to the exciting work environment at the Libraries. I am always curious to know what my colleagues are learning, what workshops they've attended, and what professional organizations they belong to. Working in an environment that has a constant stream of new information and experiences for staff to draw from allows me to think more creatively about my own work, encourages me to try new things, and helps me to maintain awareness of trends in librarianship.

At Columbia, we are aware that professional development not only builds the skills we need at work; it makes work more satisfying. "If you develop yourself as a professional, work is more interesting for you. Skill-building helps you maintain your enthusiasm about your work, keeps you engaged and excited about work," notes Columbia University Library's Manager of Training and Staff Development, Regina Golia, EdD (from an interview, November 8, 2007). By learning new skills and using my colleagues as a resource, I'm able to infuse my work with fresh concepts, build on the work of others in the same field, and ask for advice when I need it. Continued learning, information sharing, and team-building are all outcomes of staff development that make my job more enjoyable.

Staff development doesn't always require a large budget. "When faced with budgeting challenges for staff development," Golia states, "there are many low-cost ways to provide opportunities for growth. In a university setting, in particular, there are always opportunities to learn more." Inviting speakers from local libraries, from the university community, or from within the organization itself to give presentations or lead discussions on hot topics is a successful, low-cost model for staff development.

> ☑ QUICK TIP
> Look within your own library or larger institution for possible speakers or trainers to provide low-cost staff development opportunities.

People can support staff development in numerous ways without spending a lot of time or money, both of which are at a premium in libraries. Utilizing the available resources within your organization is one way to enhance staff development. Columbia library staff often

Exhibit 1.1. The importance of staff development

The following is from an interview with Patricia Renfro, Deputy University Librarian and VP for Digital Programs and Technology Services.

Why is staff development important?
Staff development is key to the ability of libraries to be effective in today's rapidly changing environment. Changes are happening in all aspects of librarianship: in technology, user behaviors and expectations, service delivery, approaches to scholarly communication, and within information markets. Library staff today must routinely update their skill sets. Staff development helps them to step outside their day-to-day jobs and home institutions to engage in an active learning experience and stay current and informed.

How do new librarians benefit from development?
It's particularly important to encourage and support new librarians who are just starting their careers, so that they can develop a network beyond their institution. One's first professional position is not necessarily indicative of one's career path; many of the leaders here at the Libraries have held a variety of positions throughout their career. It's important to continue to explore career options and interests as your career progresses. People entering the profession today have a wide range of options within the field. Staff development, such as conference attendance and involvement with professional organizations, provides opportunities to meet colleagues in a variety of positions within libraries—it helps librarians at any stage in their career identify their career options.

How do the Columbia University Libraries benefit from staff development?
The institution benefits from the ideas, new perspectives, skills, and energy that staff gain at conferences, meetings, and trainings. New professionals are particularly receptive and open to new ideas and new ways of approaching their work. They can play an important role in helping an organization take a fresh look at its challenges and goals.

lead in-house workshops based on their strengths, such as grant-writing or project management; they also attend library workshops to build or refresh research and technology skills (e.g., working with EndNote, Microsoft Excel, and Adobe Photoshop). These free workshops are primarily offered to our patrons, but staff members are welcome and encouraged to attend. Of course, working at a university with tuition benefits, staff often enroll in courses related to work out of personal interest.

New librarians may also benefit from shadowing more experienced librarians in sessions lasting a couple of hours to a half a day. Shadowing also allows librarians to learn about the daily functions of a department other than their own, for instance, the daily routines of interlibrary loan, reference, or technical services departments. New employees may also find unexpected learning opportunities by offering to help their co-workers. Helping new professionals identify these no-cost or low-cost learning opportunities is one critical role that a manager should play.

Managers should also encourage all employees to request the training they need, regardless of the library's budget. As a librarian fresh out of an MLS program with a newly created position, I had many options for what my job could be. Though initially the exact nature of my role was undefined, as time went on, it became easier to identify areas where training would be beneficial. I've since received training on public speaking, Microsoft Excel and Access, SPSS, and focus group methods—all through the support of the library and my manager. These training sessions have enabled me to enhance the skills that I need to do my job effectively.

Though Columbia is traditionally supportive of training requests, not all organizations are able to fund training at the same level. This should not deter new professionals from requesting the training they need, nor managers from supporting these requests. The act of requesting training shows an awareness of one's abilities and a desire to progress beyond one's current state. If the requests cannot be met within the current fiscal year, managers should restate their case that the training is necessary. Requesting training is one way that new professionals and their managers can advocate for professional development.

Managers and supervisors must also allow time for staff to take advantage of these opportunities. Ensuring that new staff are able to build relevant skills is crucial to their success and retention. Allowing staff to take time away from their primary responsibilities to attend a free workshop or speaker session is one critical way managers can contribute to a new staff member's development.

Network with colleagues

Before moving to New York City to attend library school, I remember hearing about the value of networking and thinking, "Hmm, I should do that." It wasn't immediately clear, though, how I would start. At the time, I was working as an intern at Rush Rhees Library at the University of Rochester. I was not aware of professional organizations or how to be involved in them locally, and I didn't have professional connections outside of my library. So before leaving for library school, I set up informational interviews with some of the directors and associate deans at Rush Rhees—something my boss had strongly encouraged me to do and facilitated through introductions to key staff members.

> ☑ QUICK TIP
> Encourage new staff to set up information interviews to learn more about the larger organization or specific areas of the library with which they are unfamiliar.

I understand now that this was a form of networking, though at the time I saw it simply as exploring my career options. These meetings enabled me to better perceive my professional options in academic librarianship before beginning the coursework for an MLS, and, perhaps more important, helped me to establish valuable and rewarding professional relationships with the staff at the University of Rochester. I still keep in touch with the librarians who welcomed me as an intern, and we find time to catch up at conferences or during visits to my alma mater. These relationships, which began with simple interviews, have grown into a well-developed support network of colleagues who share resources and experiences.

Upon moving to New York City and beginning library school, something about networking clicked. Suddenly, in my classes, I was meeting dozens of people with a wealth of experience and advice. I became exposed to the wider world of librarianship—public, academic, and special. Networking with my fellow students provided some of my first professional development opportunities. Library school offered leadership positions within the student association or the SLA@Pratt chapter as well as opportunities to attend conferences (funded by the school). The colleagues I met in library school created a strong foundation of connections, and our networks expanded organically as we began our careers. Through those relationships, I've had opportunities to speak on a panel of recent graduates and to organize tours of the Columbia University Libraries for current library school students. I brought this network into my library, where it has become a resource for my colleagues as well.

My manager encourages me to consider ways in which I could effectively incorporate library school interns into my work. Columbia has a robust internship program. My involvement with this program has included conversations with interns, advice giving, and other networking activities. (I have an "insider's" perspective, having started as an intern in Columbia's Libraries Digital Program Division.) In the coming semesters, I hope to achieve my goal of providing a valuable internship experience for a library school student, similar to the one that was provided for me.

Another way that I've kept my connection to my library school has been through providing opportunities for library school students to visit the Columbia University Libraries to explore our diverse facilities and collections and hear from our staff. Bringing students in to visit the libraries allows our librarians an opportunity to show off a bit and brings a refreshing burst of energy into our environment. These visits are simple to set up, and they allow me to provide an opportunity to library school students that was not available to me. Managers should encourage this type of activity, as it has no cost outside of staff time (which is not insignificant) and is beneficial for the new employee, the students, and the library staff.

Do you know everyone at your library? What their interests are? Who's in their network? Which library organizations they're involved in? When I started at Columbia, one of the first things I did, with the help and advice of my manager, was organize one-on-one meetings with the heads of each department or library on campus—a "meet and greet" session to introduce myself to the key players within the library system to determine how we could work together. Of the 25 libraries at Columbia, I work with 20 of them, in addition to our technical services department and our IT infrastructure team. Making the effort to meet my colleagues in the first six weeks on the job enriched my knowledge of the library system as a whole and enabled me to understand my role within the organization. Through these conversations, I learned about my colleagues' professional interests

> ☑ **QUICK TIP**
> Encourage new librarians to stay in contact with library schools. Their close proximity to the library school experience makes them an ideal liaison to local LIS programs. As they reach out to LIS programs, they build leadership skills in a more comfortable environment.

and contributions. The better I understand the nature of their jobs and the resources they can provide, the better able I am to identify and leverage valuable assets within my organization.

Managers should facilitate this type of networking—engaging colleagues and learning about the organization—as part of every new employee's professional development by identifying the key players a new employee will be working with and suggesting ways to initiate contact. Introductions and meet-and-greet meetings are a valuable part of new employees' orientation in their new positions.

These relationships naturally carry through to professional organizations. Knowing my co-workers and meeting others in their networks has afforded me many professional opportunities I wouldn't otherwise have had. Ensuring that my co-workers have a general understanding of my own job and professional interests enables them to create opportunities for me. Whether by sending me information about a fascinating symposium, alerting me to a speaker I may want to bring to the Libraries, or inviting me to a reception during a conference, my colleagues help me extend my network beyond my library.

While more formal methods of networking, such as meetings, are very effective, I also enjoy networking with my peers informally. Setting up lunch dates with colleagues with whom I don't regularly interact is an easy, casual way to learn more about their jobs and professional involvements. I often discover that I share similar interests with people or learn about entire aspects of librarianship that are new to me.

Another valuable networking opportunity with which I'm involved at Columbia is the New Professionals Round Table. In 2006, the Manager of Staff Development and Training initiated the group as a pilot project. The focus is on creating a network within the Libraries for professionals new to Columbia, although the members are not necessarily new librarians. This group consists of eight professional staff members and is facilitated by the Director for Access Services (my manager) and the Manager of Staff Development and Training. Although each member of the group has been at Columbia University Libraries for two years or less, we have nearly 80 years of collective experience working in libraries. Since its inception, the group has served as a meeting ground for those adapting to Columbia's culture and expectations by facilitating discussions about our professional needs and challenges at work. Not only have we had productive conversations about how to effectively integrate ourselves into the Libraries' structure and culture; we've also identified professional development opportunities to pursue as a team (we are currently in the process of identifying potential poster sessions and articles to work on collectively). This group has been successful in creating a comfortable, collegial, supportive environment where new professionals can openly discuss their experiences and has been valuable to me on both a professional and personal level.

> ☑ QUICK TIP
>
> Create opportunities for new professionals to come together and share their experiences. Creating this support network can help build community and provide targeted training opportunities for new staff across your institution.

One barrier to networking that new librarians might encounter is the feeling that they're novices in a room full of experts. It is important to remember that networking is a two-way street: instead of just thinking about what you can gain through networking, focus on what you have to contribute. Be confident. Be conscious of what you have to offer (we often sell ourselves short) and how you could potentially help the person with whom you're networking. Managers should help new librarians prepare for networking opportunities by verbalizing their employees' strengths, interests, and contributions to the organization. Networking is a way for other people to learn about you and your organization, so new professionals must be knowledgeable about their organization to respond appropriately to questions that will naturally come up in these conversations. Within the library community, I am networking with my peers, and although most of my peers have a great deal more experience than I do, because I'm a new professional, I can offer a fresh perspective. Librarians at all levels of experience should view themselves as partners, each able to contribute value to the networking relationship.

Of all of the professionals with whom one could network, librarians are, in my experience, among the most welcoming. Having worked in a variety of environments within academia, I've found librarians to be more open, supportive, and good-natured. Reaching out to colleagues for support can be rewarding and satisfying. In short: People are generally nice. Managers should encourage new staff to ask their colleagues for help, advice, and direction, or just to share their experiences; they will almost always say yes.

Start a book club or seminar series

Continued learning is an invaluable aspect of professional development. As a lifelong learner, similar to most librarians, I tend to enjoy everything more if I've learned something about the subject or process. Training sessions and workshops are obviously great ways to continue learning, and Columbia in particular is very supportive of those formal types of professional learning opportunities. I've also found frequent opportunities to learn within my library.

A less formal way to encourage continued learning is through a book club. When faced with a new challenge at work (for instance, working with our Libraries Digital Program Division to develop a program for Web site usability testing), I started where any librarian would—with research. I found some books on information design that are considered core texts for interface designers and knew that reading these books would help me build a foundation for understanding usability issues. After teaming up with a colleague in the Libraries Digital Program Division who had been my "go-to" usability partner, we invited the rest of the department to join us in our informal book club.

The group met rather sporadically—every few weeks, usually during the lunch hour—to casually discuss one or two chapters.

> ☑ QUICK TIP
> Find innovative and informal opportunities for training, such as book clubs, where new professionals can read and discuss information pertinent to their new positions.

Sometimes, we would develop specific questions to lead the discussion, and other times we would let the discussion develop naturally. Inevitably, we found ourselves considering how the concepts in the book applied to current projects and work flows. After two and a half months, we had finished the first book and were on to the second. By organizing an informal group that people could attend when available, with no sense of obligation or time commitment (something all working professionals are sensitive to), we were able to share a cross-departmental learning experience and develop a common language for discussing usability issues. And because many of us had copies of the books or were able to access them through interlibrary loan, there was little cost associated with the project.

This type of leadership in the workplace has multiple benefits for the organization and those involved. I developed my facilitation and listening skills, created a learning opportunity for my colleagues, and learned something practical and relevant to my work. "Book clubbing" is now an integral part of how I approach every project and team with which I work. Is there something that we could all be learning that would help us achieve our goals? What have I read in the professional literature that inspires me about the topic I'm addressing? Is there anything that my co-workers have read that is influencing their approach and perspective?

Managers can support book clubs as a staff development tool in many ways. Identifying potential subjects of interest, resources, and partners can help a new employee start a book club. A good approach might be to start the book club as co-facilitators and eventually let the new employee take the lead—choosing topics, inviting colleagues, developing talking points, and scheduling meetings. Book clubs can be casual or more formal. They can be within an already existing committee or working group or can bring together a group of employees who don't meet regularly. No matter the format or topic, book clubs are an easy, valuable way to develop leadership skills by engaging in a shared learning experience.

Other opportunities for continued learning at Columbia University Libraries include our Emerging Technologies Brown Bag Lunches, annual Reference Symposium, and regular Digital Library Seminars. These events are open to all library staff and provide easy ways to stay informed about library trends. As a new professional charged with tackling an emerging aspect of librarianship, I understand that the success of an assessment program depends strongly on the staff's adoption of assessment philosophies and practices. We are, over time, building a culture of assessment at the Libraries. To help this mission along, one of the committees I chair organizes the Columbia University Libraries Assessment Forum, an event each semester that brings guests from the greater library community, or from departments on campus, to the Libraries to share their experiences using assessment techniques. Starting a speaker series at work is a fun, low-cost way to achieve many goals. Bringing fresh ideas into your library can be a source of inspiration for the staff. Seeing new ideas applied in practical ways, with successful results, can also reduce fears about innovations and invigorate staff to try new ways of approaching their work. By bringing colleagues from other academic libraries to Columbia to share their experiences, the staff participate in a communal learning opportunity that highlights practical methods proven by our peers. These forums have led to the creation of assessment projects in three departments of the Libraries and an increased awareness of and interest in library assessment (see Table 1.1).

Coordinating a speaker series, seminar, or brown-bag lunch offers many opportunities for development to new employees. Casual environments, such as the

Table 1.1. Speaker series at Columbia University Libraries

Series	Details
Emerging Technology Brown-Bag Lunches	**Topic:** Share knowledge of new technology with one another. These meetings are an open discussion and are casual in nature. **Audience:** All staff members at the Libraries and the Columbia Center for New Media Teaching and Learning. Since the meetings are held during lunch hour, most staff members have the option to attend. They are invited to bring their lunch. **Speakers:** Staff members are invited to contribute topics they would like to present via a wiki. They can sign up to present at meetings that are convenient for them. **Schedule:** Meetings are held on the third Thursday of every month. The schedule is posted on the wiki, and brief e-mail invitations with a description of the technology topic are sent to the entire Libraries staff.
Digital Libraries Seminars	**Topic:** Promote awareness of digital library issues, programs, and innovations. **Audience:** All staff members are invited to attend. **Speakers:** Speakers are typically Libraries and Information Services staff or colleagues from nearby libraries, such as University of Pennsylvania or the New York Public Library. **Schedule:** Anywhere from four to ten seminars per year (since 2001).
Assessment Forums	**Topic:** Introduce staff to innovative assessment programs at other libraries. **Audience:** All staff members are invited to attend. **Speakers:** Speakers are typically colleagues from other organizations in our area, such as Baruch College (CUNY) and New York University. Departments within the Libraries and on campus are also invited to speak. **Schedule:** One forum is scheduled each semester (three per year). Topics and speakers are selected by a committee, although staff members are welcome to contribute suggestions.

brown-bag lunch series, provide an open forum for new staff to share and promote their ideas and work experiences. New professionals can build public speaking and presentation skills in a comfortable setting, while contributing to the professional dialogue at their organization, and meet staff with similar interests. Organizing a larger event, such as semester forums or seminars, requires more planning, networking, and brainstorming, as the coordinator or hosting group is tasked with identifying and recruiting potential speakers, but is still a manageable project. This is a great opportunity for new librarians to employ their networking skills and help their organization build meaningful relationships within the wider library community. Staff who attend these sessions may pick up a new technology, such as del.icio.us tags (http://del.icio.us), and start utilizing it at work, or, as in the case of the Assessment Forums, they may be inspired to initiate an assessment project.

Participate on committees

Committees have quickly become a central part of my professional life, being common elements of professional librarianship, both within libraries and professional organizations. As the Program Coordinator for Marketing and Assessment, I have had many chances to assume a leadership role within the library through committee work, often simultaneously creating professional development opportunities for my co-workers. Serving on a committee is a development opportunity for its members, and managers who chair or sit on committees should encourage new librarians to participate actively in the committee work.

Every working professional understands what it's like to attend meetings that are, shall we say, not engaging. As a committee chair, I aim to provide opportunities for learning and skill building to help committee members stay actively involved and interested. One particular committee I chair, the Assessment Working Group, supports the Libraries' strategic goals through developing, implementing, and analyzing assessment projects. The committee has an incredible amount of work to do, and the members must often work closely with library staff who are unfamiliar with assessment techniques. How can I help the group grow and develop as a team through our work?

As new assessment projects are initiated, I try to find productive and interesting ways for committee members to get involved. Identifying information needs, developing survey and focus group questions, designing observational studies, and gathering and analyzing information to support decision making are valuable skills that committee members are excited to learn. This group of eight people contributes a significant amount of time to committee work, and as the chair, I am dedicated to ensuring that their experience is worthwhile. My manager has been a constant support in helping me learn to engage committee members in the work of the group by providing advice, instructional resources, and feedback in our weekly meetings. After each committee meeting, we discuss what went well and which areas I can improve.

Creating leadership opportunities for committee members helps maintain their interest in, and commitment to, the work we do. I encourage committee members to volunteer to work on projects that interest them, and we work together to find ways to draw on their specific skill sets or help them build new skills. I apply the book club model in this committee as well, sharing articles and books and leading discussions on them. Bringing in examples of assessment tools and methodology from other libraries, or even from the business world, for us to evaluate as a group is also instructive. Sharing and applying what we've learned collectively often leads to lively conversations.

Managers should encourage new librarians to become active participants on committees. This entails helping new librarians understand the committee landscape within an organization (Columbia hosts nearly a dozen committees with rotating memberships), helping them apply for the committees that interest them, and staying up to date on their involvement with the committees. If the committees don't adequately tap the new librarians' skills, managers can help develop a strategy for employees to become more involved.

Working on committees allows new employees to build many leadership skills— through networking with other staff members and (hopefully) engaging in innovative work. Understanding committee structures and functions is valuable knowledge that will prove useful when new librarians are ready to seek positions on committees within a professional organization.

Be innovative at work

Doing innovative work can provide new employees with a platform on the national library scene through creating a poster session or speaking on a panel. This may seem intimidating or out of reach at first (Do I have anything relevant to contribute in a professional forum?), but new librarians might be surprised to learn how frequently their ideas and experiences can excite their peers.

Immediately after joining the Libraries, I was asked to participate in an innovative pilot project to test various ways podcasts can be used in a library setting. A team of three library staff members, including myself, tried three forms of podcasting: (1) making an image podcast of a call number guide, (2) recording audio podcasts of our many speaker events, and (3) creating enhanced podcasts (including audio and images) of a tour of the C.V. Starr East Asian Library, in five languages. This was an entirely new medium and we did not know what to expect. The pilot project achieved some successes—the call number guides are still available, and we continue to create podcasts of our speaker events— but the tour proved to be more work than we had anticipated, and we no longer pursue that type of podcast.

> ☑ QUICK TIP
> Encourage new librarians to engage in innovative projects— innovative for the organization as a whole. This new challenge and unstructured opportunity can help them grow and develop a new expertise.

My co-workers and I were able to find two outlets in professional organizations to present our project and experiences: as part of the conference "Cool Tools and New Technologies" at Dartmouth Biomedical Libraries and as a poster session for ACRL's 13th National Conference. Of course, when applying for these conferences, we had no idea whether our proposals would be accepted and so were delighted to be offered the chance to participate. This project created a sturdy platform for us to promote our work to the larger library community. It also provided my first experience with completing a conference proposal and preparing for a professional presentation. Working with a team of more experienced librarians was an advantage that enabled me to engage in these activities more confidently.

Although my manager was not directly involved in this project (I worked mostly with co-workers from other departments), he provided support by saying yes to my request for professional leave time to attend these conferences, not to mention encouraging me to be involved in them in the first place. Saying "yes" is one way my manager strives to support my interests and professional development needs. He trusts that I am conscientious of my primary responsibilities as I pursue professional opportunities, and that I do not make unreasonable requests. I trust that when he says no, he has good reason.

At the center of the discourse in librarianship lies a simple function: information sharing. By reporting on the work I do at the library, offering best practices, outcomes, and advice, I am able to find comfortable yet exciting ways to transition my work experience to professional activities. Most of the development opportunities of my first 18 months at Columbia were based on information sharing: *What are we doing, how are we doing it, and does it work?* Participating in information-sharing sessions is valuable for new professionals because we know our work well, can offer fresh insights, and report on the details of innovative strategies we're developing. By engaging in innovative work in the library, new professionals create opportunities for information sharing within the larger library community via blogs, panels, conferences, listservs, and professional organizations.

Most of the initiatives just outlined require only time and support from managers to get started. In libraries, we often find that one professional does the job of two or three, but this should not deter managers from finding time for employees to engage in professional development. Google provides inspiration in this area with its "20 percent time" philosophy (Google.com, 2004) that requires engineers to allocate 20 percent of their time (one full day each week) to work on innovative projects not directly related to their jobs, but about which they are passionate. Such a philosophy clearly has many possibilities within a library setting, but one immediate and valuable application would be to devote a percentage of time toward professional development initiatives, such as book clubs or speaker series. Google's time commitment to innovation is significant, but library managers could start by setting aside just one or two hours per week. Such initiatives will add value to the entire organization by providing exciting opportunities for new professionals.

Promote self-awareness

The New Professionals Round Table group (mentioned earlier) decided that learning more about ourselves would be a valuable way to better understand how we, as new professionals, fit into the organization. With the help of the Manager of Staff Development and Training, we participated in a Myers-Briggs Type Indicator assessment (www.myersbriggs.org) to analyze our personality types from a workplace perspective. This helped us to understand how our personality types affect our communication with our co-workers. Through this intensive self-awareness process, we were able to overcome potential communication challenges and learn to communicate with our co-workers to accomplish our goals. My manager and I continually use what we learned during that process to inform our interactions with each other and our co-workers. Our awareness of communication patterns within a work setting allows us to communicate more openly and purposefully, which has proven particularly beneficial when introducing a new service or program to our department. Communication is a fundamental part of leadership, and self-awareness is the key to communicating more effectively.

Apart from activity-based staff development, employees can develop leadership characteristics independently through self-awareness. Helping new professionals identify the characteristics that they wish to emulate is a good place for managers to start. Some leadership characteristics that I strive to cultivate include:

- Creative thinking: generating new ideas
- Good time management and project management skills: completing projects effectively and efficiently, within a set time frame, often while managing a group of contributors or partners
- Finding creative ways to work around barriers: proactively seeking solutions to challenges
- Staying open to new ideas: considering new ways to work
- Keeping up to date with library literature and technology trends: staying well-informed about the greater library world and related fields
- Supporting innovation at work: creating infrastructures and incentives for innovative work
- Being goal-oriented: establishing on-the-job goals and professional goals
- Taking advantage of opportunities: saying "yes"
- Speaking comfortably in public: taking advantage of opportunities to promote ideas and work
- Listening: encouraging others to contribute to the conversation; learning from others' experiences
- Group facilitation: working effectively in a group; maintaining motivation and productivity
- Being patient yet persistent when faced with challenges: not taking "no" too seriously; using long-term perspective to work through a challenge
- Exuding confidence and enthusiasm

One way to build a better awareness of leadership skills is to identify a professional role model who demonstrates these characteristics. Conscientious observation of professional role models can facilitate the development of leadership skills by increasing self-awareness. I have leadership role models within my organization and at libraries across the country. They are not necessarily mentors, and typically no formal professional relationship is established; they are people about whom I find myself thinking, "I would love to work for them." I make an effort to hear them speak at conferences, to engage them in conversations (in person, on blogs, and via e-mail), and to read their publications.

Evaluating my own actions is also valuable when thinking critically about library leadership. *What do I wish the leadership would do in a given situation, and how would I meet my own expectations, given the opportunity?* Analyzing current leadership situations encourages me to think more strategically about my own leadership skills. Having a role model helps me stay motivated about my work and professional development as I visualize my developing career. Increasing self-awareness is beneficial in all areas of work and encourages me to think critically and speak openly about leadership and management issues. Self-awareness can help employees communicate more effectively, understand and learn from their mistakes, think strategically about what they'd like to accomplish, and identify leadership characteristics to model.

Build leadership skills at work—strategies

1. *Network with colleagues.* New employees can tap into a deep pool of experience and expertise, acquiring well-developed networks and resources, by simply building relationships with their co-workers. Networking at work can include formal meetings, periodic touch-base discussions, or informal lunches.
2. *Start a book club.* Book clubs can be casual, temporary, and fun ways to continue learning at work. Choose a topic that interests a few colleagues. Keeping it informal reduces the pressure on already busy professionals and enables people to participate comfortably. Learning with co-workers can help employees stay motivated about keeping up with library literature, and learning collectively helps to create a collegial environment that allows for the exchange of new ideas. Continued learning also helps employees develop expertise.
3. *Get involved in committee work.* This is a great way to build leadership skills and contribute to the organization. Since many professional organizations function with a committee structure, understanding what makes a committee effective is important. Committee work may also provide opportunities to contribute to the professional development of co-workers.
4. *Do innovative work.* By striving to do interesting, innovative work at the library, new employees are not only contributing value to their organizations; they are creating a platform to get involved in the broader library community. Speaking engagements, publishing opportunities, and involvement in professional organizations are all avenues for promoting the innovative work already being done at their library.
5. *Become self-aware.* Self-awareness can help all employees work more effectively. It enables staff to improve their communication skills and become more aware of their co-workers' communication tendencies. This can help employees think more strategically about their communication. Managers should help new employees identify experienced leaders whom they can observe and learn from.

Leadership at work prepares new professionals for leadership outside the library as well. Developing leadership skills during my first years as a librarian, coupled with the support of my manager, has helped me feel more confident about contributing to professional organizations. My manager reinforces my successes by providing feedback as I progress and helps me to identify development opportunities to promote my work. Support from a manager or supervisor who is also a leader is fundamental to the successful development of new professionals. My manager continues to be engaged in the organization, contributes value to our strategic initiatives, and encourages his peers to support staff development initiatives. My manager is inclined to say "yes" to staff development opportunities, as well as my ideas for new initiatives at work. He often suggests that I attend trainings and conferences, recommends me when opportunities arise, and helps me evaluate them for potential benefits and relevance to my goals. We are able to think strategically about my career; he wants to understand my long-term goals, so that we can start working toward them today. He advocates for my continued development to the library administration and helps me secure funding for trainings and conference attendance. He has also encouraged and inspired me to promote myself within the organization and the larger professional community. A supportive manager can make all the difference when it comes to the development of new professionals.

As I continue to focus on my career outside of the library and consider some broader questions (*Which professional committees are right for me? What conferences should I be attending? Where can I learn the skills to successfully execute the new initiatives I'm hoping to start?*), I am also growing within my current position. New projects require new skills and also create new opportunities. By embracing a professional development strategy of building skills by challenging myself at work, I am able to stay motivated and create interesting opportunities, while advancing my many projects.

Knowing my co-workers leads to increased networking opportunities, continued learning helps me build expertise, committee work allows me to contribute to my co-workers' development and my organization, doing innovative work increases my opportunities for professional engagement, and self-awareness enables me to do all of this more effectively.

Engaging in professional development has also influenced the way I think about my job. I do not only have a job; I have a *career*. Professional development has fostered this sense of career by bringing skills, knowledge, and an awareness of my community to my work. These added layers help me see beyond my current position and allow me to view my career as a long-term project that I am only beginning to shape.

Since joining the Columbia University Libraries, I've also learned that "work" has a very flexible definition. "Work" is the job that I do every day when I get to the office; "work" is time spent in committee meetings; "work" is time spent reading professional literature; "work" is time dedicated to writing a book chapter or an article; "work" is time spent preparing for and attending a conference or workshop; and "work" is time spent on calls and e-mails to colleagues outside of the library. All of these things contribute to my career and enable me to continue to develop as a librarian and a leader. Understanding the broader scope of what can be accomplished in my job and how to balance all of the opportunities and demands has been a constant challenge with constant rewards.

> ## Exhibit 1.2. A manager's perspective on the importance of staff development
>
> *The following is from an interview with Terry Kirchner, Director for Access Services at Columbia University Libraries.*
>
> **Why is staff development important to you as a manager?**
> Staff development is a tool for helping individuals to achieve their goals, to discover new communication methods and problem resolution techniques, to develop their strengths, and to find new interests or untapped talents. Through staff development activities, I as a manager am able to develop a more diverse staff with a broader range of experiences and skill sets. This helps our division move forward with strategic goals.
>
> **How do you support staff development as a manager?**
> I try to lead by example. I routinely engage in staff development activities to refresh and expand my skill set. I actively encourage staff to participate in staff development activities through one-on-one conversations, making announcements at staff meetings, and communicating opportunities via e-mail. I view staff development as an important component of professional development, so I also use the performance evaluation process as an opportunity to learn about a staff member's professional goals and interests. As part of the goal-setting process I work with interested individuals to explore ways that we can incorporate staff development activities into their plans for the upcoming year.
>
> **How do you, as a manager, and the organization, benefit from investing in staff development?**
> My experience has been that staff who regularly engage in staff development activities feel more empowered to make decisions. They are often able to discover connections between their work activities and the activities of other library staff. Through developing a better understanding of the work processes of other staff members and the potential uses of technology, staff often identify improvements that lead to improved efficiencies. When we're lucky, these efficiencies free up time for staff to engage in proactive initiatives that further improve the public service experience for both the library users and the library staff.

New professionals and their managers need to work together, making time for professional development a priority. Managerial support is critical to the success of new employees' professional endeavors and continued learning. The skills gained will carry new librarians into active roles within their organization and pave the way for successful careers.

Further reading

"Bibliography of Publications Related to Women's Leadership." Institute for Women's Leadership. Rutgers University. Available: http://iwl.rutgers.edu/biblio.pdf (accessed July 9, 2008).

Buckingham, Marcus, and Oprah Winfrey. "Taking Control of Your Career and Your Life with Marcus Buckingham." Series of podcasts, release date 4/4/08 (accessed via iTunes Music Store, July 9, 2008).

Erickson, Tammy. *Across the Ages* blog. Harvard Business Publishing. Available: http://discussionleader.hbsp.com/erickson/ (accessed July 9, 2008).

Leading Effectively: Think and Act Beyond [e-newsletter]. 2001. Center for Creative Leadership. Available: www.ccl.org/leadership/enewsletter (accessed July 9, 2008).

Reading Group Guides: The Online Community for Reading Groups. Available: www.readinggroupguides.com (accessed July 9, 2008).

Tieger, Paul D., and Barbara Barron-Tieger. 1992. *Do What You Are: Discover the Perfect Career for You Through the Secrets of Personality Type.* Boston: Little, Brown and Company.

Acknowledgment

Thank you to Regina Golia, Karen Green, Terry Kirchner, and Patricia Renfro for their assistance and advice in developing this chapter, as well as their continued support for staff development.

CHAPTER 2

guidelines for knowing and showing: from good to great bosses

Mary Evangeliste

Being an academic librarian is rewarding. The profession matches nicely with many of the talents and characteristics that I brought into librarianship, mostly my intellectual curiosity about almost everything. I love having access to wonderful resources in both electronic and book form. I also love seeing students utilize the material as they develop their critical-thinking skills.

I could have very easily not become a librarian, if it had not been for the wonderful managers, supervisors, and mentors who took an interest in me. Before I became a librarian, I had been employed as a pet sitter, waitress, landscaper, rock band manager, and museum employee. Obviously, I needed some guidance. Luckily, I found mentors who were able to provide me with exciting challenges and fulfilling work. They created environments in which I could develop my skills while also taking chances; they were interested in my growth and took the time to cultivate my interest in libraries. These experiences now help me mentor new librarians and staff by treating them with respect and fairness.

This chapter is dedicated to all the great managers I have worked with, as well as the not so good ones, because although poor supervisors were difficult to work with, I still learned a lot from them—mostly how not to become them. One of the easiest ways not to be a dreadful person in charge is to be a doer, not just a talker. No one likes to sweat and get dirty while the supervisor remains stain-free and clean as a whistle. Great bosses have the talent to recognize the latent potential in their employees. Through actions as well as by example, they encourage the employees they supervise to also be doers. They provide guidance as they foster independence.

Exhibit 2.1. Lessons from my first supervisor

Sadly, my first great library supervisor is no longer with us. On the last day of 2003, she passed away after a brave two-year struggle with breast cancer. Helen R. Goldstein is now something of a legend among those of us lucky enough to have worked for her in her capacity as Associate Librarian at American University Library. She had an unusual combination of temperament and skills. She could in turn be authoritative and kind, calm and funny, decisive and inclusive. She never seemed bored or distracted when you entered her office to speak to her. Helen created an Access Services department that was exciting and respectful. She fostered an environment in which we could disagree with one another civilly. To be able to create a workplace where we could and were encouraged to participate in intellectual disagreement so that we developed a great idea or project is the skill that I would most like to emulate as a manager.

Although she worked at American University Library for more than 20 years, she met every new idea or project with enthusiasm and determination. Helen had the uncanny ability to see a person as a whole being, not merely as his or her current job function. She was able to zero in on what her staff did well and use these skills to benefit the library. She was also able to gently but firmly develop us in areas where we were less comfortable, which in turn benefited the library. In 2000, she was certain that I should pursue a graduate degree in libraries and helped guide me in the decisions I made regarding my choice of programs.

This chapter shares the many ways that leaders can motivate through their actions and examples. Before I begin, a word of caution: No amount of advice can make up for indifference toward an employee or disinterest in an organization or profession. Fundamentally, employees react to leaders who are engaged with them; no strategy or tactic can overcome a lack of interest in or curiosity about people's ideas and talents. Managers must also show respect and hope for an institution or the profession.

> ☑ QUICK TIP
> Employees respect someone who works as hard as they do.

Based on my own experience as a developing librarian, I created eight guidelines to keep in mind when mentoring new librarians and staff. These guidelines can serve as starting points for discussions that supervisors could have with their employees. I have also created two worksheets (see Exhibits 2.2 and 2.3) that can be used to track the things supervisors learn about employees. I use these worksheets to integrate ideas, facts, and knowledge.

1. Know and appreciate the talents your employees bring to the table

One frustration new librarians may face is a manager who behaves as if the employee is ignorant or completely naïve about the profession. Many people come to librarianship as a second career. They might have been journalists, public relations specialists, artists, mothers, or even marine biologists before they decided to become

Exhibit 2.2. Worksheet #1: Understand your employee's talents

What do you know about your employee's talents?

Name: _____

Past jobs:

_____

_____

Interests:

_____

_____

Studied in school:

_____

_____

Exhibit 2.3. Worksheet #2: Understand your employee's workload

What else does my employee have on his or her plate?

Name: _____

Department duties:

_____

_____

Library-wide duties:

_____

_____

Educational pursuits:

_____

_____

Other obligations:

_____

_____

librarians. We can take advantage of their knowledge by knowing what a new employee did before he or she came to the present institution not dismissing his or her past experiences. Every person who comes to work at a library brings life experience. I have experienced this as both a staff person and as a leader putting together a team to run projects.

☑ **QUICK TIP**
Take the time to understand what everyone on the staff knows and is interested in. This way, the successful manager can utilize everyone's skills and creativity in unexpected areas.

Years ago when I was starting my career, I became involved with marketing and outreach events to publicize the fact that interlibrary loan was available to deliver articles electronically. The team working on this decided that we needed to do something that would really get campus attention. We agreed that we needed a walking and talking computer and document. Obviously this was a creative group! The manager overseeing this project remembered that I and another colleague had studied art as undergraduates. She very astutely assigned us the creation of costumes. My co-worker and I enjoyed using our creativity. Our strange contraptions attracted much local press and attention, and the event was a giant success. I model the behavior of this manager when I take the time to know what people did before they came to the library and apply it to my institution's events.

As a leader I have managed people who have years of teaching, public relations, and graphic design experience. We live in a time of unprecedented invention and time compression. No one person can accomplish a large project. I learned this firsthand as the project manager of a newly created marketing team at American University Library. I wrote about the joy of working with such a knowledgeable and talented staff in *C&RL News* in my short article "You Too Can Feel Like a Rock 'n' Roll Librarian" (Evangeliste, 2006). It begs repeating. When we decided to create a marketing program at American, I wandered through the library and talked with staff. I asked many questions: Who was taking marketing classes? Who was interested in art and design? Who could do design work? Who should we consult with on a university-wide level? By asking these questions, I found two marketing graduate students who were employed in different parts of the library. I also found an excellent graphic designer who was working as a library building monitor, a job that was enabling him to complete his design degree. Combined, these people had years of marketing, public relations, and graphic design experience. Along with other amazing team members, we went on to form an unstoppable team. We created campaigns that students loved; some of our posters were even ripped down and displayed in dorm rooms. We even went on to win the ACRL 2005 Best Practices in Marketing Academic and Research Librarians @your library award. By asking questions and uncovering the talents of those around us, we can maximize our output while embracing the talents of staff.

2. Know the entire range of your employees' responsibilities

In this time of multitasking, a leader also must acknowledge that developing employees are also juggling priorities. It is part of a manager's job to make sure that his or her employees are not overworked and overextended. In order to produce a great product, sometimes employees need a reprieve from their usual duties. A great manager can help his or her employees negotiate and prioritize their responsibilities.

The need to protect an employee's time seems to be especially acute when one is creating something such as a Web tutorial or developing a product that seems simple from the outside but is actually quite complicated to complete. I have been privileged to work with flexible managers and colleagues who have given me relief time to complete large projects. This was the case when I collaborated with colleagues to create a literature review and some information literacy tutorials. In both situations, my colleagues and managers protected my time and enabled me to complete these projects. Managers who give employees new responsibilities with no understanding of how long it will take to actually bring these projects to fruition can demoralize an employee. This, of course, can be very frustrating for the employee. Managers should strive to be aware of what each staff member has on his or her plate.

Often, it was my supervisor who protected my time and watched my workload while I completed my degree requirements; she called this "money in the bank." In other words, although an organization might need to adapt to accommodate employees who wish to attain higher degrees, most supervisors will find that the dividends of creating new librarians far outweigh a short-term inconvenience to the institution. Allowing staff members a flexible work culture so they can further their education benefits the organization in the long term.

On a day-to-day level, a manager must make sure that a talented employee is not overcommitting or running himself or herself into the ground by working on too many projects simultaneously. A leader should take the time to check with the employee when assigning tasks to ensure that he or she is meeting priorities and not running scattershot through the day. Ultimately, this attention to employees' competing priorities will build confidence in abilities, pride in accomplishments, and awareness that the manager is conscious of their many duties.

> ☑ QUICK TIP
> Use the worksheet included with this chapter to take the time to understand what responsibilities and commitments the staff have to help them prioritize and remain focused on the big picture.

3. See your employees' potential—not merely their positions

In the world of libraries, we have many staff categories: paraprofessionals, interns, graduate assistants, students, part-time librarians, temporary librarians, assistant librarians, associate librarians—the list goes on and on. If we see people as their position and not as their potential, we will miss out on a lot of talent.

I was given many opportunities as a paraprofessional, including working at the reference desk for three full years before I became a "reference librarian." I was also encouraged by my managers to serve on a strategic planning team. These managers took the time to know that I was interested in reference and strategic planning. They created professional spaces with opportunities for me to develop these skills and thus fulfill some of my potential as a paraprofessional.

Of course, the idea of seeing beyond the particular job category that someone currently occupies goes hand in hand with the ideas discussed in the section "Know and Appreciate the Talents Your Employees Bring to the Table"; we must see the employee in a broader fashion. However, this concept is about what employees *want to achieve* in your institution, not what they bring to the institution. What is their potential? How would they like to use their capabilities to improve themselves professionally? By doing so, they will definitely improve the organization. Seeing beyond someone's position and into their potential is one of the best ways to retain employees, because they are invested in their own professional growth.

4. Use your experience in the field to help your employees find opportunities

Managers must mentor employees into the profession. We have to explain to them how to navigate the complicated world of presentations, committees, and exhibits. This could be as simple as helping employees navigate overwhelming conferences by going over schedules beforehand or, better yet, meeting them for coffee or lunch at their first conference. The best case is inviting them out to dinner with colleagues.

More formally, this can be realized by partnering with a new employee on a presentation or a paper. I have been on both the receiving and giving end of this equation. Supervisors have given me the opportunity to present with them at national conferences, and once I gained my footing, I began inviting newer employees to present with me. This is consistently a great experience. It is wonderful to watch employees' confidence levels grow and share their achievements with a larger community.

Just last year, I created a pre-conference session with a former intern who is now my colleague. While working together at the University of Arizona, we became fascinated with the idea of "social marketing," the area of marketing that seeks to change behavior instead of selling a product, which we believed to relate to the mission of libraries. As librarians, we don't sell products, but instead try to teach critical thinking and other more amorphous concepts. In November 2007, we presented a three-hour conference that we created from the ground up. It was well received, and since then, we have been asked to present at a public library, a regional conference, and a research library.

Another way to usher someone into the profession is to hand off a presentation to a more junior colleague or employee. This happened to me when I first became a librarian. My institution was asked to do a short presentation at ACRL, and the senior librarians discussed the opportunity with me and advised me to take on this responsibility. They helped me create the presentation and rehearse it, and they were in the audience when I presented.

Another means of offering opportunities to junior colleagues is to connect them with more senior people who can help them in their careers. As a middle-career librarian, I have seen this technique employed by many of my peers, who mentor younger librarians and staff by introducing them to experienced colleagues.

5. Trust your employees

From my point of view, nothing can motivate an employee more than feeling trusted by a manager. A manager can communicate trust in many ways. One way is to ask employees to reach beyond their normal activities and give them the support to do well. I experienced this type of trust when I was served on the strategic planning committee at American University Library. I was petrified to be at the table with the director and the assistant directors, contributing to a plan that would guide the library's future. Even when we disagreed, the leaders made it clear that they trusted my intellect and appreciated my opinions. This type of trust creates an environment where employees can truly contribute to the discussion by showing them that their opinions are respected even when they are not in alignment with those of the administration.

Feeling trusted always motivated me to research and bring educated opinions to the table. How did managers show that they trusted me? They allowed me to bring my ideas to fruition by not interrupting me. They asked clarification questions. Although they did not always agree with me, they allowed me the space to express a different opinion. They valued the news from the front line. They allowed me to question their assumptions and did so without getting defensive or becoming rigid in their ideas. These experiences taught me how to engage in "creative conflict" and

> ☑ QUICK TIP
> Trust is the key factor in eliciting honest feedback, encouraging and rewarding initiative, and sparking work that goes beyond the expected.

demonstrated that, when we foster respectful, civil collaboration, people can learn to trust one another. With trust, great things can happen.

As a project manager, I believe that a leader can show trust in his or her employees by creating a project that can be shared among many staff members. Complicated projects should be broken down into doable tasks that are delegated to employees. This enables employees to have pride in their accomplishments and gives them confidence to take on larger assignments. Knowing that a superior trusts his or her knowledge and instincts makes an employee motivated to stay the course. Having faith that an employee can succeed while giving him or her the needed support to do great things is surely one of the most vital actions a manager can take to motivate employees.

6. Give your employees specific, sincere, and tangible praise

Giving people specific praise when they deserve it could be the most important action that a manager can take. Early in my career, I was charged with leading a library-wide group for resource sharing, an offshoot of my job in interlibrary loan. This group included administrators, faculty members, and staff with whom but as yet not intensively. I took this job seriously and planned and documented the entire agenda for the meeting. Afterward my supervisor, a senior librarian, took me into her office and told me that I had done a great job running the meeting, and then she explained why: I had facilitated the meeting well, making sure that everyone had a chance to speak, and I had moved through the agenda efficiently, ensuring that we had time to address each item. This positive reinforcement not only felt great; it helped me to understand how to run a successful meeting. Colleagues have also told me that I do this well, and I have a wonderful mentor to thank for that, one who gave me specific praise.

> ☑ QUICK TIP
>
> When giving praise and compliments, take the time to explain why the person's actions worked and why they were successful.

For the past two years, I have organized, along with an amazing planning committee, a library-wide orientation event at the University of Arizona called the Amazing Library Race: Desert Edition. This event had more than 70 library staff and faculty volunteers along with staff from the Information Technology Center and the Pima County Public Library. It is a huge undertaking, with everyone taking his or her respective responsibilities very seriously. Last year, we had more than 12 stations where incoming students learned about the University of Arizona Libraries' collections and services. We also had a pizza party at the end of the event; this gives the new students a chance to meet one another. After the race, the planning committee and I wrote personal thank-you notes to each of the 70 volunteers. Each of these thank-yous had specific references to the precise work that each volunteer did to make the event a success. This was a labor-intensive process, in that we printed up special cards and the committee spent one or two afternoons writing up the cards, but I believe it was worth it. It is clear that employees enjoy being part of the event, because the first year we had 50 volunteers and the second year the number had jumped to 70.

7. Show your employees how to take risks

One of the most compelling ways to embolden those around you is to take risks. I am always inspired by when I see a superior advocate in the library or on campus for an unpopular or unsupported proposal. Managers can set a good example by taking risks while demonstrating poise and elegance as they argue their position. This behavior must also be modeled within the library. I believe that when we see a senior librarian stand up for a more junior colleague, it enables us to understand how to do this for the next generation of librarians. By modeling this behavior we can begin to understand how to use our own voices to advocate for the people in our department.

Often in the world of libraries we face shrinking budgets and competing priorities, but if we know where our focus lies and can articulate why something or someone is important to our institutions and do so in public, we will instill bravery in developing employees.

8. Show your employees how to get things done

Of all the ideas I have talked about throughout this chapter, I believe that this may be the most important. For me, the most motivating and inspiring thing to see a manager doing is getting something done. Helping with an important job that needs to get done will gain a manager a good deal of respect from his or her staff. If employees perceive their manager as someone who will roll up his or her sleeves and get dirty in the everyday business of the institution, they will also get dirty. It was always a joy to see Helen R. Goldstein, Associate Librarian at American University Library, staffing the circulation desk. This usually happened at the beginning or end of the semester when Circulation was swamped. I also have fond memories of administrators who stuffed bags of candy and other welcome treats for students. Finally, it made the day of the entire crew of the Amazing Library Race: Desert Edition when the Dean of the University of Arizona Libraries and Center for Creative Photography, Carla Stoffle, staffed the welcome table, staying for two hours in 100-degree heat to speak to the incoming students.

Conclusion

As we go through our busy days, it is easy to forget fundamental strategies that will help us to be great managers. I believe from personal experience that if we keep these eight principles in mind we will foster an engaged and proud workforce. We must remember to take the time to find out what talents our employees have to bring to the table and their professional goals. We must remember to use our leverage in the profession and in our professional organizations to help new employees. We have an obligation to know the responsibilities they have before asking them to take on new ones. We must always make the time to tell employees what they did right. We must look beyond position to the employee's potential. Most important, we must model

---

Exhibit 2.4. Questions for managers

Questions to ask ourselves about our employees as we develop as managers:

- Do you know the talents that your employees bring to the table?
- Do you know what else is on their plates?
- Do you see your employees as their position or as their potential?
- Can you give them specific, sincere, and tangible praise?
- Can you show them how to get things done?
- Can you use your experience in the field to help develop your employees?
- Can you show them how to take risks?
- Can you trust your employees?

behavior that shows employees that it is okay to take risks and be willing to pitch in to bring projects to fruition. I know how important these eight guidelines are because many managers took the time to use them while mentoring me. Their good example has helped me to become a leader, and I want to continue to emulate the great supervisors who have helped me along the way.

Reference

Evangeliste, Mary F. 2006. "You too can feel like a rock 'n' roll librarian." *C&RL News* 67, no. 7 (July/August): 425.

Dedication

This chapter is dedicated to Helen R. Goldstein, who fostered my love of the library profession by seeing my potential and allowing a space for a loud, goofy, slightly disheveled newbie like me. To watch someone as skilled and knowledgeable as Helen conduct herself with such grace while seemingly enjoying her position was truly one of the best lessons of my library career.

CHAPTER 3

the power of trust in cultivating new leaders

Kim Leeder

As a young academic librarian in my first year of a true professional position, I am perhaps an unlikely individual to provide insight into management strategies to cultivate new leaders. Yet, I find myself already chairing an Association of College & Research Libraries (ACRL) section committee, serving as co-chair of a second, and beginning my participation as one of the American Library Association's (ALA) second round of Emerging Leaders. I use the phrase "find myself" consciously, as I am still surprised to have this much leadership responsibility in the library world so soon.

Although it felt at the time like a natural (if accelerated) progression, I now realize that my success so far in the library profession has not been coincidence or luck. In my work and in my ALA service, I have been provided at each step along the way with opportunities and responsibilities that seemed, to me, to exceed my experience and knowledge of librarianship at the time. Yet through these opportunities, I gained new knowledge and new skills at a pace that could not have been duplicated in formal learning situations. These challenges drew me forward into the field and into the leadership positions I now hold. I have been fortunate to have my work recognized, appreciated, and rewarded with what I consider the most valuable asset of all: trust.

In using the word "trust," I am thinking of the great confidence invested in me by many of the library leaders with whom I have been fortunate to serve. These remarkable people have employed my skills, sought my advice, and never expressed a moment of hesitation in handing me increasingly challenging projects and tasks. Without any apparent concern for my newness to libraries, they have brought me seamlessly into the world of librarianship by recognizing my abilities and finding new ways for me to expand and grow into the role of a librarian and a leader. They benefited from my energy and desire to fulfill their expectations, while I have flourished under their tutelage. Their trust in my ability to rise to each new challenge has inspired my own greater confidence and ambition.

I am speaking on some level about mentoring, but a type of mentoring that goes beyond the practice as I have generally seen it in action. Trust is the foundation upon which true mentoring is built. Without it mentoring can certainly take place, but it will be a mere shadow of its potential self. A mentor whose behavior and actions reflect trust in a mentee, and a mentee who is conscious of and returns that trust, will be tied together in a symbiotic relationship from which both parties benefit. This is a reversal of the way we typically speak about trust in manager-employee or mentor-mentee relationships, in which the concern is with inspiring the employee's trust in the manager. Supervisors will always find that employees who trust them will perform better and be more productive; hence, this trust is often a focus of books and workshops on the subject of management. However, in terms of cultivating leadership potential, the concern should be with building the employee's trust in himself or herself in various ways. As a manager or leader wishing to train new leaders, the first step to enabling employees to trust themselves is to trust them.

When I speak about trust in this context, I mean trust as a principle of management—not the type of trust that comes from employees earning trust over a long period of time. When a manager can take a leap of faith to trust the staff to make decisions, creating a self-directed workforce, this both frees the manager to spend her or his time leading and fosters an environment of risk taking. Managers must go beyond trusting just those employees who have earned their trust; they must utilize trust as a general business principle. This will lead to greater achievements, an environment of experimentation, and a more productive and satisfied team of people.

Once an employee feels trusted by a leader in the field, his or her response will be to act in a way that fulfills the expectations of that sentiment. As Bibb and Kourdi (2004) describe in their book, *Trust Matters: For Organizational and Personal Success*, "If someone says to you . . . 'You can do it', your natural response is to prove them right, to throw yourself into the task and justify their support" (16). Employees who feel trusted will be inspired to take on new challenges, work harder, become more ambitious, and strive for greater accomplishments.

> ☑ **QUICK TIP**
> Self-confidence can be developed by giving someone your trust.

So what can library leaders do to express their trust in a new librarian? Trust is an abstract concept, and much of its power comes from an everyday demeanor that reflects confidence in the abilities and knowledge of the individual in question. Yet some concrete actions contribute substantially. These include:

- creating opportunities for the individual,
- actively referring the individual to others for projects, appointments, and other tasks,
- involving the individual in high-level brainstorms and projects,

- confiding in the individual about the challenges, successes, and frustrations of a leader's role, and
- treating the individual as an equal.

Though not a complete list, it provides a few examples of ways current library leaders can foster leadership qualities and ambition in the individuals who must eventually replace them. These examples are reflective of an attitude toward new librarians that is generous, respectful, and caring. Later in this chapter, I discuss these strategies in more depth and explore how to create trusting relationships that inspire new librarians to rise into leadership roles in the field.

Leading Generation X

Important to the concept of trust in this context is making a distinction between the *ability* to lead and the *desire* to lead. A far greater number of individuals have the skills and capability to lead than will ever accept a leadership role. The generation into which I was born, Generation X, is characterized by a reluctance to accept— maybe even an aversion to—management positions. In one article on the topic, the author describes a situation in which a city manager discovers that her Gen-X assistant, whom the manager was grooming as her eventual replacement, had no interest in a promotion. "Thanks but no thanks," said the assistant. "I wouldn't wish that on my worst enemy!" (Lancaster, 2006: 34). I have heard this same sentiment expressed by my peers and colleagues who have watched their parents and/or supervisors consumed by their careers to the exclusion of time for fun and family.

Compared to previous generations, Generation X is characterized as striving for a greater quality of life. They desire a balance between family, fun, and work (Meredith et al., 2002). Based on my own perspective and those of my friends and contemporaries, this appears to be a largely accurate stereotype. It is also the source of our reluctance to take on leadership roles, a reluctance causing some consternation among current managers. Leadership is a tremendous time commitment that many Gen Xers fear would throw their lives out of balance. Current leaders should be aware of this concern among their younger colleagues and address it in their efforts to cultivate these individuals as future leaders. The key to inspiring Gen Xers to lead is

> ☑ QUICK TIP
> Modeling and encouraging a healthy personal-professional life balance is key to inspiring others to take on leadership roles.

to show them that leadership can be compatible with a healthy lifestyle. Managers can have fun (at work and outside of work) and they can make time for vibrant personal lives. By acknowledging this need of Gen-X individuals, trusting them to get the job done, and allowing them space for a personal life beyond the nameplate, managers can reach these potential library leaders and inspire them to achieve.

The benefits of trust

The *Academy of Management Review* in 1998 published an issue with the special topic of "Trust in and between organizations." In the introduction to that issue,

Denise M. Rousseau and colleagues (1998) summarize the articles in the issue to define trust as "a psychological state comprising the intention to accept vulnerability based upon positive expectations of the intentions or behavior of another." It is the vulnerability inherent in trust that can make it so difficult to give to others, particularly those such as new colleagues or employees who have not yet earned it. What if they don't complete the task well? What if they don't know enough yet? However, the more generously trust is handed out to those individuals, the more quickly they will respond by rising to the challenge and returning the sentiment. Granted, risk is involved, and certain individuals may fail to live up to expectations. However, the great majority of people will respond in powerful ways to the trust placed upon them by others. "To wait until someone proves that they are trustworthy does not work," explain Bibb and Kourdi (2004: 123). "If you start by assuming that they are, they will invariably prove you right. Trust is reinforced by trusting."

> ☑ QUICK TIP
> Feeling trusted is key to job satisfaction and a productive and positive work environment.

By giving their trust to employees, managers can yield a whole range of benefits even beyond the cultivation of new leaders. Employees who feel trusted by managers will be happier, more productive, more relaxed, and will contribute to a better working environment. The impact of trust in the workplace, as described by Bibb and Kourdi (2004), can encompass a wide range of benefits. The following eight points are paraphrased from Bibb and Kourdi's research:

1. Trust inspires employees to greater performance and accomplishment. People who feel trusted with certain responsibilities will be more invested in meeting the demands placed upon them.
2. Trust helps employees focus on their work, providing increased productivity. A trusting workplace reduces the need for gossip or conjecture about what is going on "upstairs."
3. Trust enables better customer service by allowing employees to be more independent. Trusted employees will think of creative ways to make people happy with the services provided by their organization.
4. Trust improves communication and idea sharing. Those who feel trusted will trust in return, and be more inclined to speak and brainstorm freely.
5. Trust reduces stress by eliminating frustration with management. It makes people happier with their jobs and more likely to be relaxed at work.
6. Trust increases employee effectiveness and reduces turnover. Happy employees don't leave! With less time spent on searching for, interviewing, and training new people, managers can put more effort into their actual jobs.
7. Trust can reduce costs by facilitating employee buy-in on cost-cutting measures. People who trust their managers are more likely to support efforts to cut costs rather than complain about them.

8. Trust enables employee risk taking and innovation. Managers who trust their employees to try new things will reap the rewards in innovative ideas.

These factors will be identical for manager-employee, mentor-mentee, and library leader-new librarian relationships. The first benefit listed is perhaps the most important in the context of cultivating new leaders in the profession, but every increase of trust will have a ripple effect throughout the organization. "When you trust people, you can inspire them to be all they can be," explain Bibb and Kourdi. "The result is invariably sustained commitment and a virtuous cycle, with trust leading to great effort, which in turn results in great trust and a higher chance of success" (16). People who feel trusted will be happier, more motivated, and more invested in the results of their work. Building trust in the next generation of library leaders will result in a myriad of positive effects on the profession.

Cultivating new leaders through trust

I attribute my own career growth to library leaders who have trusted me with an array of responsibilities beyond my station. During my second year of library school, I began a position as Special Assistant to the Dean in the Administration Office at the University of Arizona Libraries. I was new to the field and very conscious of being "just a student," so I was surprised when the associate dean, Janice Simmons-Welburn, immediately befriended me. During my first days on the job she showed me the ropes, gave me advice, made sure I met the people I needed to meet, and took time to get to know me. At first I was hesitant. Soon, however, I was flattered, and eventually I became comfortable with the idea that, despite the gulf of experience and knowledge between us, a mere student could be friends with a dean.

As the months passed, our working relationship developed in concert with our friendship. We collaborated on projects and learned each other's working strengths. We also escaped to each other's offices for humor breaks to dispel the stress that occasionally built up. We shared stories about our previous jobs, our families, and our plans for the future. From the beginning of our working relationship, Janice treated me as if we had been colleagues for years; as if we were equals. She helped me when I needed guidance on projects, asked me for help when she needed it, offered advice about my career path, and shared stories about her life and career. She took me into her confidence and shared her ambitions and frustrations and was always available to hear mine.

Just as important, she took the time to learn about my individual skills and talents and put them to work. I had come to libraries after several years of working as an editor, and Janice relied on me to review and wordsmith important administrative documents. We reviewed her e-mail messages together. In addition, as she worked on committees within ACRL, she encouraged me also to participate. From there, the ball has just kept rolling.

At my first ALA Annual Conference, before I had joined any section or committee, I spent the bulk of four days in steamy Chicago just trying to keep my head from spinning. I was overwhelmed by the size of the event and the fact that I didn't yet know what direction my career would take. I had to look up every acronym in the conference guide (repeatedly), and was not sure if I would be welcome at any given committee meeting or discussion group. I observed The Stacks with wide-eyed amazement as groups of librarians with large bags swarmed like dog packs upon the ready vendors. I wandered the conference center halls as if I had just been dropped from outer space and was trying to determine on what planet I had been abandoned. If not for the encouragement of those I worked with, I may not have returned the following year.

> ☑ QUICK TIP
> Becoming involved in professional service makes attending conferences more rewarding and more purposeful.

My second annual conference was the opposite experience. I was a committee member. I started with the University Libraries Section (ULS) of ACRL and kept busy with committee meetings, meals with new people, and other networking opportunities. This time my attendance had a purpose, and I enjoyed the sense of contribution to a larger goal. I was sold. After being a member of the Communications Committee for one year, the chair left for other commitments, I decided to fill the role. After hearing my supervisor, who was also involved in ACRL, speak highly of me, other leaders in ULS began to approach me for committee positions, section projects, and freelance work. I agreed to join a Program Planning Committee, and then found myself stepping up to be co-chair. Because I knew how to build a Web site (no matter how minimal my skills), I was drafted as Webmaster for the Greater Western Library Alliance (GWLA), the ULS Advocacy Toolkit, and even an ALA presidential candidate's campaign.

It all happened so quickly, but I always felt confident and ready for the next step. I realize now that my confidence originated, in large part, from my relationship with Janice. Her implicit trust in my abilities, my knowledge, and my sense of responsibility made me trust myself to fulfill each new demand placed upon me. Whereas before I was merely floating in the world of libraries, I now have purpose, goals, and commitment. Suddenly, the idea of being a dean doesn't sound impossible. Being a department head sounds even more feasible. Although I recognize that I still have much to learn about leadership, I find that I am eager to learn it. Even better, I now have a role model: a library leader who is generous, caring, and professional.

Of course, not every dean or manager needs to develop a personal friendship with their young librarians to cultivate the same effect. However, they *will* need to develop a relationship that involves actively giving trust, even unsolicited, to their younger colleagues. Above all, it means treating them with generosity and respect. "The Golden Rule of managing people is: treat others the way you would want to be treated. When supervising people, it is important to treat them as adults who are capable of making good decisions" (Norton, 2007: 78). When cultivating new leaders, managers can—and should—treat them with even higher expectations. The following five strategies are examples of the infinite number of ways that mangers can give and express trust in new librarians and cultivate their leadership potential.

Creating opportunities for the new librarian

Perhaps the most obvious manner of expressing trust in a new librarian, and probably the most common, is by creating opportunities for the individual to learn new skills, take on new responsibilities, and advance in their work. Everyone at the start of a career path needs to have a door or two opened for them so they can begin to gain experience and build a reputation. Library leaders who want to cultivate leadership qualities among their younger colleagues will need to open those doors by helping them gain appointments to committees and other organized project groups. Providing new librarians with the chance to work with more experienced colleagues on concrete projects is an invaluable contribution to their careers.

> ☑ QUICK TIP
> Creating opportunities for staff to take on more responsibility and new projects is a straightforward mechanism to show trust.

The most significant experience for me, in terms of becoming invested in the field of librarianship, was being appointed to an ACRL section committee while I was still in library school. As a student I was inclined to hover backstage, still a little shy and awaiting my chance to step into the mainstream of library culture. I was content to help others with their work, fulfill my duties as an assistant, and collect knowledge and experience that I could use later. I believed that my chance to get actively involved in librarianship would come *after* graduation, once I had been officially initiated and could show that little piece of paper to anyone who doubted my abilities. Maybe it was my own insecurity coming out, or maybe most library school students share the belief that professional involvement in the field is, well, for the professionals. Regardless, when I heard I would be appointed to a committee, I was very surprised and a bit uncertain. What would others on the committee think about working with someone who was still a student? Would I have anything to contribute?

Of course I did. When I joined ULS's Communications Committee, the chair handed me the reins of the section newsletter, whose editorship had been on the rocks for the previous few years. It was my pleasure and responsibility to bring the newsletter back from the edge of extinction, redesign it, and make sure it actually came out on time each spring and fall. It was a very familiar and comfortable place for a former editor to start in the maze of ACRL committees and groups. Working on the committee gave me a sense of my place in the larger organization, offered me purpose and concrete goals to accomplish, and allowed me to meet and develop relationships with new colleagues. Better yet, it gave me a foothold from which to look out at other opportunities in librarianship and consider, from a slightly more elevated perspective, how else I might like to participate in the field.

Referring the new librarian to others

As I began to grow into my new role on the Communications Committee, my biggest surprise was how quickly other leaders in ULS came to know me. As editor of the newsletter, I attended the Executive Committee meetings at the ALA conferences, and at the first meeting I attended I introduced myself and then remained silent for the rest of the time. Janice took the lead, praising me profusely in front of anyone who would listen, introducing me to her friends and longtime colleagues, convincing me to join them for dinner without any apparent awareness of or concern over the potential awkwardness of such situations. She took it upon herself to make sure I met the people I needed to meet and they met me.

Her efforts paid off; her trust in my abilities seemed contagious. Several librarians I had met through Janice contacted me to help them with other projects. The opportunities presented to me multiplied, and my involvement in the field grew. I was soon on a second ULS committee, held roles as chair and as co-chair, and led various Web site projects. Most recently I was given the honor of creating a Web site for and assisting with the campaign of an ALA presidential candidate. In just a few years, I went from wallflower library student to working with a potential ALA president.

A trusting leader will believe in a new librarian's abilities enough to actively refer him or her to other leaders with the goal of providing the young colleague opportunities for growth, development, and challenges. When colleagues ask for the names of individuals who are available to fill a particular post, help on a project, or take on other tasks, such a leader will not hesitate to name their young colleagues and share their talents, thereby advancing their future in librarianship. From these opportunities, the young librarian will grow in abilities, knowledge, and leadership potential.

Involving the new librarian in high-level brainstorms and projects

In my work on the Web site and campaign of the ALA presidential candidate, and in the case of a second campaign for ACRL president entered into by another respected mentor, I have been somewhat surprised to find myself being consulted on brainstorming language and content for important campaign events and publications. What do I know about the critical national issues in librarianship, after only four years in the field (including schooling)? I was slightly intimidated at first, but soon embraced the excitement of addressing the big questions that my mentors would face in their campaign debates. I felt connected to ALA and ACRL in ways that I had not before. In addition, seeing campaigns for high-level ALA office from backstage stripped the process of its mystery and gave me a larger understanding of the organization and the people who lead it. *Perhaps*, I began to think, *I could be one of them someday*. Perhaps I could even want to.

Perhaps the best way to give people a sense of importance and investment in an organization or project is to involve them in top-level discussions about it. Let them feel that they have a voice in the goals, direction, or management of the project and they will immediately become invested in its purpose and success. This is similar to a strategy advocated by management experts as a means to improve the performance of middle managers in an organization. Top-level managers may find a gap between their perspective and that of the

> ☑ QUICK TIP
> Involve early-career librarians in top-level discussions about issues important to the library.

middle managers—a gap that can be resolved by giving those in the middle a sense of ownership of the organization.

> That can only be done, says Mass Mutual CEO Tom Wheeler, by giving managers more freedom to speak up and participate in solving organizational problems. He says, "I think it is a matter of *bringing them into the loop* so that they feel they can speak their piece in an environment that promotes some risk taking." (Horton and Reid, 1991: 178–179)

In essence, it means giving them a role in the leadership of the organization. This can be easily applied across the board to individuals in any type of organization or project group, including those in libraries and library organizations.

Confiding in the new librarian

For those just entering the library field, it can be difficult to imagine what life at the top is like. A new librarian who has had little interaction with deans, directors, or managers will see only the administrative façade: the manager's public face at staff meetings, the announcement of new rules and directives, the yawning chasm of a large office. A few of these new people may already be thinking that they'd like to see their careers take them to that office someday. But most will not. Most new librarians feel a little intimidated when encountering library leaders and will be nervous about initiating even the most mundane conversations, lest they say something "stupid." They therefore allow an opportunity to slip by that might have expanded their knowledge and understanding of leadership.

The impetus therefore falls upon library leaders who wish to cultivate these new librarians to trust them enough to share some personal stories and give them some insight into what goes on behind the façade. Tell them about the demands of a leader's work: the challenges, successes, and frustrations. Be candid, honest, and, when appropriate, even critical. Invite them to occasionally participate in the personal or social life of a library leader. Allow the new librarian to see that the leader is a regular person, and let them get to know about that person's experience as a leader.

Working in a library administration office and getting to know several library deans at once made a big difference in my perspective on library leadership. Going out to dinners with colleagues at ALA conferences was even more powerful, because it allowed me to see these leaders when they were relaxed, enjoying one another, and having fun. That is not to say that they were in any way less aware of their important roles in the field, but they were taking a break from the demands of those roles. Being invited to share their free time, eat and drink with them, and get to know them on a more personal level helped me believe that eventually I could be "one of them." In truth, I began to feel that I was already halfway there.

Treating the new librarian as an equal

In my interactions with Janice and her peers, I have been pleasantly surprised by the manner in which I have been treated. At the start I was admittedly uncomfortable— a bit nervous and self-aware among librarians with vast experience and important titles. I was a new face among people who had been friends and colleagues for many years. Yet those generous men and women never so much as blinked at my appearance among them. They appeared content to include me in their meals, personal conversations, and jokes. Even when I was a student, they asked me about my projects and showed interest in my thoughts on library issues. They spoke openly about their work, opinions, and ambitions. Among them I gained the sense that, despite my newness to the field, I was already accepted and expected to rise to their level in a few years.

The previous four strategies described in this chapter all culminate in the idea of treating the new librarian as an equal. That involves trusting the new librarian to *act* like an equal, a trust which the great majority will fulfill with pleasure. It can be difficult for a busy dean or director to take the time to include a new employee in discussions about topics about which the new person will have little knowledge. It may be tougher still to make a point of spending personal time with that individual. However, if the goal is to cultivate new library leaders, the most important step in that process is to help the new librarian *feel* like a leader. The skills of leadership can be taught and the knowledge passed on, but the awareness of oneself as a person capable of leading others can be far more elusive. It is also far more important when dealing with a generation that tends to be hesitant about taking on leadership roles.

Treating a new librarian as an equal encompasses the previous four strategies and extends beyond them into various aspects of one's daily demeanor, such as the manner of conversation with the individual and the manner of assigning and reviewing tasks. It means consciously speaking to the new librarian as one who is likely to understand the complicated duties of a leader. It doesn't mean pretending that the younger person has the same role or experience, but simply acknowledging that they will in the future and dealing with them according to that expectation. Perhaps it might be more accurate to advocate not treating them as if they are already professional equals, but treating them as future equals, people whose respect and friendship will be of value in return.

Conclusion

Jan Carlzon, respected former CEO, once observed,

> You can manage an organization by fear, but if you do you will ensure that people don't perform up to their real capabilities. . . . But if you manage people by love—that is, if you show them *respect* and trust—they start to perform up to their real capabilities, because in that kind of atmosphere, they dare to take risks. (Quoted in Lauer, 2005: 24)

This tenet is equally applicable to leadership in general, and to any leader-protégé relationship in which the individual in power wishes to cultivate the potential of the younger individual. Those who have led by fear—in organizations just as in nations—have inevitably been successful only to the point at which their followers have gained enough power to remove them from their leadership role. Leaders who give and inspire trust will be respected long after they have been replaced, and their legacy will be the trail of younger colleagues who have been motivated to follow in their footsteps.

Giving trust to new librarians is not always easy, and it does require effort. It demands a strong concern for the future of the field, a desire to see that future in capable hands, and the wish to contribute to that future long after one's own retirement. Above all, it demands the constant cultivation of each new leader through the five strategies described in this chapter as well as other, similar strategies that will contribute to their skills and knowledge, provide them with networking opportunities, and imbue them with self-confidence and ambition. Based upon my experience as a developing leader, I consider the strategies presented in this chapter as the primary principles for cultivating new library leaders. However, creative leaders will find additional ways to cultivate new leaders through trust, possibly on a daily basis as circumstances change and new opportunities arise.

The philosophy behind the strategies presented is one based upon simple human nature. Experienced library leaders often forget what it's like to be new to the field, as they are far removed from their first days as librarians. It is natural that this will happen. Those leaders who hold on to those memories and remember the path they followed to the top, including the contributions of those individuals who played a role in their professional development, will be more successful in their efforts to do the same for others.

Cultivating new leaders is not scientific or formulaic; each individual has different needs and different strengths and weaknesses that need to be addressed in order for him or her to advance in a career. For instance, new librarians such as me, who fit into the characteristics of Generation X, will need to be shown how leadership can fit into a balanced lifestyle. We don't need to be convinced or argued with; we just want to see models of how to simultaneously be happy and successful. Many good examples can be found among current library leaders who enjoy their work and share that enjoyment with those around them. New librarians with other values or characteristics will want to know how they fit into leadership as well. Current leaders can address those issues simply by getting to know their younger colleagues' opinions, hopes, and ambitions.

During the past four years, I have evolved from an uninitiated library school student to a first-year academic librarian with the ambition to achieve and become a leader in my field. Already I am chairing committees and participating in a leadership training program to work toward those goals. I am thirty-one years old, and a few of my colleagues still refer to me as "a child," but there is nothing immature in my perspective, my skills, or my sense of confidence. I am always aware that a number of library leaders whom I respect trust me to fill their shoes someday. Every year they present me with expanded opportunities, greater responsibilities, and a range of new ways to learn and grow into the role of a leader.

Trust alone will not create a library leader out of a first-year librarian. Combined with the strategies above, however, it will go a long way toward inspiring younger colleagues to step up to more demanding roles in the field and will provide them with the skills and ability to do so. To a certain extent, we are all driven for better or worse by those around us. New librarians who are treated with confidence *will* be confident. New librarians who are challenged to achieve *will* achieve. New librarians who are trusted to accomplish great things *will* accomplish great things.

References

Bibb, Sally, and Jeremy Kourdi. 2004. *Trust Matters: For Organizational and Personal Success.* New York: Palgrave MacMillan.

Horton, Thomas R., and Peter C. Reid. 1991. *Beyond the Trust Gap: Forging a New Partnership Between Managers and Their Employers.* Homewood, IL: Business One Irwin.

Lancaster, Lynne C., and David Stillman. 2006. "If I Pass the Baton, Who Will Grab It? Creating Bench Strength in Public Management." *Government Finance Review* 22, no. 4: 34–41.

Lauer, Charles S. 2005. "The Mark of a Leader." *Modern Healthcare* 35, no. 25: 24.

Meredith, Geoffrey E., Charles D. Schewe, and Alexander Hiam, with Janice Karlovich. 2002. *Managing by Defining Moments.* New York: Hungry Minds, Inc.

Norton, Lee. 2007. "Be a Good Boss." *Canadian Consulting Engineer* 48, no. 6: 78–83.

Rousseau, D. M., Sitkin, S. B., Burt, R., and Camerer, C. 1998. "Not So Different After All: A Cross-Disciplinary View of Trust." *Academy of Management Review* 23: 1–12.

CHAPTER 4

coaching from the ground up:
building goal-oriented relationships

Scott Collard

Remember when you were a kid? You were involved in many different activities. For me it was swimming classes, music lessons, soccer practice, and so on. You might have looked forward to them (or not) in different ways, and you might have learned different kinds of skills and values from them, but they were nearly ubiquitous, at least in my life. I measured summer by the time it took to learn the breaststroke; fall, by the time spent learning how to play defender instead of midfield; an entire year, by the time involved in making the transition from playing concert snare to drum set. I now know how to do all those things pretty well. I worked at it for a while and came out on the other side with a skill set that allowed me to move to the next level—to learn the next swimming stroke, to pick up another instrument a few years later, etc. In retrospect, it seems natural—not always easy, but part of learning, growing up, and progressing. Now in my adult life, in my adult job, I can't help but wonder: What made those experiences and skills stick? What made their acquisition so successful? And, what do they all have in common? The answer: *Coaches.*

That's right: the people—more experienced, more skilled at the activity in question—who guided you toward improvement, showed you how to advance, how to erase your bad habits, and how to, if not always excel, at least become better than before. They may not always be called "coaches" (my music teachers probably would've rolled their eyes at that label), but they all do the work of a coach: they help you acquire a clearly delineated set of competencies, through regular focused interactions, in an understood and finite amount of time. They had the knowledge that you needed to succeed, and they transmitted that knowledge to you in ways that made it (somewhat) easy to learn, apply, and build on.

Now, in my very adult life, I look around and wonder: Where have all the coaches gone? I'm not talking about those things we do for our own edification at the end of the workday; we still take our music lessons, learn to speak a new language, and so on. I mean right here, right now, at work, *where are the coaches*? When, during my day, for example, do I meet with that master collection development librarian and absorb his or her skills? Where do I find that person to walk me through a large software implementation start to finish, so that I can, if not set up one on my own, at least talk intelligently about it? How do I structure my relationship with that talented manager so that I not only work for him or her but also learn to become a better manager myself?

Where are the coaches? might seem an odd question, but as our jobs become more wide-ranging, more technologically complex, and more fast-paced, it is the one we should be asking. I learned this when, a few years ago, I took part in a prototype coaching program that remains one of the most valuable learning experiences I have had since I became a librarian.

Introduction to the coaching process

You may say, "But we have mentoring relationships," and that is true. We're pretty good in the library world at developing long-lasting relationships that can serve as touchstones throughout our career, give advice, connect us with other people, and get us through bad spots. We even enshrine these relationships by making mentoring committees at our libraries, or assigning new employees a mentor. Obviously, we see the need for the kinds of structures that help more junior members succeed (although the efficacy of "assigning" a mentor honestly escapes me). But what I would suggest is that these relationships are not the end all of the desired structure. Not by a long shot. In many cases, they may be too dependent on other factors such as personality, geographic distance, or the participants' areas of expertise to be effective. More often what we really need is someone who knows a lot about a particular topic or task who can work through a problem or interest with us over a short time span, after which we can tackle the situation with newfound skills. We may again turn to that person for advice in the future, but that also might be the end of the relationship; the skills transmitted, we move on.

My own coaching experience began when I was accepted to the Teach Model Coach (TMC) program via the Chicago Library System (now the Metropolitan Library System), the interlibrary coordinating and learning organization for libraries in the Chicago area. As a prototype, grant-funded project, Teach Model Coach was designed to take the precepts of the coaching movement and apply them in a library setting, with a special focus on transmitting the wisdom and leadership skills of more experienced librarians to those newer to the profession. The basic outline of the program was simple on paper: junior librarians and paraprofessionals applied to the program with a specific problem, topic, or issue that they wanted help with, while more senior, and even retired, librarians applied to become coaches in the program by enumerating their strengths, skills, and interests. Paired coaches and learners, once selected and matched, would work together intensively on the proposed issue for a three-month span. After a fairly rigorous review and interview process (particularly for the more senior librarians) the program director, Kathryn Deiss, and her colleagues began to winnow the pools of applicants, carefully matching coaches with learners. Because of the scale of the undertaking (about 30 matched pairs participated), this was an intensive undertaking, and the directors worked very hard to find pairings that would be mutually beneficial and satisfying. At the end of the process, both coaches and learners would report back with outcomes from their meetings and qualitative analyses of the program.

Once selected, both groups underwent an initial training period. For the learners, this training was a simple one-day workshop designed to tell us what to expect from the program and what our role in it would be. We did quite a bit of talking and thinking about what it means to enter into this kind of relationship, and why and how it might help us solve the particular issues we each had enumerated. Most important, we explored the ways in which we could effectively elucidate our goals for our coaches, and provide them with the kind of background, feedback, and context that would help them understand what we hoped and needed to get from our pairings once we finally met. We topped some of this very concrete work off with some more playful activities designed to spur creative thinking and processes.

For the coaches, the training was more demanding. It required an initial three-day immersive institute designed to make well-versed, solid coaches out of the participants, and to impart a "toolbox" that they would use to help their learners work through their chosen topics. Halfway through the first year, the coaches met for another day of training, and at the end of the year they participated in a two-day capstone learning event. Although obviously I was not present at the coaches' sessions, my own coach later told me that she came away with a concrete, yet nuanced, way of thinking about her role in the program. Coaches learned that they shouldn't simply tell a learner what to do, but rather help the learner be able to do it; they must not really give advice, but help the learner "practice" skills and modes of thinking that would be helpful. In other words, it was very similar to learning that new instrument. Through this session, coaches learned (in truth, they, too, were coached) how to help their learners get there on their own, and thus truly meet their goals on their own terms. (See Exhibit 4.1 for more on what coaches learned.) My coach frequently expressed to me how surprised she was at what she learned in the sessions, and of the high value of the skills she acquired.

At the end of all of the preliminary training it was finally time to meet our coaches. The other learners in the program shared both my excitement and trepidation at meeting the people with whom we had been matched. I later learned the same was true for many of the coaches. We were invested in the project by this point, and really very hopeful for using it to achieve the goals we had set for ourselves. The bar was set pretty high. My worries proved unfounded as, within about the first ten minutes of conversation, I understood that the process had worked and the right

Exhibit 4.1. Interview with Kathryn Deiss, Project Coordinator

How did you originally get the idea for creating a program based around the precepts of coaching?

Alice Calabrese, the Executive Director of the then Chicago Library System, a multitype system serving hundreds of libraries in Chicago, wanted to tap the knowledge and wisdom of professionals on the verge of retirement or actually retired. I began thinking about what they could bring to others and thought of coaching specifically because there are many mentoring programs and coaching could provide assistance with actual work content and growth in a professional or paraprofessional position. I had had experience with the curricular material related to coaching while at the Association of Research Libraries (ARL) so had that experience to draw upon.

Can you describe the general qualities and skills that an ideal coach would strive to have?

In the Teach Model Coach Program, a very strong emphasis was placed on coaching as a helping relationship. This means that the skills of asking questions and helping the learner find their own way and come to their own conclusions are primary. Effective listening skills, the ability to not appropriate problems, the ability to guide without telling the learner what to do, and a strong conceptual and practical foundation in the principles of consulting were the key areas of skill and knowledge development. Finally, for me, the biggest asset for a coach is the ability to be present and in the service of their learner—to not fall prey to one's own ego nor to the distractions that can interrupt dialogue.

What do you think makes coaching a good option for nurturing newer librarians?

I think anyone at any level and at any point in their career can benefit from effective coaching. Newer librarians may have had other careers and typically have rich life experience upon which to draw so the premise of coaching newer librarians should not be to "train" them but to provide them with assistance from someone whose only interest is that newer librarian. For me the strongest benefits of effective coaching have to do with the development of independence, self-awareness and reflection, and confidence in one's own ability to sort out questions, challenges, and opportunities.

What advice would you give to library administrators who might want to try out a coaching model in their organization?

I would love to see coaching more prevalent in all types of libraries. It is important for administrators to understand that experience alone does not make an effective coach. Coaching is a discipline in and of itself and requires training, reflection, and practice just as any other discipline does. So firstly I would say be ready to invest in the development of coaches. Secondly, slow down and carefully structure how you are going to offer coaching. For instance, is this going to be a program where

(cont'd.)

Exhibit 4.1. Interview with Kathryn Deiss, Project Coordinator *(continued)*

---

people find one another or where the HR department or some other group helps create the pairs? How will you create a program that is not too controlling—because over-control is in opposition to the concepts of the helping relationship and effective coaching? It is possible to share the coaching concept across several institutions so that learners may have access to a coach not at their institution; this helps release some of the political tensions and power relationships that could exist between people who work for the same organization. Though, to be clear, effective coaching within one organization is certainly possible. It just requires good training of coaches and learners and the development of an ethos and philosophy that drives the program.

If people wanted to read one good work on coaching, what would you recommend?
This is so easy for me because I do have a favorite coaching book. It is *Coaching: Evoking Excellence in Others* by James Flaherty. There are many, many good books on coaching and books that provide neat tools and processes. Flaherty's book is simply fundamental for me because it assumes the learner or person being coached is a strong, intelligent adult and the philosophy is one of support but not control. It is entirely in keeping with the concepts of the helping relationship. That said, I have dozens of coaching books on my bookshelf that I draw upon for different needs. But Flaherty is my "go-to" guy!

---

coach had been selected. Not only did we get along personally, but she seemed to share many of my desires and goals in terms of work, and, most important, she tried to create and sustain a kind a certain "can-do" perspective about the process that helped to keep my goals front and center. The match had been made, and the real work could begin.

Walking through the coaching process

We very quickly got down to business. We arranged a weekly schedule that set aside meeting time as well as time to work individually on my central problem (which in my case had to do with learning how to better create and sustain momentum for new projects, given my relatively low level in the organization). Because of the clearly delineated time frame, we knew that our meetings needed to be fairly intensive and frequent, so we usually spent about two to three hours per week in meeting, and another hour or so in individual activities. We met outside of our library settings, instead opting for a location (in our case, a nearby coffee shop) where we could feel unrestrained by our usual day-to-day responsibilities and work without interruption. This core meeting schedule was one of the main keys to the success of the program for me and my coach. Having a designated place and time to work together made a massive difference. As a newer librarian, learning to balance a portfolio of new duties with the need for reflection *and* the desire to continue educating oneself can be a daunting task. This process created enforced reflection and growth time, devoted to picking up things that I had missed, filling in holes in knowledge, and most important, analyzing my own assumptions and preconceptions about my work. Moreover, being outside of my usual routines and spaces freed me to think of novel approaches and solutions.

> ☑ QUICK TIP
> Including time for reflection and growth is a crucial and often neglected step in the development of a new librarian as leader.

To further our work, we also designed a set of mini "assignments"—"thought experiments" actually—to help guide me through my process of exploration. These assignments I completed on my own for discussion or revisiting at the next meeting. The assignments generally emerged directly from the discussions of one of our meetings, and included a range of activities, from the familiar and standard literature review, to more open-ended writing, to very concrete goal- and plan-development work. Most important, these assignments were conceived of in the close consultation of the meeting; during our conversations, when we discovered an interesting or seemingly fruitful avenue, we would collaborate on creating an assignment to help explore it further. In fact, most of the time, this collaboration would reveal that my coach also needed an assignment, be it further mulling over a topic, bringing some useful materials to our next meeting, or reading up on an issue. This made both coach and learner responsible for the continued learning in the relationship, and made the course of the work highly dynamic and creative.

One of the most striking aspects of our work together was how it worked on both explicit and implicit levels. That is to say, on one side, we had the explicitly stated goals that formed the basis of my application and project. Every week we would progress further toward meeting these goals and fulfilling our work. However, almost more important were the *implicit* aspects of our sessions. My coach's leadership style was different from many others I had experienced (again, probably thanks to the care with which we were matched), and observing an alternate way of thinking about the role of leadership, of motivating colleagues, and of setting priorities was extraordinarily eye-opening. Looking back, this was partly a function of my coach, to be sure, but it is also intrinsic to the role of the true coach.

Because coaching is designed as an exercise in *practice*, rather than one focused on advice or hierarchical maintenance, good coaches display a style that is open, responsive to the learner, and, to a great extent, selfless. This "selfless" leadership style illustrates perfectly what many institutions seem to struggle to understand: If you give your staff room to grow, decide, and innovate, and let them practice these skills, you create more dynamic interactions and more dynamic librarians. In the end, my coach, and the coaching itself, exemplified a leadership model—open, flexible, problem-oriented, and highly collaborative—that should be the

> ☑ QUICK TIP
> Openness and flexibility—almost to the point of selflessness—are vital characteristics for coaches to maintain.

basic requirement of leading and excelling in an environment of disruptive and constant change.

Why coaching works when other programs fail

Looking back on the experience (and reentering my reflective learner zone) makes me want to take stock of exactly what made the program so effective for me. I tend to come back to a number of themes, and although I really have only myself to judge by, I think that many of these themes would hold true for other participants.

The first, and possibly most important, aspect is that it is a *goal-oriented process*. Because coach and learner both know, from the first meeting, what the goal of the sessions will be and what the expectations on the part of the learner are, this program is a very efficient way to acquire new skills and knowledge. A good coaching relationship can span a flexible time period, allowing for work to begin and end appropriately, depending upon the progress of the sessions. Moreover, because the goals and understandings are set at the outset, course correction becomes very easy. The relationship exists expressly to deal with the goals at hand and can be easily reined in or refocused in the course of the work. In a world where we frequently find ourselves at the helm of more and more projects that seem to continue ad infinitum, it is extremely gratifying to know that this project will begin at the point of need, continue until it has served its purpose, and *then stop*.

Indeed, coming into the environment of the modern library, I remember feeling like every day brought a new project, a new undertaking, a new service. I don't think I am alone in this feeling, and it is only enhanced by the suspicion that as a newly minted librarian, you might be instantly seen as the go-to resource for all things technological. Flattering as it is to be needed and wanted for your skills (actual or not), what gets lost in that tumult of continuous growth is *dedicated time for reflection*. We may not have the space or the energy to sit back and enjoy our progress, much less try to think about priorities and direction. The coaching relationship is predicated on this very notion: we build into our work structures and processes that help us refine and refocus our thinking. Moreover, because the coaching relationship is by its nature devoted to a clearly defined goal, it can be extremely helpful in understanding what, in a project or in your own approach, just isn't working. We tend to continuously add to our work "plates," and we jettison projects (not to mention behaviors) only rarely, so having a way to identify what needs to go or change becomes a valuable asset.

> ☑ QUICK TIP
> Coaching is about building reflection and refinement into the day-to-day work process.

Of course, the other side effect of this continual accretion of projects that many new librarians might feel is a loss of *space to focus*. In fact, the built-in, logical conclusion of creating a well-defined, goal-oriented process that assumes time for reflection is heightened focus (that is, Goals × Time = Focus). The chance to drill down into one thing I do—without e-mail, without the other projects, without going to the desk or teaching a class—created an almost Zen-like state that is often missing in our usual hubbub. In addition, the focus that it allowed for my project at hand had side benefits as well: I knew that no matter what, when I got to Friday at 2:00, I would be working on my learner's work and only my learner's work, so I put that time aside guilt-free for the rest of the week. It meant that when I encountered something useful or relevant to my learner's work during the week, I had a convenient mental "box" in which to file it away. I could then revisit it on Friday. Last, it provided me a model to follow for those non-learner projects for which I knew some concentration was key, but for which I struggled to find the time and space to dig deep.

One aspect of the process that I was particularly eager to benefit from was the chance to *build on one's professional network*. Because the Teach Model Coach program was a multi-institutional effort, learners were paired with others outside of their institutions. We all know the value of getting a different perspective in our professional lives, and, as expected, taking advantage of a distinct voice was very useful. In my case, in which learning to navigate some of the intricacies of my organization was the goal, the neutral observer was obviously key. But our rapport provided me with new perspectives on other fronts, too, and gave me an outlet to explore my project with a less confined perspective. I could see other styles of leadership, other ways of doing things, and other modes of working that could be explored. I also think the chance to see outside of my own somewhat delimited world strengthened my commitment and connection to the profession. If "every organization is unhappy in its own way" (to heavily paraphrase Mr. Tolstoy), it was great to see that those aspects of my own institution that I didn't like could be different, or better, or improved upon, and that I could apply that knowledge in my current position and those to come.

The final reason that the coaching program worked for me is different in nature, having more to do with my conceptions of the workplace and organizational culture. Much has been written of the *different expectations many newer librarians bring to their work environments* (more fluid career paths, greater variation in work structures, no "cradle-to-grave" employment, etc.), and coaching seems to be an ideal way to acknowledge and embrace these expectations. Because coach-learner relationships are by their nature short-term and goal-oriented, they give librarians a way to enhance skills and create that desired fluidity and flexibility. They also can give organizations a way to keep their staff interested, keep them learning, and harness their energy and skills for the good of the organization. Imagine if an organization's newer employees were constantly acquiring valuable skills and work methods, bringing them back into the organization, and using them to help pursue the library mission. Further, imagine the goodwill

> ☑ QUICK TIP
> Not only is coaching beneficial to the individuals involved, but it can significantly impact the organization.

(and, one hopes, commitment to the organization) that sponsoring such an activity would create in those librarians searching for organizational kismet. Coaching, then—particularly via inter-institutional structures (more on this topic later)—can be a boon to the librarian, but more importantly, a catalyst for great change and advancement when harnessed by the organization.

How to implement a coaching program

So what can other organizations learn from this experience? What can they take into their own settings and to their own employees? How can they, in essence, "get coaching"? Replicating the experience that I had would require some work and coordination, but coaching can also start on smaller levels than the full-blown, grant-funded experience that I had. Keeping in mind a handful of specifics, and opening your organization to the possibilities created by more involved models further down the road, would pay dividends. Some of these are easier, and some will require more investment, but the short list of requirements would include the following:

1. *Start your program and get training.* Copious books and articles focus on initiating a coaching program and creating training opportunities for your coaches-to-be, some from the business world and some directly related to the library world (see the Further Reading section at the end of this chapter), but there is no substitute for some truly in-depth training. Once you have dedicated your organization to the concept of starting a coaching program, find out what options are available to build up the coaching skills of your first crop of coaches. Some library organizations (like ACRL, ARL, ALA, and others) will contract for coach training, as do some larger library systems, and many skilled facilitators will bring training to you (for a cost, of course). Explore the possibility of training a core group of implementers who can take coaching global at your institution, and offer opportunities to involve those in supervisory roles so that they may incorporate coaching into their repertoire of management skills.
2. *Clearly define what your coaching program is, and what it is not.* Don't let people confuse coaching with mentoring. They are distinct processes and use different tools and approaches, and librarians who may want to explore an alternative to the mentoring relationships they already have might find coaching appealing. (Of course, I think this goes doubly true for many newer librarians.) With a clear understanding of what kinds of skills and training can be acquired through the coaching process (and how the process differs from and complements the mentoring relationship), members of your institution will start finding more and more ways to use it. (See Exhibit 4.2 for differences between coaching and mentoring.)
3. *Set aside the time and space for coaching opportunities.* This is probably the single most important thing to do; without it, we have no room for the creative, deep processes that coaching can create. Whether it is an ongoing, formal library program, an application-based model, a tenure/promotion requirement, or simply a Friday morning scheduled block, the coaching program needs time and space to grow and function. Consider adding the planning, implementation, and marketing of the program to the bailiwick of your staff development committee (if you have one) and begin to create a pool of coaching expertise within your organization.

Exhibit 4.2. Coaching versus mentoring

Coaching and mentoring are closely related. Indeed, both relationships interrelate and may even be used for similar situations. Where they differ, however, is in their processes and structures. How do you know which kind of relationship is which? Here is a brief encapsulation of some of the most important differences:

MENTORING IS...	COACHING IS...
An ongoing relationship	A finite relationship
Broadly ranging on many topics or issues	Focused on a single goal or task
A relationship defined by participants	Often facilitated through third parties
Informal and sporadic in terms of meeting	Structured with a regularized meeting schedule
Focused on advice and guidance to the individual	Focused on skills and performance of the individual

---

4. *Pick coaches and learners with care (at least at first).* The coaching relationship won't work without committed coaches and learners. Creating and then sustaining this special relationship requires not only a certain set of skills and understanding, but also a definite mind-set. A certain selflessness on the part of the coach is necessary; above all, coaches need to be mindful of not acting for their own ego, to prove they're right, or to enforce their mode of work on their learner. Rather, coaches should act as co-conspirators in helping the learner formulate a problem statement, work through an approach, and reach his or her goals. At the same time, learners need to bring a focus and desire to the relationship, as it is their energy that moves the process forward; they must also be ready to examine their preconceptions honestly and challenge their own modes of work. Most important, both individuals must bring an open-mindedness and spirit of discovery to the process.

5. *Work on goals, not advice.* Remember: This is a temporary arrangement, designed to be deployed until it is no longer useful. The purpose is to help the learner fulfill the goal at hand, rather than to tell him or her what to do. Advice doesn't necessarily create the learning that a coach should strive for; helping the learner figure it out on his or her own (giving the learner time to "practice," that is) does. This is the most difficult distinction to make and the hardest thing about being a coach, which is why to be most effective, the organization should find ways to get participants the training they need.

6. *Consider partnering with other institutions.* Coaching can be made extra effective by allowing your staff to take advantage of wider resource networks. If you belong to a consortium or local library community, think about convening a group of interested individuals from across your organizations to get the ball rolling (and split the cost of the coach training you got in number 4). This inter-institutional cohort can steer the program and match learners and coaches across

the spectrum. Learners will have a better chance at learning skills that might not exist at your institution, and they can in turn bring these skills home to your advantage. Because the program is designed and clearly understood to be about short-term skills training, you don't have to worry about participants creeping too far outside of the program, and you have a way of generating beneficial activity and goodwill. Last, remember that there is often an eager group of solo librarians out there in the corporate and special library world, and many of these librarians may possess unique and valuable skill sets as well as the desire to interact with their peers outside. Tap into the offerings of your library system that are aimed at these professionals.

Learner's lessons

My Teach Model Coach experience is already four years past, but I come back to certain lessons regularly, lessons that have permanently changed the way I approach my work. First and foremost among these are, of course, those skills that we worked on explicitly in our session. Better understanding how to navigate organizational structures, how to create buy-in, how to move a project forward—these are skills that I have leaned on heavily as I have moved forward in my career, and all are facets of my original TMC project. My coach helped me understand the need to step back and question the assumptions and perceptions I bring to a project, and try harder to, in the words of Peter Senge, "balance advocacy with inquiry." She also helped me think through what it means to bring a group together around a project, and what it takes to harness that group's collective and collaborative energies and strengths to improve the outcome. In addition, her insight into how to recognize and nurture teams involved in focused and nascent projects (the "Hot Groups" that can help create innovation in organizations) was useful by helping elucidate what I (as a frequent Hot Group member) could do to take my projects to the next step; and also by illustrating what I (as an administrator in the future) would do likewise to nurture this vital development space. Although I was not made an instant expert on the intricacies of navigating this difficult leadership terrain, without the TMC work to draw on, I know I would be far more vexed.

However, as I alluded to before, the experience also provided a host of implicit lessons. Chief among those lessons was just seeing the aforementioned style of leadership that is engendered by the coaching relationship. The more facilitative style of interaction made me aware of the power of allowing work to cohere through co-exploration and open discussion. The questioning-rather-than-telling approach used in the coaching relationship can help inform decision making when dealing with diverse expertise and know-how. In addition, the importance of creating spaces and time for focused work, as well as for more exploratory, playful work, cannot be overstated. Having an umbrella of shelter from day-to-day tasks and necessities under which one can explore and reflect is a key to creating (and keeping) energetic and innovative staff, and is one element in creating the kind of "learning organization" that libraries desire themselves to be. Indeed, it is no mistake that so many of my explicit *and* implicit lessons learned are centered on learning new, more open and learning-focused ways of working; coaching is at its heart an open process, and using it tends to highlight these modes, tends to make one a "true believer."

Last, a number of things that I took away from the experience are specifically about the coaching model itself (see the previous section). To me, these are the bread and butter of what makes coaching work: the intensity of time and goals (what I like to call *memento momentum*); the focus on the efficacy of personal practice; and the selfless exchange of ideas and questions between coach and learner. Seeing how these facets of coaching produced results made me understand the usefulness of creating an open framework that is built to be flexible, but also built to autocorrect and change course appropriately and quickly. Although I haven't gotten to formally coach, I can and do use some of these very techniques in other settings, and find them very effective. I have had many formal (re)learning opportunities in the library world, but this is the only one that really made me stop, step back, and really come at my development in fresh ways.

Coaching is not a silver bullet. It will not teach all skills, or fix all organizational woes, or create the perfect staff of 100 percent-innovative go-getters. It is, however, a useful discipline for helping to create the kinds of organizations that libraries need to become to stay relevant and vital, and to attract and retain the kind of people that ensure that vitality. A coaching program means that your staff learning activities can meet the needs, styles, and desires of almost anyone in the organization, as long as a coach can be found for them. Surely, it is but one tool of many, but a tool that when used puts us in the good company of some of the most innovative and interesting companies and institutions in the world. Any tool that does that deserves a closer look.

Further reading

There is an overwhelming amount of coaching literature in the business and executive training world. Here are a few suggestions for some of the highlights of that literature, as well as some applications directly to the library world. For a more comprehensive look at what is available, see the first item on the list.

Douglas, Christina A., and William H. Morley. 2000. *Executive Coaching: An Annotated Bibliography*. Greensboro, NC: Center for Creative Leadership.

Flaherty, James. 1998. *Coaching: Evoking Excellence in Others*. Boston: Butterworth-Heinemann.

Hunt, Karen. 2003. "Executive Coaching: Application to Library Management, Reference, and Instruction." In *Managing Library Instruction Programs in Academic Libraries: Selected Papers Presented at the Twenty-Ninth National LOEX Library Instruction Conference*, edited by Julia K. Nims and Eric Owens, 91–96. Ann Arbor, MI: Pierian Press.

Lubans, John. 2005. "Coaching: A Musical Illustration." *Library Administration & Management* 19, no. 4: 206–208.

Lubans, John, Jr. 2006. "Coaching for Results." *Library Administration & Management* 20, no. 2: 86–89.

Rogers, Jennifer. 2004. *Coaching Skills: A Handbook*. Maidenhead, Berkshire: Open University Press.

Senge, Peter M. 2006. *The Fifth Discipline: The Art and Practice of the Learning Organization.* New York: Doubleday/Currency.

Sheppard, Blair H. 2006. *Coaching and Feedback for Performance.* Chicago, IL: Dearborn Trade.

Voyles, Jeanne F., and Carol A. Friesen. 2001. "Coaching for Results." In *Staff Development: A Practical Guide,* edited by Elizabeth Fuseler Avery, Terry Dahlin, and Deborah A. Carver, 98–100. Chicago: American Library Association.

Whitworth, Laura. 2007. *Co-Active Coaching: New Skills for Coaching People Toward Success in Work and Life.* 2nd ed. Mountain View, CA: Davies-Black Pub.

CHAPTER 5

mentoring new librarians: the good, the bad, and the ugly

Antonia Olivas

According to the Association of College & Research Libraries' Ad Hoc Task Force on Recruitment and Retention Issues (2002), a significant percentage of librarians plan to retire in the next decade and the number of MLIS graduates is declining; therefore, retaining current librarians is extremely important: "Such individuals not only need to be retained, but also need to be mentored, coached, and developed for future leadership roles in the academic library community" (16). With 45 percent of today's librarians possibly retiring by the year 2010 (Lynch, Tordella, and Godfrey, 2004: 28), the new leaders of tomorrow need your expert advice and guidance today in order to ensure longevity and success in the profession you helped cultivate.

For years American libraries have been recruiting new librarians to the profession, but retention efforts have fallen short. In "The Five Year Itch: Are Libraries Losing Their Most Valuable Resources?," Markgren and colleagues (2007) note that exactly 50 percent of the new librarians they polled admitted they have thought of leaving the profession. Too many early career librarians do not have the right mentor (or any mentor at all) to provide encouragement and supportive feedback when they need it most. Unfortunately, they are usually the ones who have a difficult time dealing with the stresses and demands of their new jobs, and who eventually leave the profession altogether. The authors of "The Five Year Itch" also note that 57.9 percent of new librarians agree that libraries are generally welcoming environments, but many of those same librarians have said that "it takes huge doses of openness and affirmation [from their leaders] to overcome . . . feelings of being overwhelmed, underappreciated, disillusioned and underpaid" (Newhouse and Spisak, 2004: 44).

Think back to your first days as a new librarian. Did you have anyone who helped you along the way? Did having a knowledgeable guide to lead you through the maze of your first career steps provide some comfort and assurance? You gradually began to feel comfortable in your new career and felt a little more confident in your journey. Over time you probably began to possess some of the same professional qualities and ethics you admired so much in your mentor(s). You chose to carry on their legacy in the quality of your work performance and are now a successful leader yourself. You now have the opportunity to offer the same gift to someone else. What a great way to honor the mentors who chose to invest so much faith and time in you!

In researching different mentoring strategies, I came across a book called *Be Your Own Mentor* by Sheila Wellington and Betty Spence (2001). In it, the authors claim to reveal helpful secrets of success, and the publisher goes so far as to call it a "mentor-in-a-book." Interesting concept, but it's just not that easy. Mentors cannot be found in a book because a book can't create and nurture relationships. Nothing can replace human compassion and understanding.

Naturally, we can do certain things for ourselves (after all, we are resourceful professionals), but new librarians need all the help they can get. Thanks to constant technological advances, high patron expectations, and the changing social climate of the world today, librarians face more stress than ever. They need someone who will tell them that what they are feeling is normal when they express doubts and fears. They need someone who will show them that becoming a good librarian is a journey that takes time, patience, and much practice.

As librarians we are trained to find the most useful tools and resources to help our patrons get what they need. Numerous studies and success stories have proven that mentors are one of the most valuable information tools that *we* need for ourselves. Mentors not only serve as guides and cheerleaders; they are important institutional resources valuable to any new librarian's career.

I hope that this chapter will convince veteran librarians to take a more active role in shaping the future of our profession. However, choosing to become a mentor is not a decision to take lightly. This is why I decided to discuss what did (and didn't) work best for me in my own experiences with mentors and mentoring programs. No single book can fully replace the special relationship between you and your mentee, but the ideas presented in this chapter should help you to develop and nurture your own mentoring relationships. Not all of the ideas discussed here will work for everyone, but you should feel free to take what speaks clearly to you and build on that. Whether you find yourself in a formal mentoring program or you naturally gravitate toward new librarians in an informal setting, know that the time and effort you devote to these individuals benefit both you and your library's productivity (Burns, 2004: 32).

Elements of a successful formal mentoring program

Whether you are thinking of putting together a mentoring program from scratch or you're trying to revitalize a program that isn't working very well, consider the following suggestions and conduct further research on the subject before you follow through with all of your best intentions. Much of the literature discusses the importance of "buy-in." That means that the key element for your program's success is to make sure that library administrators and potential mentoring librarians are enthusiastic and sincere about the program. If they don't endorse it wholeheartedly, the program will fail miserably.

> ☑ QUICK TIP
> No mentoring program can make up for a lack of enthusiastic, sincere participants.

Administrators need to see the bottom line. How will a mentoring program benefit *their* library? I would suggest creating a sound business plan that shows not only your potential for productivity but also your estimated retention numbers of new librarians who join your organization. Library leaders want to keep turnover rates low because training new employees is both a time- and a money-consuming project they can't afford to keep repeating. Show that you can keep spending down by retaining new hires and that will help your case immensely.

Next, study programs at other institutions (not just libraries) that have formal mentoring programs already established. What are they doing that works? What specifically isn't working (and how would you improve it)? Explain clearly what will you do differently, and what will make your program special from other mentoring programs. Administrators and participants need to know they aren't just falling into "another mentoring program," because many of them may have already been through one that didn't work so well. Change their minds! Get those skeptics on your side and they will be your best allies when implementing your program.

After your administrators accept your proposal, and you've identified new librarians who would like to participate in your program, you need to put together a list of potential mentors. You may not get very many candidates if you simply ask for volunteers (who wants to volunteer for extra work?), but you will get a better pool of candidates if you ask for nominations from your staff. After all, these are people who work together on a daily basis and know one another's quality of work. Peers are more likely to nominate well-qualified candidates who may otherwise be too modest to volunteer themselves (Burns, 2004). A word of caution: Make sure to ask the nominated candidates if they are willing

> ☑ QUICK TIP
> Instead of asking for volunteers, consider soliciting nominations for those who would make great mentors among your librarians.

to participate in your mentoring program before you match them with new librarians. A candidate's time and talents are precious and should be respected. They need to have the final say regarding whether they want to take on the additional responsibilities of being a mentor. Remember that you want only the best people for this important job. People who are forced into the position will only breed resentment and could possibly sabotage your mentoring program.

If you're still having trouble finding qualified candidates, consider giving incentives for people who participate, but never punish your staff for not taking part in your program. The mentors you bring on board deserve positive recognition for their leadership roles (Burns, 2004). Involvement should always be voluntary and incentives for participating as a mentor should not be seen as bribery. For example, you could offer release time from some regular duties or provide extra development training to a person devoting his or her time to a new librarian. Never offer cash incentives; it may attract the wrong crowd to your pool of candidates. Mentors who participate in your program should have the best interest of new librarians at heart—not their own pocketbooks.

> ☑ QUICK TIP
> Incentives and rewards for acting as a mentor can have the opposite effect of replacing or shadowing the true and inherent value of being a mentor.

Once you have enlisted potential mentors, you will want to make the best matches possible for all participants. The new librarian and the mentor should have similar professional *and* personal interests. You will likely never find a "perfect match," but both parties need to feel comfortable and safe with each other in order for the mentorship to be successful. If a new librarian is stuck with someone he or she doesn't feel a connection with, it altogether defeats the purpose of establishing the mentorship. Give mentors and mentees a chance to provide feedback on each other and periodically evaluate the effectiveness of their mentorships. If a match is not working for either one of the participants, provide alternative mentorships, if possible.

Finally, make sure to train your mentors and mentees so that they have a clear understanding of their roles and expectations for the mentorship. "Training could include reflective interviewing, effective listening and questioning skills, coaching, techniques for giving and receiving feedback, goal setting, conflict handling and negations" (Miller, 2006: 14). Even though you've created a formal mentoring program, keep it flexible and avoid too much red tape. The mentorship should grow and evolve from the foundation you have laid. The rest is left up to the participants.

What to avoid in your mentoring program

My first professional library job was as a resident at a large research institution. The most attractive selling point for me in taking this position was that although I was going to be considered a professional librarian, the position was also viewed as a learning opportunity and had a structured mentoring program that included assigned mentors in each department. The idea was for me to rotate among the various library departments and eventually choose one of interest for more detailed and focused training. Ideally, a department chair would act as my mentor, and that person was responsible for creating projects for me to work on while he or she monitored my work and made sure I met objectives that were set at the beginning of each rotation.

Unfortunately some of my assigned mentorships didn't work out that way. While everyone did their best to make me feel welcome and comfortable in my new position as a library employee, some departments were ill-prepared for my arrival or obviously didn't want me around. In those situations, I found myself without clear learning objectives and spent my time doing clerical work or quietly observing staff members doing their everyday jobs. I enjoyed learning how each section of the library worked and appreciated the time people spent with me, but sometimes I didn't feel like I was using the master's degree I had worked so hard to earn.

In some cases, I was reassigned to non-librarian mentors because some department chairs decided not to participate in the mentorship and rarely checked in on the progress of my projects. This was the case when I took initiative in organizing and implementing a large project on my own. Once the project was complete, the department chair (who did not assist or guide me during the assignment) took all the credit for my work. This person was a tenured librarian and well-respected in the community. Having no recourse, I left that department feeling betrayed and disillusioned with the entire program.

Fortunately, a majority of the departments and department chairs I worked with in that library were happy to assist me and allowed me to contribute fully to their areas. The residency's mentoring program had been established a few years prior to my arriving, and it was clear most people involved wanted to see participants succeed. Unfortunately, the program was a victim of its own success and didn't grow with the changing times. As the years passed, the program was handed from person to person to manage and coordinate, and I think it eventually got lost in the shuffle. Not all administrators were on board with the program, and participants were not properly recognized for their efforts. The people who decided to take on the task of coordinating the program, though well-intentioned, were not prepared to deal with the needs of the program firsthand.

Supervising this residency when I started was a library administrator who acted as the lead mentor. The program was designed to have weekly meetings with this lead mentor and talk about my developing interests and research ideas. Unfortunately, our meetings were sporadic at best and not very effective. The administrative mentor, though kind and supportive, simply did not have the time to devote to the program or to me. After three years at this institution, I left, feeling unchallenged and underappreciated. To my knowledge, the program has yet to hire any new residents and the supervising mentor has not been named.

The "accidental mentorship"

If formal mentorships are not possible in your organization, consider forming "accidental mentorships" with new librarians. Spontaneous or "accidental" mentoring relationships work very well for most people because they are more personal and relaxing. Although these mentorships tend to develop through already established friendships, as well as professional relationships, they still need to have some structure in order for them to work. The new librarian and the mentor must discuss clear expectations and outcomes before the mentorship begins. Regular meetings

> ☑ QUICK TIP
> Establish regular meetings, clear outcomes, and a feedback system in order to build mentoring relationships that are productive and rewarding for both participants.

during which feedback and guidance can be given need to be planned and conducted. Once these formalities are taken care of, the mentorship can be set in motion.

Some of my best mentor experiences were the ones in which the mentor and I just happened to form a mentoring relationship out of an already existing acquaintance. I didn't always want to be a librarian, but lucky for me I had great mentors recruiting me from the beginning. The ones who inspired me to make this career choice for myself were the people who shared their enthusiasm and passion for their jobs. They guided me to the right schools and helped me get financial aid when I needed it. They even welcomed me into their homes when I was in graduate school so that I could concentrate on my education and graduate with as little stress as possible. These were the individuals who helped make me the librarian I am today, and they each found themselves "accidentally" taking on an important role in my life. These people were not a part of any formal mentoring program, but they paid attention to my life and helped shape events that led me to where I am now.

At one point in time I had hoped to be a high school teacher. Unfortunately, reality set in and I became disillusioned with the idea of teaching in a traditional high school environment. By the end of my senior year in college and after many semesters of student-teaching hours, I decided that teaching high school was definitely not for me. When I came to this realization, I felt disappointed and lost. I was trapped in a career I no longer wanted for myself and couldn't find a way out. Fortunately I worked part-time in my hometown library while earning my bachelor's degree, and I enjoyed my job immensely. Once the director and other librarians discovered I didn't want to pursue a career in a traditional classroom, they jumped at the chance to sell their profession to me. They told me how fulfilling their careers were and how much they enjoyed helping their community. Since I already worked in a library environment, they said, it would be a fairly easy transition for me to make a full-time career in libraries.

Each librarian took an interest in my future and shared their stories of how and why they became librarians. Most important, when the director saw that I was seriously considering library school, she put me in contact with people at the university who could answer my questions and help me with the application process. Many of these librarians offered to write letters of recommendation and introduce me to people involved with specific ALA scholarships. As a result of their guidance and encouragement, I no longer felt lost. I had a purpose: get into graduate school and become a librarian.

Throughout my graduate studies, I befriended several veteran librarians who worked at the university and who taught some of my classes. We would meet periodically to discuss my educational goals and future plans over coffee or lunch. Getting together in personal, informal settings helped me feel like I had more of a connection to the profession (and especially to my professors) and helped me focus on my studies. As a result, I was able to graduate sooner than I expected and quickly found myself in the library profession because of the networking connections I had already made.

Leaders in the library field can encourage potential or new librarians in many ways. If you are in a leadership position at your library or are a veteran librarian who has been working in the profession for a few years, talk to the people who work around you and see how their lives are going. You don't have to set up a formal mentoring program with each of them, but take the time to let them know you have an interest in their lives and care about what they're doing professionally.

> ☑ QUICK TIP
> Beyond the bounds of formal mentoring relationships are many ways that you can express your professional interest in the career path of early-career librarians in your organization.

Lead by example. Model how much you like your job, because the best way to recruit to the profession is to show potential librarians just how much you treasure the profession yourself.

Most important, once a potential librarian "takes the bait," be prepared to answer questions about getting into library school and funding. It may have been years since this person was in school, and maybe he or she is intimidated by the prospect of entering a graduate program. Perhaps the potential librarian is coming fresh out of a bachelor's degree and just needs a little encouragement for taking the GRE. Consider setting up appointments for potential librarians with graduate school officials and offer to write letters of recommendation. Once the person is in graduate school, continue meeting with him or her in person (or virtually) to discuss how things are going. Help that person acclimate by introducing him or her to helpful librarians connected to his or her program.

Again, the key purpose in "accidental mentorships" is to foster guidance without all the bureaucracy of a formal mentoring program. You and your mentee each set up your own schedules and decide what works best for your mentorship. Always maintain professionalism and lead by example.

The mentor in *you*

When you find yourself in a mentorship, whether formal or accidental, don't feel pressured to be someone you're not, and don't impose a lot of unrealistic expectations on yourself. Be the best mentor *you* can be and share your valuable time and energy with someone who appreciates your efforts. There is no such thing as a "perfect mentor," but an ideal mentor should have the right combination of knowledge and skills regarding the library profession as a whole and her specific work environment. She or he should also be trustworthy and emotionally stable. That being said, effective mentors are not arrogant or self-absorbed but have the humility to show their faults and acknowledge they have some growing to do as well. That's not to say these faults are a sign of weakness and you're not a competent librarian. It just means you are a well-rounded mentor who isn't afraid to show that you're human.

Be a mentor with a positive attitude toward the profession. The most contagious disease in "library land" is a negative attitude, and you don't want to pass that on to someone just embarking on this career. If you honestly think you can't maintain a positive attitude about our profession or your specific work environment, perhaps you should consider not becoming a mentor. Mentors should practice what they preach and show a level of professionalism that any new librarian would want to emulate.

The librarian I wanted to emulate was Claudine Arnold Jenda. As an established librarian at an academic research library, Claudine was Agriculture Librarian and Assistant Head of Reference and Instruction Services at Auburn University. She was an ideal mentor for me because she took a genuine interest in my success and was always willing to help me learn. She helped me navigate the political waters of a large research institution and oftentimes guided me away from professional suicide. And she did all of this with a sincere attitude of giving and a genuine interest in seeing me succeed.

Claudine was an "accidental" mentor who started out as a colleague who occupied the cubicle next to mine. I found myself asking her advice and opinion nearly every day, and eventually our professional relationship grew into a strong mentorship. Before Claudine agreed to be my mentor, she and I discussed our differences and similarities in work ethic and my learning objectives for our mentorship. We met weekly to discuss my goals and expectations for the immediate and long-term futures, and she helped me draft realistic plans for the projects I was working on. Sometimes I would meet those goals and other times I wouldn't, but Claudine never harshly judged and never made me feel as if I had failed. Instead, she helped me adjust my goals to match the reality of my growing work duties. As an academic librarian, sometimes I would be asked to teach extra classes or cover extra hours at the reference desk. This would require me to rearrange my priorities and goals, but Claudine was flexible and encouraged me to be flexible as well.

Claudine was the main reason I chose to focus on Reference Services and Instruction. She had already established herself as an excellent reference and instruction librarian and was patient with those of us who were new to the field. She knew exactly when and where to step in to "rescue me" and when to let me fly solo. Part of the reason our mentorship was so successful was because we genuinely enjoyed each other's company both in and out of the library. Away from work we sometimes met for lunch or shopping, and in the library she guided me with the utmost professionalism.

I was lucky to have found Claudine when I did because she filled an important role for me in my early career by just being who she is naturally. She was respectful and patient with a lot of neophyte librarian mistakes I brought to the table, but most of all, she was a friend with whom I remain in close contact despite several states and two time zones between us.

> ☑ **QUICK TIP**
>
> Mentoring relationships can work well when focused on a specific aspect of professional life; everyone should have several different mentors who bring different qualities and life experiences to the table.

Not all mentorships will lead to lasting friendships, but remember that a good mentor serves a purpose for a specific time and allows the protégé to grow and move on (Fiegen, 2002). Your job while mentoring is to be yourself. Remember that your mentee has a master's degree and is a professional, so don't spread yourself too thin by trying to be everything to your new librarian. He or she should be expected to solve professional issues on his or her own, using the techniques you've been teaching him or her. You are expected to be the best mentor you can be while continuing with your everyday responsibilities as a librarian.

When a mentorship goes wrong

As I mentioned before, I have been in situations in which some of my mentors and I were not well-matched. Hopefully this experience is an exception to the rule. However, if you find yourself in a similar predicament, my advice is to bring in a third party to help manage the situation and get out while you still can.

The worst mentoring experience I had fortunately did not happen to me as a librarian, but I think the events described will translate perfectly to any professional mentorship. It was a mentoring relationship full of conflict, dissatisfaction, and misunderstandings that ended bitterly, and both participants involved were left feeling let down and abandoned.

During one of my undergraduate student-teaching experiences, I was paired with a mentor with whom I seemingly had common interests. We both enjoyed literature and liked being around students. Regrettably these similarities could not salvage the inevitable wreck that became our mentorship.

Naturally a student teacher is expected to have good and bad days, but on a particularly bad day I expressed my doubts regarding my career choice to my mentor. In general I would expect my mentor to talk with me about my doubts and help me see my value as a new teacher. That didn't happen. When I told my mentor that I was having doubts, she took it personally and vented her frustration and disappointment out on me in front of our students. She proceeded to take the classes away from me and told me to sit in the back of the classroom so as not to disturb *her* class. It was at this humiliating point I knew I had to bring someone in to help.

The university's mentoring program coordinator came in to mediate a discussion between my mentor and myself. The mentor admitted she was upset and felt as if she was wasting her time and energy on someone who didn't care to learn what she had to teach. She said she didn't think I should be a teacher and wanted me out of her classroom. The coordinator and I tried to clarify to the mentor that my frustrations and doubts were natural for a beginning teacher to experience and that my doubts in no way were a reflection of the mentor's own teaching style. In the end, we simply agreed to disagree; the mentor reluctantly agreed to give me some control of our classes.

Unfortunately, our mentorship completely changed after this incident. My mentor no longer offered any more outside help or constructive criticism of my lessons, and she stopped eating lunch with me or communicating anything at all except for my final written evaluation. Of course, I was frustrated and angry with her for turning on me, but I walked away from that experience knowing that I had made the best decision for myself by bringing in help before it escalated into something I could not control.

My advice to library mentors is to not take yourselves too seriously and not be offended if your new librarian decides this particular line of work isn't the right path for her. If she expresses discontentment with her career choice, don't shut her out completely, because you may end up shutting her out of the profession altogether. Instead, listen to her frustrations and encourage her by sharing your own new librarian stories. Your self-disclosure may help foster more trust and understanding between you and your mentee (Johnson and Ridley, 2004).

What you give is what you get

In my experience, the right mentors don't just pour knowledge into a person's brain but instead encourage active learning and growth. Through mentor coaching and guidance, new librarians learn to build on their own strengths and weaknesses, thus becoming confident and successful professionals themselves. I no longer need to be held as tightly by the hand when I deal with difficult library issues. I know I have mentors all over the country to call upon when I need them the most. My mentors have also instilled a strong work ethic and a desire to maintain a sense of pride in the profession I have chosen. This is why I decided to become a mentor myself. Hopefully, I can be half as good as some of my mentors have been, and continue to be.

Exhibit 5.1. Interview with my mentor

The following is from an interview with Claudine Arnold Jenda, Agriculture Librarian and Assistant Head of Reference and Instruction Services at Auburn University.

What specifically made you choose me as a protégé? Where there certain qualities you liked or was it just a natural gravitation for you?
Most mentoring relationships develop naturally. Even where the formal and institutionalizing of mentoring occurs, at the core a mentoring relationship develops from an informal, voluntary, mutually agreed-upon relationship that is not done for a fee. From this, I would conclude that the mentoring relationship developed from a natural gravitation. Before the relationship, there was the recognition of similarities in experiences, underlying values, and professional goals.

Do you think we worked well together? Why? Why not?
I see we were able to have an open and trusting relationship. We also knew that we have the best interests of the other person at all times. While the relationship was developed in our professional work, there was the awareness on both parties that the relationship involves the total person. In the relationship, efforts are made to treat each other with respect, dignity, and treat the other person or their information the way you would want to be treated.

As mentor and mentee, there was the willingness to walk together side by side on this life's journey, and also to create the space boundaries when time apart is best. Meanwhile, when an issue arises we each knew we could call on each other for direction, support, or simple listening.

As a mentor you come into a relationship with more experience. For example, I saw skills, abilities and opportunities that could be utilized to meet professional and

(cont'd.)

Exhibit 5.1. Interview with my mentor *(continued)*

---

personal goals and aspirations and potential in a mentee. I saw my job as one of constantly holding up a mirror to a mentee for them to see who they truly are. You constantly have before you the image of the mentee in the present moment, and another image in the "near" future where the mentee is fully developed, accomplished, actualized, and highly successful! With shared goals and aspirations, the day-to-day time is spent with mentee leading as they make choices, follow through on advice, develop additional skills, or gain needed experience.

As a mentor, there were times when challenging the mentee was the right thing to do, oftentimes if they are falling short of their potential, when you feel they are settling. In this role, I have to be willing to "make my mentee uncomfortable," and to know that we will not agree; and that this is all right.

As a mentee, you were a quick study and did most of the work. As such, all the growth that has happened personally, spiritually, and professionally are in truth a result of choices and efforts that you made. And you have much to be proud of!

Yes, I think we worked well together. Notice though that the relationship, while it may change, is truly ongoing in that I will always have a vested interest in knowing at all times how you are doing, how you have developed. Though there will be new mentors in your life at different times, I will still want to know how you are doing, through periodic checks.

How could current librarians and administrators provide similar mentorship experiences for their protégés? In other words, what words of wisdom do you have for new mentors?

We are all constantly being called into a "teacher/student" relationship. Each one of us has gone through life experiences that have made us grow into stronger and better persons professional or spiritually. If we are open to the needs of people around us, we will realize that the life's lessons we have can benefit someone who is facing an experience that was similar to ours. To discover these needs, we need to be willing to encounter and care to know as many people in our workplace and other places as possible. Make efforts to widen your circle of friends, and include those that are new or may fail to belong for various reasons. With a caring attitude, great listening skills, and a genuine respect for the other person as a "colleague," each person will have the joy and privilege of watching up close the development of a future leader.

References

Ad Hoc Task Force on Recruitment & Retention Issues. "Recruitment, Retention & Restructuring: Human Resources in Academic Libraries: A White Paper." Association of College & Research Libraries Personnel Administrators & Staff Development Officers Discussion Group. (May 20, 2002). Available: www.ala.org/ala/acrl/acrlissues/acrlrecruiting/recruiting-wp.pdf.

Burns, Mary. 2004. "Both Sides Benefit in Business Mentorship." *Crain's Chicago Business* 8 (August): 32. Available: http://find.galegroup.com/ips/start.do?prodId=IPS (accessed December 14, 2007).

Fiegen, Ann Manning. 2002. "Mentoring and Academic Librarians: Personally Designed for Results." *College & Undergraduate Libraries* 9, no. 1: 23–32.

Johnson, W. Brad, and Charles R. Ridley. 2004. *The Elements of Mentoring.* New York: Palgrave MacMillan.

Lynch, Mary Jo, Stephen Tordella, and Thomas Godfrey. 2004. "Retirement and Recruitment: A Deeper Look." *American Libraries* 36, no. 1: 28.

Markgren, Susanne, Thad Dickinson, Anne Leonard, and Kim Vassiliadis. 2007. "The Five Year Itch: Are Libraries Losing Their Most Valuable Resources?" *Library Administration & Management* 21, no. 2. (Spring): 70–76.

Miller, Marcus. 2006. "Developing an Effective Mentoring Program." *CMA Management* (March): 14–16. Available: http://find.galegroup.com/itx/start.do?prodld=GRGMS (accessed December 14, 2007).

Newhouse, Ria, and April Spisak. 2004. "Fixing the First Job." *Library Journal* 129, no. 13: 44–46.

Wellington, Sheila, and Betty Spence. 2001. *Be Your Own Mentor: Strategies from Top Women on the Secrets of Success.* New York: Random House.

CHAPTER 6

from paraprofessional to department head: lessons in cultivating a new professional

Stephen Brooks

N ew librarians come from diverse career backgrounds. Some of us went to library school to escape a previous career, others to enhance library careers we had already begun. My story is the latter. For the 12 years before I entered the MLIS program at the University of North Carolina at Greensboro, I was a student assistant in the graduate library, a full-time classified staff member of two acquisitions departments, and a part-time library clerk at a community college learning resources center. Ostensibly, I was qualified to be the head of the Acquisitions and Gifts Unit in the University Libraries at George Mason University when I accepted the job, by virtue of my extensive hands-on experience and an American Library Association–accredited MLIS. This chapter provides an account of how my experience did and did not prepare me for the challenges of my first professional position, a middle-management position. I hope that library managers can glean useful information about how to help librarians following a similar path to succeed in technical and/or management positions.

An accidental librarian

During my first 12 years of working in libraries, I was neither trying, nor hoping, to become a librarian. In fact, my library career began by accident. Having received a federal work-study grant, I worked in the library, shelving, sorting, and discharging library books for a few hours a week for three and a half years. By the end of college, I was familiar enough with Library of Congress classification that I occasionally found typographic errors on call number labels. (I probably also incorrectly identified and

---

Exhibit 6.1. Lessons from my first supervisor

I spent a great deal of time one-on-one in the office of Janet Flowers, the Head of Acquisitions at the University of North Carolina–Chapel Hill, when I was an ordering supervisor. She set an example of a confident manager and leader. There were power struggles in a very large academic library that I could not observe firsthand, which impacted my daily work. She brought a calm demeanor to quell interpersonal conflicts between librarians in her own and other departments. She managed by meeting regularly with the two librarians, who were searching and ordering section heads, respectively, and their assistants (my co-worker and me), leaving the day-to-day supervision up to the managers who answered to her. I learned about the history of the Acquisitions Department from her perspective and took that back with me to my cubicle.

Now, as a head of Acquisitions myself, I strive to follow her example: I make time to talk to my staff one-on-one, I try to appreciate my staff's perspectives and augment them with my own in ways that I hope are helpful to my staff, I honor confidentiality and encourage my staff to speak freely to me, and I keep a cool head in a crisis. Janet and I still "talk shop," more like colleagues now, although I still consider her to be a mentor.

Perhaps it is not coincidence that several editorial board members of the ACQNET discussion list began their acquisitions careers as classified staff members in that very department. We all had the same supervisor early in our careers who inspired us to become heads of acquisitions departments.

---

pulled some works in numbered series, believing they were erroneously cataloged journal volumes, so unfettered was my enthusiasm for bringing order to the world of knowledge!) Upon graduation with an English degree, I accepted my first full-time job as bibliographic searcher in the same library. Previously, I had no concept of technical services. At my first technical services interview, I was shocked to discover that the expansive cataloging, acquisitions, and serials departments existed in the same building. And I had thought I knew it so well from combing its nooks and crannies for misplaced books! I fell in love with collection development. I received a promotion to order supervisor and a position upgrade in three years.

Encouraging staff involvement at UNC

At UNC, I was encouraged to participate in library activities beyond the scope of my regular duties. In my second year of full-time employment, I agreed to serve on the Library Staff Development Committee, which sponsored a couple speakers annually and sponsored the very popular Interdepartmental Awareness Program. I worked on an Acquisitions "Sets" Committee and Space Planning Committee. Most large organizations offer similar chances for staff to participate on a broader scale. This

☑ QUICK TIP
Involving staff in departmental projects can benefit the staff in a deep way, helping them become involved and invested in the library.

helps entry-level employees connect to the organization on a personal level, in a deeper way than simply showing up for work.

Library managers can involve staff in departmental projects, benefiting the staff in a similar way, with the added benefits of helping them feel more involved and invested in the library as an institution unto itself. In return, staff perspectives are deeply rooted in the tasks that keep the organization functioning; such perspectives are critical when changing work flows, vendors, or software packages.

In my second year at Davis Library, we sent out a request for proposals to library materials vendors to provide approval plan and firm order services. As vendors competed for our business, I sat in on presentations and meetings during which bibliographers and technical services librarians discussed profiles, used words such as "non-subject parameters" and "coverage," and compared online collection development tools. Acquisitions staff members were encouraged to participate in these meetings. We utilized our technical familiarity to help managers make informed decisions. This made us feel more valued, as if our opinions mattered; it was reassuring to be asked to stand up from our workstations and participate in decision making. Finally, the experience informed my view of how my job fit into the bigger picture, the organization's mission.

Through the lens of this exercise in approval plans, I saw collection development as an organized, deliberate endeavor. Although I had never articulated the question of how a research library's collection is built, I had received the answer.

Lessons learned as a part-time staffer

After college, I worked part-time at the Learning Resources Center (LRC) at Asheville-Buncombe Technical Community College (A-B Tech). Here I got a break from acquisitions, returning to my circulation roots. However, a small library means broader responsibilities and less specialization for staff. The LRC was small—minuscule, to my way of thinking at the time—which permitted me to perform tasks outside of the rigid world of circulation transactions. In addition to technical processing, I troubleshot networked computers and printers, assisted with microfilm, and oversaw a periodical shifting project. I met numerous public services librarians who were working on pathfinders, presentations, and classroom instruction—not just answering reference questions. Working in a small library, I had more direct contact with a variety of library functions. I built on and applied the technical skills I had already acquired. As my understanding of the roles libraries play in academic institutions grew, I became content with working in libraries. When a full-time staff position at the LRC became available, I sought it, and soon found a job as the acquisitions assistant at UNC Asheville's (UNCA) Ramsey Library.

I enjoyed returning to library technical services full-time. At UNC my work had been very specialized; at UNCA, I found myself more greatly involved in all aspects of acquisitions. With a materials budget that was a tiny fraction of the one at my previous acquisitions post, and a staff of two full-time library assistants in the Acquisitions Department, we could not have the separation of duties that were in place at Chapel Hill, where no one could be involved in two of the following acquisitions functions: ordering, receiving, and invoicing. Even with multiple responsibilities, I was never very busy. I had ample time and leeway to improve upon our processes in a way that provided better stewardship of the taxpayers' money. The acquisitions team leader and I negotiated better firm order discounts with one vendor and then leveraged the discounts by more deliberately choosing from among the three vendors with whom we did business. At the time, we stretched the university's materials budget by about $10,000 per year. I also successfully lobbied for the elimination of a tiny approval plan for playscripts and for a new budget structure that allowed separate tracking of monographic and subscription funds. My experience at Davis Library had directly informed my practice at UNCA.

Library employment as a real-life laboratory for MLS students

Library managers can enrich the experience of their staff and realize morale and performance benefits simply by encouraging and supporting staff members who seek an MLS. A year and a half after I began working at Ramsey Library, UNCA hosted a cohort of distance-education students in the UNC Greensboro (UNCG) MLIS program. The coordinator for the UNCA cohort happened to work two offices over from me and strongly encouraged me to apply. It was time for me to move forward in my career. The convenience of continuing my day job while attending evening classes in an adjacent building made the UNCG program very appealing. I applied to and was accepted into the MLIS program. During my first three semesters, I got married, bought a house, and had a child. If it had not been for UNCG's distance-education program, library school would not have been a viable option at that time in my life. Furthermore, the free class and in-state tuition to which I was entitled each semester were significant motivating factors in my decision to start the program at that time.

> ☑ QUICK TIP
>
> Encourage and support staff seeking to further their library education, especially through the MLS degree.

Simultaneously working at the library and attending school greatly contributed to my education and skill-building. Because Ramsey Library is so small, I knew all the librarians and would regularly engage them in discussions about being a librarian. I discussed my assignments and topics that interested me, such as intellectual freedom and collection development, and applied the knowledge I was gaining in school to build networks for information exchange. Library managers may be able to further encourage and assist staff in graduate programs by fostering this kind of interaction.

> ☑ QUICK TIP
>
> Develop a mentoring program among librarians and graduate students in library science working at the library.

I suggest library managers allow librarians, as part of their professional development requirements, to mentor graduate students at their own libraries. Both parties' professional development would benefit, as librarians can be exposed to current theory in librarianship while students can work outside the boundaries of their staff positions.

The institution benefited as well. The theoretical, academic world in which I was thriving enriched my day-to-day job experience, providing me with a new context in which to understand my work. For example, during the semester I was taking a general reference class, our materials budget was slashed so horribly that the Acquisitions Department had very little work to do. While a reference librarian was on extended leave and I was taking classes a couple nights a week, I worked four hours a week at the reference desk and 16 hours at the circulation desk. I realized that reference is fun and rewarding. Library work helped me in library school too. For example, my years in acquisitions departments allowed me to become very familiar with MARC records as the basis for library catalogs. I had a working knowledge of Library of Congress classification. When I took the required cataloging class, many of my classmates had never been exposed to cataloging before. While many of them were confused, bored, uninterested, or lost, I already knew something of the mechanics of cataloging.

Getting the most out of motivated staff

Motivating staff is an ongoing challenge for many library managers. Bored staff may not seek out new challenges, but may benefit from them, with a little push and direction from their managers. During my time in library school, the head of technical services in my current library asked me to do a collection analysis report on our psychology holdings, although I had no psychology background or collection development expertise. This was a major project through which I would learn and apply new skills, helping my development as a budding librarian. This also benefited UNCA, as no collection development was actively being undertaken in psychology at the time. He gave me collection age and circulation statistics, broken down by LC classification ranges for the BF class. I also had analogous data for the other members of the consortium (in which shared collection development actually was practiced to a degree). Knowing something of the campus academic climate, and inferring student interest in specific topics, I was able to put together a summary of where the gaps in our holdings were and where our holdings were outdated. I recommended specific resources to update and complement our holdings. I received positive feedback from my supervisor, as well as from the librarian who was eventually hired and had responsibility for developing the psychology collections. I became more enthusiastic about collection development and my confidence grew. The project had also been a valuable use of my ample unstructured time.

The orientation of a new librarian

When I assumed leadership of the Acquisitions and Gifts Unit at George Mason, I represented at least the fifth change in that position in ten years. I had joined a unit that had floundered and struggled under a massive workload and external pressures without consistent, experienced leadership. This had stifled innovation. The library had no accurate, up-to-date procedure manual; procedures were taught to new employees by the long-time employee and the director of Technical Services, who worked closely together and managed by a hands-on, expert-centered approach.

Working in its favor, the Acquisitions and Gifts Unit had one person who had been with the unit for a number of years and with the University Libraries more than 20 years; she was acting as the interim head of the unit when I arrived. Also, the director of Technical Services is highly organized, extremely professional, and attuned to the politics of GMU. The two of them knew how to do practically every task in the Unit.

Believing I had the skills and experience to bring this unit into the twenty-first century, I arrived ready to take the reins. I understood that I was expected not just to manage, but also to perform some basic tasks as needed. I was not afraid to get my hands dirty. This requirement of the job had been communicated to me explicitly during the interview process.

Becoming a middle manager

When I came to George Mason, I had a "knight in shining armor" approach to my new position: the library, the Acquisitions and Gifts staff, everyone needed me to come in and rescue Acquisitions and Gifts. I expected to be lauded and thanked, received with great admiration. Please indulge my slight hyperbole, because this point is important: How mistaken was I! This knight in shining armor was received more like a traveling salesman than a savior. No, I was not lauded but received by my own staff with skepticism, suspicion, doubt, and uncertainty about my ability to manage the unit, as well as my commitment.

To manage the Acquisitions and Gifts Unit, I needed a week-by-week, step-by-step orientation to working at GMU, being a librarian, and supervising my unit. Moving into this job was a greater transition than I had ever before made in my career. I would have liked an introduction to each function of my unit, with scheduled lessons in performing each of the tasks I was expected to supervise and in which I would occasionally participate. I would gradually assume responsibility for supervising the functions of my unit, taking them from my supervisor or from the interim head, as needed. At the end of this period, I would have had the tools I needed to supervise the unit, and would then take full management responsibility.

Instead, I spent my first year in this position "putting out fires." I have learned on the job largely on my own, addressing what seemed to be the most pressing problems—or fastest-approaching deadlines—and figuring out the rest as I went. Outside of the unit's daily work, I needed to know what else would be expected of me in my various collaborative roles.

As a new librarian, I failed to heed my own advice. During the interview, I had given a presentation about implementing Electronic Data Interchange (EDI), with an emphasis on how to effect change by getting staff to buy in to and take ownership of the change that would impact their work. Instead of asking staff what changes they thought should be made, I tried to insist upon making changes *I* wanted to make. I should have approached the job humbly, striving to understand each of my staff's perspectives and job responsibilities. I should have shown appreciation for the hard work my staff performed daily, especially the ones who had remained in their positions through several unit heads.

To say that the learning curve going from detail-oriented, perfection-oriented staff member to unit head is steep is a gross understatement. Managing people is nothing like managing data. Data behave the same way every time you do the same thing to them. People, on the other hand, respond one way to a stimulus today and unpredictably to the same stimulus tomorrow. These observations are probably self-evident to a seasoned manager; the point I belabor here is that technical services experience, although necessary for a beginning manager of a unit in technical services, is insufficient. The skills I continue to learn on the job cannot be recorded in a procedures manual; they cannot be articulated in a series of if-then statements. Every day, the most important aspects of my work are building relationships, listening, educating myself about other people's responsibilities (and other people very gradually about mine), team-building, and collaborating.

> ☑ **QUICK TIP**
> Focus on the relationships between people on the team more than on systems.

Making lemonade out of lemons: my first conference presentation

One ongoing challenge I work with in my current position is dealing with the purchasing system mandated by the Commonwealth of Virginia, eVA. In short, eVA requires all vendors who do business with Virginia agencies must pay a fee to register as an authorized vendor. Many of the vendors with whom the University Libraries at GMU do business are upset about this requirement and refuse to join. GMU incurs a fine for doing business with vendors outside eVA. On top of irritating rare-book dealers and database vendors, eVA also adds a great deal of record-keeping and data management to already-strapped library staff, as well as the university's Purchasing and Accounts Payable staff. From a professional standpoint, eVA has been the bane of my existence at times, and is representative of the struggles I have encountered as a new librarian in a new library.

I would never have considered eVA to be a blessing to my career. However, in 2006 Polly Khater, Director of Technical Services (and my supervisor) approached me about doing a presentation on the topic of eVA. We spoke to about 25 librarians and vendor representatives at the 2006 Charleston Conference, Issues in Book and Serial Acquisition, about how we work with eVA. At the conference, it was listed as a "Lively Lunch," and it lived up to its billing. For what I consider a very dry topic, we entertained numerous questions from vendors about why we ask for their participation (and what happens if they refuse it) and from librarians about how to manage the process at their own institutions. Our seven PowerPoint slides carried us through more than an hour and a half of discussion and helped us improve our relationships with some of our vendors. Also, it gave me confidence that we were managing eVA as well as can be expected and that I had knowledge worthy of sharing with other librarians.

The presentation topic and forum were suggested by my supervisor as a joint project. As we developed the presentation, Polly took responsibility for submitting the proposal and making the PowerPoint slides. She let me develop much of the content for the presentation, as well as the overall structure of the program.

Thanks to Polly's experience and willingness to work with me, I was able to get over a major professional development obstacle: my first conference presentation. Without her participation, I would have been bogged down and stressed out about minor details, such as formatting the slides and working out logistics with the conference organizers. With Polly's experience and help, I was able to get my name on the conference program and contribute significantly to a successful presentation. This gives me confidence as I progress in my career. I also learned that the key to a successful presentation is not necessarily being passionate about your topic; having information that is of use to others and finding an appropriate forum in which to transmit that knowledge is also extremely important. Not many other librarians would be able to talk about eVA! New librarians often lack confidence and would benefit from seasoned colleagues' guidance and leadership. New librarians who have fresh, cutting-edge ideas they just learned in library school and that they have applied in the real world will need direction in sharing these ideas. Library managers can help new subordinate librarians get their feet off the ground in professional circles by collaborating with them on projects, similar to how Polly did with me.

> ☑ QUICK TIP
> Help staff get their feet wet in professional circles by collaborating with them on presentations and scholarship.

Library school and the real world

I have often commiserated with fellow technical services librarians and staff that library school graduates do not emerge with an understanding of technical services. For example, GMU will hire a new reference librarian with no track record in collection development, leaving it to me to explain approval plans, standing orders, budget cycles, and how to select titles in their areas of expertise. In retrospect, I realize that, just as my graduate program did not prepare me to be an acquisitions librarian, it also did not prepare me to be a reference librarian, even though reference was heavily emphasized in the curriculum. Reference librarians in academic libraries are asked to do so much more than provide reference services, including collaborating with departmental faculty to build library collections and integrate library instruction into departmental curricula. Even though our program was in the School of Education, reference classes were geared toward teaching about useful resources, which they did very well. What they omitted was practical instruction on providing reference services, such as how to conduct a reference interview or how to develop a lesson plan.

My MLIS degree represents an education deeply grounded in the theory and ethics of librarianship, but also the practical application of some specific skills many librarians need, such as evaluating and using reference resources to answer questions and application of communication technology. Management is difficult to address practically in a classroom setting, but I received a whole semester of case-based library management education, in which we applied the textbook theories to realistic management situations in a variety of library settings. Managing real people when problems arise is very different from the case-based approach in one regard: feedback from those one manages. This echoes the offhand observation I made earlier, that managing people is much different from managing data. I may come up with a management solution that works "on paper." However, real-life situations are not discrete enough to fit into a scripted scenario. What if the staff members I want to help do not trust me? What if my boss tells me to take a different approach? What if I have misread the problem itself? Management and leadership improve with practice, just like technical work. Neither can be adequately covered solely in library school. As with reference skills, they may be addressed in the classroom, but they must be refined through application in the context of the job.

Lessons for library managers

Library managers can realize tangible benefits from supporting staff development within their institutions. Creating a culture of development that reaches professional and classified staff builds collegiality and loyalty. At GMU, classified staff in Technical Services regularly take classes offered by OCLC Eastern, and staff across the University Libraries have held offices in the Virginia Library Association's Paraprofessional Forum. Librarians at GMU—as with most academic institutions—are expected to participate in local, regional, and national professional organizations. Not every organization can afford to support extensive external professional development, but a great deal can be done to foster it in any library. Nurturing classified staff whom pursue MLS degrees, formal and informal mentoring for MLS students and new librarians alike, and offering opportunities for cross-departmental collaboration are efficient and effective ways to improve morale and achieve desired professional development benefits. The immediate payoff manifests as staff are more engaged with their work and aware of how their roles benefit the organization. Over the long term, MLS students share with classmates their positive experiences at their employing institutions and bring back academic knowledge from their graduate programs to the workplace laboratory; new librarians learn from experienced colleagues how to succeed professionally; and seasoned librarians prepare for management roles as they help newer colleagues navigate the open seas of professional responsibility.

Libraries as institutions share a history of helping people to expand their horizons at little cost to themselves. By pooling resources, libraries make information accessible to many people and, as a place, bring people together in the spirit of exploration and discovery. As employing institutions, libraries are well-positioned to provide the same environment to their employees, and realize benefits of an informed, engaged, energetic workforce.

Further reading

American Library Association (2008). *LSSIRT: Library Support Staff Interests Round Table.* Available: www.ala.org/ala/lssirt/lssirt.cfm (accessed July 13, 2008).

Baldwin, D. A., and D. C. Barkley. 2007. "Staff Development for Student Employee Supervisors." In *Complete Guide for Supervisors of Student Employees in Today's Academic Libraries,* 233–244. Westport, CT: Libraries Unlimited.

Black, W. K., and J. M. Leysen. "Fostering Success: The Socialization of Entry-Level Librarians in ARL Libraries." *Journal of Library Administration* 36, no. 4: 3–27.

Garber, G. 2006. "Making the Leap from Paraprofessional to Professional in an Academic Library." LIScareer.com. Available: www.liscareer.com/garber_para.htm (accessed July 13, 2008).

Oud, J. 2008. "Adjusting to the Workplace: Transitions Faced by New Academic Librarians." *College & Research Libraries* 69, no. 3: 252–266.

CHAPTER 7

the librarian as researcher:
support for research and modeling a research mind-set

Cat Saleeby McDowell

I remember the revelation quite clearly. I was on the phone with my mother, describing the events of the preceding weekend. I had been invited to speak before a group of publishing executives at the National Press Club in Washington, DC. The invitation had come somewhat last-minute, so I had not had the time to really think about what I was getting myself into, or to let it sink in. In truth, it was my first experience with complimentary airfare—the very concept that someone would fly me in just to hear me talk was completely foreign! And then there was the hotel—a far cry from the usual budget hotels I was used to staying in at conferences. Already feeling more than a little like a fish out of water, I was honored—and slightly terrified—to find that I would be sitting next to the Acting Surgeon General of the United States of America, and speaking right after him! How do you make small talk with the surgeon general? How do you follow up the surgeon general's plea for greater access to medical information for all mankind with a talk on institutional repositories?

If I had thought too much about these things at the time, I might have spent the whole day hiding in the bathroom. But I was focused on my mission, and my relief afterward. It wasn't until my mother asked a simple rhetorical that day that I really began to reflect on the meaning of it all. "Cat," she said, "how many twenty-eight-year-olds do you know who have spoken at the National Press Club, following the surgeon general on the program?"

The truth is, I didn't know any. I didn't really know anyone in my profession who had received so many great opportunities at such a young age. Why was that, I wondered? Why did I have a full dance card of speaking engagements lined up all over the country, when so many young librarians are happy to attend even a regional event? While tempted to chalk it up to my own abilities, dedication, and efforts, I soon realized that the highlights of my career were really not much of my own doing. In reality, none of it would have been possible without the support of my supervisor. He got a ball rolling that didn't stop at the door to the library, or the edge of campus, or a regional event, or even the National Press Club. That ball, and my career, have the momentum to keep on moving uphill, thanks largely to him.

Hiring practices for the twenty-first-century library

I came to the University of North Carolina at Greensboro (UNCG) as the University Libraries' first Digital Projects Coordinator in October 2005. The position, which reported to the head of Electronic Resources and Information Technology, was something of an enigma to me, since my employment in similar positions elsewhere had always been in archives. Being neither a librarian nor an IT specialist (I hold an MA in Public History with a concentration in Archival Administration), it was an unusual fit. In addition, because it was a new position for the library, there was no precedent for what I would be doing, only a vague paragraph in a job description and the hopes that whoever was hired would know what "digital projects people" do.

In hindsight, I am very thankful that UNCG was willing to think outside the box a bit when it came to hiring me. As colleges and universities increasingly create interdisciplinary programs that blur the lines of traditional academic disciplines, so too are academic libraries becoming a place where customary, well-defined fields and functions are blended, stretched, and rethought. The same is occurring in library schools, where curricula now regularly incorporate courses in information science, instructional technology, and all manner of technical skills, while providing training in emerging cross-disciplinary niche fields such as metadata, digital curation, scholarly communications and digital publishing, assessment, usability, data services, and repository architecture. Rather than requiring an MLS degree or demonstrated course work in computer science, UNCG sought a digital projects coordinator with a particular skill set, regardless of whether those skills were acquired in school, on the job, or just "picked up," and regardless of whether past library experience was in cataloging or acquisitions or systems or archives.

> ☑ QUICK TIP
> Consider the whole picture when making hiring decisions, even if that means veering away from someone who has an MLS degree, so that you can include a broad range of qualified individuals with the aptitude and skills needed for the work at hand.

More important, as I learned later, my future employer put a premium on character and personality, purposely advertising a job that was largely free of specific skill and experience requirements so as to cast a wide net. Demonstrated aptitude, ability and eagerness to learn new things, flexibility, accomplishment, and proven mastery of something—even in an ancillary field—were considered critical for new professional library hires. They were characteristics that would translate well to any library position, and will become increasingly crucial as rapidly changing technology dictates changes in library operations. As libraries face an uncertain future, one in which it is hard to predict what we might be doing next semester, let alone next decade, it makes sense that tomorrow's leaders will be those that have a solid foundation of knowledge, talents, competence, and initiative with which to embrace the new services, technologies, and challenges that will surely come.

My employer acknowledged that character is sometimes a better indicator of job performance than years of experience, and that the right fit for a position may have more to do with teamwork mentality, enthusiasm, and creativity than a checklist of qualifications that might be obsolete tomorrow. In particular, my supervisor later confided that chemistry is probably the most important quality he looks for in applicants. "A great working environment," he notes, "leads to higher productivity in the long run."

> ☑ QUICK TIP
> Allowing staff to investigate areas of their professional interest may lead to striking innovations and great accomplishments.

I was able to tailor what was a somewhat vague description of my duties to my particular interests and skills. As a new position in a cross-departmental field, the intentionally generic job description left the day-to-day details to be fleshed out by the new hire. My supervisor gave me the latitude, and even encouraged me, to pursue activities and research in areas of personal interest to me, even if they were not specifically noted in my official responsibilities.

Characteristics of a great manager

It did not take much time to realize that the head of Electronic Resources and Information Technology and assistant dean of the University Libraries (my supervisor) was different from most of my former bosses. His approach to leadership and to managing library resources was decidedly distinctive. For one thing, he frequently included the entire department in decision making. Many times we would all sit around a table and discuss a new initiative that the library administrators were contemplating, or a service some other library department was considering. He would ask us to brainstorm on the strategic direction of the library, or for feedback on a new technology or hot topic in the library world and how it might affect UNCG. We regularly got

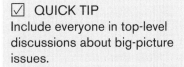

> ☑ QUICK TIP
> Include everyone in top-level discussions about big-picture issues.

summary reports of his meetings with other administrators and were kept apprised of campus-wide technology initiatives. To be certain, there was no information hoarding, and he always gathered as much concrete information and as many informed opinions as possible before making an important decision.

My supervisor, Tim Bucknall, is a librarian, woodworker, chef, artist, soccer player, and *Library Journal* "mover and shaker" (2006). Bucknall is well-known in certain circles as a forward-thinking, innovative technologist, librarian, and administrator, and his efforts have put UNCG on the map. Among other achievements, he is the inventor of Journal Finder, a homegrown integrated search interface and link resolver that competes with commercially created products like Serial Solutions. After successfully implementing Journal Finder at UNCG, he shared it with others, with more than 40 colleges in six states now subscribing to the service. Bucknall regularly mined aggregated Journal Finder usage data for information that could be relevant to library operations, including subscription purchases, improvement of the interface, or streamlined functionality. Journal Finder was recently sold to a commercial vendor for a six-figure profit.

He is also the brains behind the Carolina Consortium, a group of 60 libraries in the Carolinas convened to leverage their combined buying power. Bucknall has negotiated with publishers, saving the consortium members a combined $80 million dollars in 2005 alone. Begun as a group of 12 schools participating in four deals, the Carolina Consortium now functions as one of the nation's most efficient "Big Deal" negotiators, with the work of less than one full-time employee (himself) resulting in savings currently upwards of $100 million a year. Bucknall pours over every detail of every deal and crunches all the numbers to get the best total product for the best price. The result of this work, according to him, is a project that "exceeded far beyond expectations in all measures of volume" and continues to do so.

These two most heralded projects, as well as many of the smaller, lesser-known ones, have several important common factors. They all spring from Bucknall's desire to take a data-driven approach to decision making, his belief in the value of metrics and assessment, and his embrace of new technologies and inevitable change. Time and time again, I have seen him analyze data sets, looking at usage statistics and dollar amounts, making graphs and charts, seeking concrete evidence of trends. If it can be quantifiably measured, Bucknall wants to see the data before coming to a conclusion. If the best way to address the results means going against the grain or suggesting major adjustments to the status quo, any fear of change always yields to his drive for improvement and efficiency.

Bucknall's advocacy of "the facts, just the facts" has made him a popular speaker. A perusal of the 90-some publications and presentations he has authored in the past 15 years reveals titles such as "Cost-per-use Data for Electronic Resources," "Responding to the Results of the Journal Finder Usability Test," "Getting More out of your Electronic Collections Through Studies of User Behavior," "Evaluating the Effectiveness of Sharing E-Journals via a Consortium," and "Data-Driven Approach to E-Journal Acquisitions." His evidence-based approach, still a cutting-edge concept in the library world, has had important ramifications for those of us who work with him.

Assessment and evidence-based librarianship

Although use of measurements and statistics is a hot topic in the library and in academic realms, it is still a somewhat new trend, and one that is rarely utilized to its full potential. Bucknall was espousing assessment long before it became a buzzword in higher education or academic librarianship. According to the libraryassessment.info blog, the term encompasses "any activities that seek to measure the library's impact on teaching, learning and research as well as initiatives that seek to identify user needs or gauge user perceptions or satisfaction, [with] the overall goal [being] the data-based and user-centered continuous improvement of our collections and services" (Ryan, 2006: 78).

The concept of quantifiably measuring and benchmarking libraries and their services has a history that dates back at least to 1908, when James Gerould began collecting statistics, and became more visible in the 1960s when the Association of Research Libraries (ARL) began publishing his data and created its own Statistics and Measurement Committee. In 1994, the ARL committed to having in-house capability for collecting and analyzing statistics and hired its first full-time Statistics and Measurement employee. The practice of library assessment saw a huge boost with the introduction of the SERVQUAL survey by ARL in 1999. The following year, plans were made for its successor, LibQUAL+, with the symposium's announcement of this new tool prophetically titled "The New Culture of Assessment in Academic Libraries." By 2003, more than 308 institutions were participating in the survey, and in 2007, the 1,000th library used LibQUAL+ to quantitatively measure library services. The success of LibQUAL+ and the growing popularity of assessment have led to the creation of DigiQUAL, a project that repurposes the existing protocol to specifically address the services provided by digital libraries. More information is available from www.libqual.org and www.digiqual.org.

Of course, ARL has been a leading force in the push to "measure the continuing and the emerging realities of the modern research library" (ARL Statistics and Assessment Committee, accessed 2008). Initiatives of the ARL Statistics & Measurements department include annual member surveys addressing more traditional measurement of collections, expenditures, staffing, and salaries; SPEC surveys; the Measuring the Impact of Networked Electronic Services (MINES) online survey, and, in 2005, the launch of the Effective, Sustainable, and Practical Library Assessment service, in which Visiting Program Officers Steve Hiller of the University of Washington and Jim Self of the University of Virginia perform on-site consultations for a small fee. The year 2006 also saw the commencement of an annual library assessment conference and a companion blog, both supported by the ARL.

Closely related to the rise of library assessment is the emergence of evidence-based librarianship, or EBL. In a movement concurrently arising with the ARL's launch of LibQUAL+ and announcement of a "new culture" in libraries in 2000, a call for greater evidence-based librarianship was issued by the Medical Library Association (MLA), which that year created an Evidence-Based Librarianship Implementation Committee (EBLIC). The practice of EBL was soon adopted by librarians of all types, and defined as "a means to improve the profession of librarianship by asking questions as well as finding, critically appraising and incorporating research evidence from library science (and other disciplines) into daily practice. It also involves encouraging librarians to conduct high quality qualitative and quantitative research" (Crumley and Koufogiannakis, 2002: 62).

In 2001, a group of primarily health sciences librarians held the first EBL conference in Sheffield, United Kingdom, with a fourth biennial conference convened at the University of North Carolina in 2007 to meet the "increasing interest in using the best available evidence to improve library and information practice in all types of libraries" (EBLIP4, accessed 2008). In 2006, *Evidence Based Library and Information Practice* was launched. This was the first journal dedicated to EBL and "how it affects the decisions we make, how we look at and perform research, and how it allows us to make more informed decisions based on the best available evidence" (Glynn, 2006: 1).

The approaches just described are clearly reflected in what I observed from my supervisor. From him, I learned that the tools of library assessment could be applied not only to information literacy learning outcomes and goal-oriented strategies, but also to larger issues of accountability, transparency in expectations and performance, and return on investment. I watched as he compiled research that could help direct the library's strategic future, its planning for and use of physical space, its financial allocations, and its concrete goals for improvement of the library's physical and virtual resources. He exhibited commitment to assessment as part of an essential ongoing process, not just a biannual study done in a vacuum. I witnessed concrete examples of evidence-based librarianship at work—and I liked it.

My experience in evidence-based librarianship

My observations of Bucknall's data-driven approach and his management style were a formative influence on my career. As a lawyer's daughter, rational decision making based on hard evidence was somewhat preprogrammed in me. Seeing firsthand how effective quantifiable measurements, documentation, and statistical data could be in libraries was simultaneously eye-opening and totally predictable.

When I was appointed to the library's Institutional Repository (IR) Task Force in late 2005, it seemed only natural to me that this group would approach IR implementation at UNCG in a similar manner. I was assigned to the task force primarily because IRs are by definition digital, and I was the digital projects coordinator, and also because I had some previous experience in open repositories and metadata. There was never any intention of the IR becoming a digital project that I would manage; many members of the task force were aware even then that the most crucial elements of IR (content recruitment and description) probably were best handled by the library liaisons, catalogers, and the scholarly communication officer.

Nevertheless, as an IT department representative on the committee, I delved into whatever research I could find on the more technical aspects of IR implementation. As I looked at specifications of potential platforms—operating systems, supported file formats, interoperability, authentication and administrative access control, metadata, storage and backup requirements, etc.—I realized I really needed more data on which to base a recommendation. I wanted to find out what current users thought about those specifications and how they rated certain functions. In fact, I wanted to know just how many people were implementing these IRs in the first place, and who they were. So I went looking for answers in true evidence-based fashion.

In fall 2005, discussion of IRs usually revolved around three applications: the open source platform DSpace, from Hewlett-Packard and MIT; free software GNU Eprints, developed at the University of Southampton, United Kingdom; and Digital Commons from commercial vendor ProQuest (now managed by bepress). I decided that my research would begin with the compilation of a list of users for each; before I could start contacting implementers to find out what they thought, I first had to figure out who they were. Perusing the Web sites of each of these applications, it did not take long to find lists of subscribers or user groups, and patterns quickly emerged. Eprints user institutions were largely located in Europe and the British Commonwealth. The list of DSpace implementers included more American libraries but was surprisingly short. Likewise, Digital Commons subscribers seemed to be largely smaller American institutions, and there were far fewer of them than I had expected.

My interest was immediately sparked. Despite repeatedly hearing about how IRs were the new "it" thing for libraries, reading about their importance in literature, and essentially operating under the widely held impression that "everybody was doing it," even a cursory look at *Open*DOAR (www.opendoar.org) or lists of libraries using specific open access (OA) repository platforms revealed that this really wasn't the case, at least in America. I wondered where these ideas I kept hearing were coming from, and what concrete evidence one could gather to document the true status of IRs in the United States. Although originally seeking only a list of contacts who might answer questions about their chosen IR platform, I realized that this list might also be used in other ways, including as a measure of the popularity, or lack thereof, of institutional repositories in America.

Thus, from a small question (What IR platform should we use?) sprang a larger, much more difficult question: Why should we have an IR at all, if they aren't succeeding as everyone seems to think they are? I knew that for our IR task force, and especially for my supervisor, answering this question meant making a persuasive argument based on data and documentable facts. I also knew that to take a data-driven approach to this decision we were going to need a lot more data than a simple list of IRs in the United States. We needed to know more about the schools that had them, and to look for trends in which had them and why. We needed to know how many items were in IRs, and what types of materials they tended to be. Put simply, we needed to know many things that fell outside the scope of my duties as a digital project coordinator or my responsibilities with the IR task force.

> ☑ QUICK TIP
> Employees will pick up on those themes that you value: in this case, the importance of data in making decisions.

I spent a considerable amount of time those first few days formulating my study and researching the initial data before informing Bucknall of my activities. As a new employee, I was unsure about whether or not this kind of research was an acceptable on-the-clock activity for a non-tenure-track faculty member, especially since it was not an assigned project and could be viewed as irrelevant to my daily duties. But more important, it was largely because I found the research so engrossing that I forgot about almost everything else, including letting my supervisor in on what was going on. I knew he would be interested in and supportive of what I had already done but was less sure of what he might say about the future of my little project because I had a much bigger vision for what that little project might become.

I soon learned my supervisor shared my vision. When I discussed the activities of the IR task force with Bucknall, he immediately shared his hunch that many American library administrators were basing their enthusiasm for IRs on anecdotal information and hearsay, caused partially by the dearth of applicable "real data" to go on. We both suspected that the success and popularity of institutional repositories in Europe was being applied universally, since there was virtually no literature specific to America. What did exist seemed to apply mainly to MIT, a school with which we at UNCG had little in common. The remainder of American authors primarily addressed very general topics such as what IRs were and the theoretical benefits of having one.

One highly notable exception, however, was a recent article by Clifford Lynch and Joan Lippincott, both from the Coalition for Networked Information, which reported the results of a survey sent to 205 American colleges and universities the previous winter. Published in the September 2005 issue of *D-Lib Magazine*, "Institutional Repository Deployment in the United States as of Early 2005" reported, among other things, the existence of only 41 IRs (mainly in large research universities), tracked the types of content currently contained in them, acknowledged "confusing relationships at many institutions among digital libraries, digital research collections, and ... institutional repositories," and called for analysis of repository size as an evaluative metric (Lynch and Lippincott, 2005). The article seemed to validate our hunch that perhaps IR success in America was being overestimated, that perhaps European efforts were not necessarily germane to IRs in American academe, where OA mandates didn't exist and faculty culture seemed more entrenched in traditional publishing models. The article undoubtedly helped me understand the pressing need for more research and just how much data were out there waiting to be gathered.

I knew I wanted to be the gatherer. Instead of counting IRs by sending out surveys in the manner of Lynch and Lippincott, I wanted to go hunting for them—every single one of them. I wanted to decrease the potential for confusion over what was or was not an IR by creating and applying my own definition. I wanted to know what, if anything, these IR implementers had in common, and I wanted to know exactly how many items were in their repositories. Fortunately for me, my supervisor did too. He immediately and unquestionably saw the value of this type of research not only for our university's IR Task Force, but for libraries all over the country faced with the same decisions. Wanting to "weigh the potential costs of an IR against the probability of success," he wholeheartedly encouraged me to go in search of any statistical data that might serve as predictors of success.

Reasons to use research assistants

In hindsight, I vastly underestimated the amount of time this research would take. Starting with IRs that I found on Web pages for DSpace and Digital Commons, I had already created spreadsheets listing all the institutions using each. However, finding all the data I wanted about these institutions quickly proved problematic. Then there was the issue of tracking down institutional repositories running on different platforms or simply not listed on the various platform Web sites. Worse, the list of criteria with which to compare institutions with IRs was growing. My simple spreadsheet listing the total student body size, number of faculty, ARL membership, and *US News & World Report* ranking of universities soon grew to include additional categories such as physical location, number of undergraduate and graduate students, Carnegie Foundation classification, and American Association of Universities membership. My initial two- or three-day estimate for this data-gathering phase was rapidly becoming untenable.

Realizing that I wasn't going to get this research done without help, I turned once again to Bucknall. I was hopeful that letting my undergraduate student assistants double as research assistants for a few days wouldn't be out of the question, and it wasn't.

I absolutely could not have completed this project without the help of my student assistants. Hired primarily to scan unique archival documents and photographs, they threw themselves into this new project with enthusiasm. Counting the number of items in an IR didn't seem as tedious for the students as I had found it to be, and they came to look forward to an "IR day" as a welcome break from their usual routine. Several students were publicly credited for their work on the project, which is a nice addition to any recent graduate's résumé. I was proud that they came to feel very personally involved in the project, discussing among themselves which universities were "lame" because they hadn't added items since the last count, and exclaiming praise or surprise over those that posted large growth. The student assistants asked increasingly thoughtful questions and progressively demonstrated critical thinking about the data they were gathering. I overheard them discussing potential explanations for universities that were statistical outliers and pointing out trends among a small group of colleges.

> ☑ **QUICK TIP**
> Give credit where credit is due, at every level of help on a project.

The research assistants learned a good deal from participation in the project. I was surprised that several of them were specifically impressed with the idea of open access and new models of publishing. This was a theme that had always framed the study, but I was not aware my students had picked up on it. More predictably, several students noted what they learned about "how to conduct research" and "sources and technologies available when doing a project like this," skills which hopefully will prove useful in future classroom assignments. Finally, and somewhat humorously, at least one student commented on what she learned about "time frames involved in project planning," perhaps because this particular project seemed always to require more time than was initially allotted.

I am fortunate that my boss felt that having students do some of this work for me, even if it wasn't in their job descriptions, was justifiable. He could have pulled the plug on the project at any point, deciding enough library time and expense had been put into research unrelated to digital projects, but he didn't. He could have asked for a firm time estimate or cutoff date, but he didn't do that either. What he did do is remain supportive as my one-time-only data-gathering project evolved into a year and a half of monthly data mining, requiring several students to devote a full day every month to the project. The project had grown to include examination of incremental growth rates, which could only be documented by multiple item counts of every IR in America, as well as the prevalence of specific formats among these items, which similarly required tedious and time-consuming analysis of IR contents.

> ☑ QUICK TIP
> Many hands are needed to accomplish the work of important research studies. Supporting and encouraging high-quality quantitative and qualitative research may mean allocating resources toward an individual research project.

Benefits of research projects

As word about my study spread throughout the library community, it was generally greeted with both curiosity and enthusiasm. Some wondered why I would undertake such a project, since I was not tenure-track and thus didn't have to. Some simply wanted to know more about what IRs were and why they were being talked about so much at library conferences and workshops. Others wanted to know how soon I could report my findings so they could "save the date," a response that both terrified and flattered me.

Once again, much credit has to be given to my colleagues in the Electronic Resources and Information Technology department for spreading the word about my forthcoming data set. I was quickly put on the program at the Charleston Conference, a large gathering of librarians and vendors known for introducing fresh ideas and producing lively discussion. Despite being a complete unknown, I was given my own session and assigned to a room with a 100-person capacity—and all of this before any part of my data set had been analyzed. That would have to wait until a week before the conference, in order to have a full 12 months of numbers to report.

I must admit I was very pleased with the capacity crowd that attended that first presentation. I surely benefited from all the "buzz" surrounding IRs in fall 2006 and also from the promotion of my session by my many UNCG colleagues in attendance. In the end, most of my data did not shed a favorable light on the IR deployment in America up to that point, which I feared might deem me persona non grata for the rest of the conference. I was also concerned that 45 minutes of charts, graphs, and numbers would be excruciatingly boring and mind-numbing to the poor unwitting souls who attended.

Instead, my presentation was met with overwhelming enthusiasm and interest. Many positive responses came from those who had always suspected the trends I reported, but were grateful for evidence to take back to their own libraries. Some were stunned and even angry that the reality of IRs did not match with the hype, while others, including IR proponents, were at least curious to hear more about IR metrics and benchmarking. A line of people formed, waiting to ask questions and find out what more I could tell them. I left that conference room in Charleston with a stack of business cards and invitations to do just that.

From that point forward, each event or presentation spawned a request for another. From an attendee at the Charleston Conference came the National Press Club event invitation. After that, I went on to the International Open Repository Conference in San Antonio. There I met Chuck Thomas and Robert McDonald, who were involved in a research project that related closely to mine. From that meeting came a two-part article summarizing our findings, which, like the article that first opened my eyes, was published in *D-Lib Magazine* (Thomas, McDonald, and McDowell, 2007). News of that forthcoming article led to presentations in California, Texas, and throughout my home state of North Carolina, where I enjoyed a reputation as a leading expert on IRs and was unanimously elected chair of a statewide advisory committee on their deployment.

Once again, I must give credit to the library administration at UNCG, which generously supported this extensive travel. For invited engagements, reimbursement for expenses not covered by honorariums was supplemented by my library's travel fund. My supervisor and the University Librarian have both showed a tremendous commitment to funding travel for any employee on a conference program, regardless of the presenter's status as support staff, non-tenure track professional, or tenure-track librarian. This generous financial support allowed me to personally present my research all over the country, long before it was made freely accessible to anyone in the world through publication in an OA journal.

> ☑ **QUICK TIP**
> Funding travel at high levels for those presenting their scholarship is a strong signal of support for the research agendas of librarians.

Conclusion

In the end, Bucknall decided that, given my statistics, the chances that UNCG could recruit a sufficient quantity of IR contents to justify a substantial commitment of resources were not promising. Instead, he proposed creating another homegrown application as part of a consortium of peer institutions, something that could be done more economically and that could be easily scaled up if our IR program was met with great success. That custom IR system has now been deployed at four other universities, saving each of them thousands annually. My article on IRs was one of the first submissions to that repository.

For me, however, the decisions concerning institutional repository deployment were less important than how those decisions were made. Through my research, I knew that I had given my supervisor, and others around the country like him, reliable data on which to evaluate current and future IR initiatives. I knew that I had given my student assistants a learning opportunity that would serve them well in future classroom or office environments. And I knew that I personally had been exposed to

Exhibit 7.1. Suggestions for promoting research in your library

- *Hire new young employees with previous experience or demonstrated interest in research.* This is easy to gauge simply by asking in interviews about the applicant's thesis or capstone project topic. Enthusiastic, detailed responses will sound quite different from vague, labored ones!
- *Use young, enthusiastic employees to help find answers to specific library issues.* Consider assigning background research projects to these staffers before creating a committee to investigate. Not only will the investigator learn valuable lessons, but the potential committee members will be saved a significant amount of time.
- *Assign new and young employees to committees.* These experiences can help individuals learn about approaches to problem solving, the value of documenting processes, and how to best effect team-based decision making.
- *Actively seek and suggest outlets for publication.* Let employees who have engaged in any level of personal research know that there are a range of options, from regional newsletters to national peer-reviewed journals, and use your contacts to help facilitate the submission process.
- *Lead by example.* New librarians will be more likely to methodically search for answers if library administrators display transparent, evidence-based decision making rather than appearing to follow whims, gut feelings, or the pressure of internal or external politics.
- *Reward young employees who take initiative.* Create a fund and a policy that subsidizes travel related to or presenting research at 100 percent, on top of standard travel allowances. Provide bonuses or raises to non-tenure track employees who exceed expectations for contributions to the profession.

people and places that would provide the basis of a network from which would, and have, come other projects, invitations, and opportunities. I also know that most of the credit for all of this lies with a supervisor who inspired me, encouraged me, and supported me through the project that got me on the map, at the library for which he did the same.

References

ARL Statistics and Assessment Committee. Available: www.arl.org/stats/aboutstats/statscmte.shtml (accessed July 25, 2008).

Crumley, Ellen, and Denise Koufogiannakis. 2002. "Developing Evidence-Based Librarianship: Practical Steps for Implementation." *Health Information and Libraries Journal* 19, no. 2: 61–70.

EBLIP4. Home page. Available: www.eblip4.unc.edu/index.html (accessed July 25, 2008).

Glynn, Lindsey. 2006. "Editorial." *Evidence Based Library and Information Practice* 1, no.1: 1.

Lynch, Clifford, and Joan Lippincott. 2005. "Institutional Repository Deployment in the
    United States as of Early 2005." *D-Lib Magazine* 11, no. 9 (September). Available:
    www.dlib.org/dlib/september05/lynch/09lynch.html (accessed July 25, 2008).

Ryan, Pam. 2006. "EBL and Library Assessment: Two Solitudes?" *Evidence Based Library and
    Information Practice* 1, no. 4: 78. As quoted at http://libraryassessment.info (accessed July
    25, 2008).

Thomas, Chuck, Robert H. McDonald, and Cat S. McDowell. 2007. "Repositories by the
    Numbers" *D-Lib Magazine* 13, no.9/10 (September). Available:
    www.dlib.org/dlib/september07/mcdonald/09mcdonald-overview.html (accessed July 25,
    2008).

CHAPTER 8

getting the big picture through participating in library-shared governance

Toni Anaya

U pon graduation from library school, with diploma fresh in hand, I was enthusiastic to go out, conquer new lands in my first professional position, and make my mark on the library world. However, like many other recent graduates receiving their MLS, I was completely in the dark about how libraries were run. In theory, I knew all about budgets, collection development, and library politics, but my practical experience was slim to none.

Thankfully, during the course of my work in a university library, I had the opportunity to change all of this through hands-on practical experience in decision making at the highest level of the library. I was selected to serve as a member of our library's Cabinet (our decision-making body), and this experience changed everything for me. Throughout the time that I served on Cabinet, I learned about budget allocation, fielding requests for additional staffing, making the case for the library at the campus and national levels, and the ins and outs of library administration. Because the library took the opportunity to welcome an early-career librarian into the decision-making process, my career changed and the library benefited from having someone's fresh eyes on problems. This experience was one of the most beneficial elements of my early career because it gave me a big-picture perspective on libraries and helped develop my leadership skills. At the same time, I believe that I was able to give back to the library almost immediately through my work on this committee.

My background before academic libraries
While working as a paraprofessional at the public library, I enjoyed helping people find information and being a readers' adviser. I ultimately came to the conclusion

that becoming a librarian was the career choice for me. My position at the library had taught me the basics: issuing library cards, learning how to do a basic reference interview, the difference between a reference and a directional question, evaluating damaged materials, and dealing with difficult customers (which would definitely come in handy for years to come). I also learned how to put together programming that was timely and appropriate to the customer group we were hoping to serve; I primarily helped with story time for preschool children by deciding on a theme, finding books, and prepping the craft for the day. What I didn't realize at the time was that doing story time would help me learn how to project my voice, gauge my audience for their reaction, and adjust my presentation accordingly. This also helped me in public speaking; once you have danced around with a stuffed animal on your head while singing Hap Palmer's "Beanbag Song," the fear of making a fool of yourself while speaking to a group diminishes.

I began taking classes at the University of Arizona School of Information Resources and Library Science. In fall 2002, I became a member of the first cohort of Knowledge River, a program funded by the Institute of Museum and Library Studies (IMLS), which recruited Hispanic and Native American students to become librarians. With financial help from Knowledge River, I was able to work part-time and enroll in more classes to finish my degree in December 2003. The classes offered by Knowledge River built awareness of the challenges facing Hispanic and Native American groups that are sometimes very different from other ethnic groups. These issues include language and cultural barriers, access to a library from remote areas, and lack of telephone and/or Internet service. As I learned about these issues, I became much more aware of how the programming topics I chose would be received by some members of the community, and the possible discomfort some might feel about the content. I also came to the realization that for some communities, going out and making personal connections with the community would be the most effective way to bring some groups into the library. Looking back, all of this training helped prepare me for my future participation in governance and leadership.

My first academic library position and its responsibilities

In February 2004, I was offered the Library Specialist position at the University of Arizona Libraries on the Materials Access Team. Life in a large ARL library was very different from working in a medium-sized public library. This team, composed of more than 20 team staff members, was responsible for the day-to-day customer service operations for the library's five branches. This work included training, hiring, and supervising student shelvers; providing circulation and basic reference services; maintaining and processing course reserves; and maintenance of the book stacks. The basic duties of the position offered to me were to provide customer service and basic reference to customers at the circulation desk.

Because of my previous experience with the public library I was able to take on more responsibility. I was promoted to a Library Information Analyst approximately two years after starting with the University. A major part of my position was to coordinate the work of five other staff members and manage the fees and billing process. This included training staff on the Materials Access Team and, most important, developing new policies and systems regarding billing and collections. As anyone who has ever had to deal with unhappy customers getting billed for items they borrowed and never returned could tell you, developing policies that were fair and acceptable to the campus while keeping the library in a good light was a fine line to tread. This proved to be a lesson I learned quickly as I began to write policies for new billing processes. This type of leadership role taught me the art of balance and tact, and the ability to receive and evaluate criticism and defend and explain the reasoning behind the need for a new policy while addressing the needs and concerns of those affected. Suddenly I began to realize that this work called for a totally different set of skills that I hadn't realized I possessed. As discussions became more involved, my facilitation skills improved; the ability to guide and keep a discussion focused suddenly became less of a challenge. My confidence in public speaking also gained an additional boost as I developed my facilitation skills.

Increasing assignments

Along with these title changes came the opportunity to see how the many cogs in the library machine work together. One especially interesting new role for me came through a library project designed to re-envision our reference desk services. Previously, the reference desks in our largest branches, the Main and Science libraries, were staffed by professionals and a student assistant at all hours. A task force in the library took on the work of re-imagining how reference services could be offered, and designed a plan for staff to take over many of the hours that faculty librarians were providing. I was one of the first staff members to take advantage of the opportunity, excited by the promise of learning more about our collections and resources while providing more direct in-depth research service to our patrons.

Taking on new responsibilities in the library was a combination of my own initiative and my supervisor's flexibility and willingness to re-imagine my work. My supervisor in this position often worked with me to allow and even encourage me to step up to the plate when new tasks needed to be assigned. For example, shortly after I began with the Libraries, one of the mid-level supervisors went on an extended leave of absence; my supervisor offered me the opportunity to fill in for my absent colleague. My position suddenly transformed from part-time service desk person to a full-time position dealing directly with other units on campus, such as the Bursar's and Registrar offices. This opportunity gave me experience and insight that few staff got to experience. Not only was I dealing with other campus agencies, I was also learning student information software required to deal with student accounts as well as acquiring a new set of skills that would prove beneficial for years to come as my role evolved into a policymaking position. Not

> ☑ **QUICK TIP**
> As new opportunities emerge within the library, consult new employees and gauge their interest in taking on new tasks. Their openness and eagerness to learn may be exactly what the task requires.

only had I developed relationships with other departments, I had the skills and knowledge necessary to take on the responsibility of training new library staff to use this software to complete the work unique to the Libraries. Over the years, I was encouraged and supported when I expressed interest in taking on more responsibility and learning new skills.

Professional involvement

Not only was I encouraged to assume more responsibility in the workplace, I was also supported and encouraged to participate in professional development activities. During my tenure at the University of Arizona Libraries, I became active in local and national professional organizations. I attended American Library Association (ALA) winter and annual meetings (holding committee appointments) and local conferences such as the Arizona Library Association (AZLA) annual meeting and the Living the Future conference, which were informative and useful to my career.

During my time working in a staff position, I held appointments on two national committees and officer positions in my local REFORMA chapter. REFORMA, an ALA affiliate, is a national organization committed to the improvement of library and information services for Spanish speakers and Latinos in the United States. The group has a very active local chapter in Tucson, which provides funding for events such as the annual El Día de los Niños events as well as Nuestras Raíces, a literary arts festival. Taking a leadership role in a smaller local organization helps a new librarian learn how to lead a group, introduces her to other local librarians, and teaches her how to organize events. For example, during my tenure as an officer, I organized welcome dinners for the local library school and coordinated volunteers for a large literary festival held at the local public library. These activities would not have been possible had I not become active in the local chapter of REFORMA.

When library supervisors encourage their staff in this way, not only does it provide an opportunity to learn new skills, but it also gives staff the confidence to take on new responsibilities and think of innovative ways their positions can change. It also promotes increased job satisfaction. Encouraging staff to work with professional organizations will help individuals develop relationships with librarians and staff from other types of libraries. These colleagues can provide a new vision, which may lead to improvements in current services as staff begins to gain new perspectives of the profession and libraries in general.

Staff governance: my first chance to get involved

Soon after the start of my new position, I was elected to represent my work team on the University of Arizona Libraries Staff Governance Association (SGA). Established in 1993, the Staff Governance Association of the University of Arizona Libraries addresses concerns of staff and works with various groups in the library to ensure that staff concerns are treated fairly and taken into account when decisions are made. The SGA board consists of one elected representative from each functional team and two elected at-large representatives, for a total of eight people on the board at one time.

During my two-year appointment, our SGA worked on a variety of issues including the Staff Travel Guidelines and Shared Governance issues. Not only is the SGA board involved in library issues, it has a representative on the Campus Staff Advisory Council, which allows library staff to be aware of issues facing staff campus-wide. My work on the SGA board provided me with an introduction to the creation of library policies and the politics that surround those policies. This is one of the most difficult lessons for new professionals to learn as they navigate through the murky waters of office politics.

Having an SGA working in a library helps staff become involved in projects that are outside of their personal work team while introducing and exposing them to the different experiences of other staff members. In a large library, it's easy for staff members to become isolated and only get to know the other members of their team, never reaching out to other teams or even knowing about the other projects and initiatives going on in the organization. This also holds true for staff members learning of common issues faced by other staff in a college campus setting. When isolated and focused only on the issues faced by one group, the broader field of issues facing colleagues and the campus can sometimes be missed. The existence of a staff governance organization, run by staff that has the authority to make decisions and advocate on a range of staff-centered issues, helps employees become more invested in their work, sensitive to issues being faced by others, and willing to participate and become involved in governance issues.

One example of how a staff governance association can increase participation in discussions on important staff issues was when the SGA board was charged with revising the library staff travel guidelines. The UA Libraries had provided financial support for travel for many years, encouraging both faculty and staff to be active in local, state, and national professional library organizations. With the dissolution of the Travel Committee, both the SGA board and our partner, the Library Faculty Association (LFA), were charged with creating guidelines for the approval and allocation of travel funds for our respective groups. Not only was the board charged with finding a way to streamline the funding request process, but we also had to ensure that the budget supported as many staff members wanting to travel as possible. The task required many hours of work with individual functional teams, open membership meetings, and soliciting feedback from individuals.

> ☑ QUICK TIP
> Find opportunities for new staff to look at the entire library's structure and organization.

One of the challenges SGA was facing was the amount of staff this funding was to support; classified staff make up close to 65 percent of library employees, so developing a fair policy that gave us the "most bang for our buck" was vitally important. The lessons learned during our work on the travel guidelines proved beneficial when I was working in the Analyst position and trying to draft policies that were fair to all user groups while addressing the concerns of everyone who provided feedback. This served as the best lesson learned from my governance experience; I gained experience in how to address those concerns and justify my decisions while not feeling obligated to take all that feedback to heart and change the entire policy to the satisfaction of a few.

My big chance: serving on Cabinet

Although my work responsibilities were constantly changing and increasing, what proved the most beneficial were the opportunities I was given to develop my leadership skills by participating in policymaking, staff governance, and the distribution of the library budget. This opportunity came from my being appointed as the staff representative on our library's decision-making body, Library Cabinet. It was this appointment that kept me working at the UA Libraries and gave me an inside view of the realities facing a large research library.

The organizational structure at the UA Libraries is known for being a flattened organization with a team structure. The staffing structure has been flattened and most teams have only two layers of management: a team leader and a work team leader. This allows a more flexible work environment in which individual work can be changed or reassigned based on customer need. Staff are given the opportunity to be members of actual decision-making committees and cross-functional teams where the strategic direction of the library is decided, giving them the feeling that their voices have been heard and their work has made an impact on the daily operation of the Libraries.

The Cabinet group contained approximately 14 members and was composed of the Dean, Associate Dean, Assistant Dean, Team Leaders from each of the functional teams in the Libraries, a representative from the Center of Creative Photography, a representative from the Library Faculty Association, and a representative from the Staff Governance Association. As the consensus decision-governing body of the library, Cabinet discussed and made decisions on a broad variety of topics, from the library participating in consortia groups and positions to be filled to one-time funding requests and appointments to decision-making committees. This group was also responsible for creating charges for cross-functional project teams and committees, appointing people to complete this work, and assigning Cabinet members to serve as liaisons between the team or committee and the entire Cabinet group. Other topics that were discussed were the development of new services and staff, strategic planning, and budget issues. The topics we discussed gave me a realistic view of the issues facing large libraries on a daily basis. I also learned how to evaluate a topic and look not only at the local impact, but how it would affect the library as a whole. It's easy to forget that some issues, although beneficial to one group, may impact another and cause problems not so easily solved. I developed an understanding of how to determine budget implications when considering requests as well as how to evaluate which positions would be most beneficial to the organization when looking at permission to fill requests.

The Library Cabinet is the University of Arizona's way of ensuring and encouraging a more democratic decision-making process. All teams have equal representation and staff members have the opportunity to express their opinions and concerns on decisions that will impact their work. This type of decision-making process encourages staff to pay attention to what discussions are happening in the Libraries and understand how those discussions will affect the role of their team.

My experience on Cabinet made me aware of how important it is to keep current on what is happening in the Libraries. This transparency and the variety of ways I could provide feedback really made me believe that unless I spoke up and asked questions, I had no cause for complaint later when decisions were made that personally affected my work or that of my team. My supervisor did a great job of making sure the team was aware of issues and understood what was happening in the Libraries, and encouraged feedback so she could communicate the team's concerns to Cabinet.

Her example of how to communicate to our functional team helped me formulate a strategy on how to clearly communicate with staff when there was an issue about which I needed to solicit feedback from the staff members I represented.

> ☑ QUICK TIP
> Encourage new staff, whether they serve on decision-making bodies or not, to become aware of the system-wide issues facing the library. Consider circulating minutes of advisory meetings, announcing open sessions, or providing background documents.

My appointment to participate as a member of Cabinet during my second year on the SGA board came after a year of learning the culture of the Libraries. I was relatively new to the organization and had a steep learning curve, but I was excited and had the enthusiastic support of my supervisor. During my weekly mentor meetings, my supervisor would make sure to ask if I needed any help or background information for any of the topics on the upcoming Cabinet agenda. Not only would she ask if I had questions, but she would forward background documents to me and schedule additional meetings to discuss agenda topics for which I needed more help. She understood the challenges I was facing and was sure to keep that additional work in mind when job descriptions and functional work changed and new tasks were allocated. Most important, my supervisor listened to my concerns and any problems I may have had to make sure that my workload was manageable. This awareness really reinforced the idea that she truly cared and wanted to make sure I was successful in my new role.

> ☑ QUICK TIP
> Make time in weekly or monthly meetings to touch base with new staff about both the responsibilities of their jobs and the responsibilities of their outside professional activities. It will help keep you abreast of what they are active in and may help in creating a schedule beneficial to both you and the employee.

The activities taking place in the shadowy world of the Dean's conference room where the closed-door meetings of Cabinet were held were generally communicated to staff through weekly meeting notes and updates from individual Team Leaders. As the SGA representative, it was my responsibility to make sure the voices and concerns of staff were heard and taken into consideration. During my one-year appointment as SGA Cabinet representative, I was required to attend and participate in the weekly three-hour meetings of Cabinet and prepare accordingly. Preparation included reading proposals, agenda items, and background documentation in advance. Due to other functional work responsibilities, I often had to "make" time to prepare, so I would sometimes find myself reading over lunch or taking my papers to an empty conference room. More often than not, I would take the paperwork home. I quickly learned that this was not ideal and developed ways to remove myself from my desk so I could get some uninterrupted time to prepare for my meeting. The sheer amount of preparation for these meetings taught me how to prioritize my work and keep a realistic view of what can really be accomplished in a regular 40-hour workweek. It also helped me learn that sometimes it's okay to say no to a new project or assignment. Learning how to say no was a challenge, and I'm very happy that I had a supervisor who was able to help me see the big picture and allowed me to keep a realistic workload while leaving the door open to new opportunities.

Part of how I prepared for meetings was by reviewing the Cabinet agenda for the week, then discussing the issues that were unclear or for which I lacked sufficient background information with my supervisor, who also served as a member of Cabinet. Having a supportive supervisor helped me understand not only the issues but also the political aspects of topics as they related to the campus environment. This assistance proved invaluable as I began to realize that decisions made in Cabinet not only guided the Libraries but also established its validity as a "Place" on campus as well as defined its image in the national arena of academic libraries.

My supervisor was especially helpful to me during the formation of the strategic planning team of the Libraries and appointment of team members. Being new to the Libraries, I did not have the institutional memory of others who had worked there for years. Instead, I had to learn not only the institutional history but also the politics and roles of the different teams in the Libraries. My supervisor and her willingness to help me proved invaluable as she provided the background documents that I needed to begin understanding where the Libraries were, how they had developed the current strategic plan, and what steps were required to take the Libraries into the future. Some of the things that I had to learn were how and why an environmental scan was done, what steps were needed to create a planning timeline, and how stakeholders are identified. Most important, I was able to experience the strategic planning process from a staff perspective as well as the Cabinet perspective of being the management review team.

How serving on Cabinet helped shape me as a leader

Serving on Cabinet helped shape my leadership skills in many ways. It may seem obvious why sitting at the table during important, top-level discussions would help enlighten the mind of an early-career professional. However, some benefits are not so obvious and they include the following.

Relationship building: getting to know smart people at the top of their game

One of the most important things an employer can offer a new employee, regardless of position, is the opportunity to develop relationships with people in the profession who can help guide their careers and act as a sounding board. I personally have never formally sought out mentors but rather developed relationships with various individuals who have helped me understand the new waters in which I was venturing. Having the confidence to ask for help in understanding the issues as well as working closely with administrators in the library provided the opportunity for me to learn from and have conversations with library leaders about the future of our profession. It also helped that, as I sat at the table with these individuals, I was treated as a colleague. It made me realize that everyone, at one point or another, had been new to the profession, asked the same questions, and needed the same help.

Learning budget and finance: budget decisions as a precursor to leadership roles

It may seem too early in someone's immediate post-MLS career to be learning the details of budget allocation and library finances, but that is exactly what this opportunity provided. During my second year in my staff position, I was appointed to serve on the Library Budget Advisory Group (BAG) as a member of Cabinet. This group was composed of more than 20 individuals and required more than 30 hours of meeting time to allocate the library budget. The process was complicated and involved reviewing the different funding requests that had been submitted, discussing the benefits of each, and then ranking them in order of importance and impact. Since this was a consensus decision-making group, it took many hours of discussion to come to agreement on many of the different items. This challenging task was one that really forced me to take a look at the proposals, weigh the impact on the library, and decide which should be funded.

The experience I had gained from my assignment in Cabinet proved beneficial, as I could recognize which proposals would make a larger impact to the services the Libraries could provide in the long term. As a new employee, I found it difficult to understand how a library budget works with endowments and other funding sources. Being involved in the budgeting process gave me a real-life example of how these funding sources are used to provide a wide range of services.

Effective meetings: developing the facilitation skills necessary to lead

My tenure on Cabinet helped me develop facilitation skills. Sitting through hours of meeting time, I learned a variety of skills that have taught me how to lead a meeting and tips on how to keep it on track. The efforts of the Libraries as well as my supervisor fostered the development of these skills by providing me with training and opportunities to practice, and constructive feedback helped me identify problems and possible solutions on how to run a meeting more effectively. These skills have helped me lead meetings not only on a functional team but also at a professional level while serving on various committees.

Learning from your surroundings: environmental scanning to improve your library

During my role as the SGA Cabinet representative, I was offered the opportunity to play a role as part of the environmental scanning group for the Materials Access Team. This experience taught me the skills needed to conduct an environmental scan, know where to look for trends, and compile information and identify opportunities. This work made the strategic planning process much easier to understand, and I was able to read documents, comment on the planning timeline, and ask questions regarding the process with a much clearer understanding than I had before. This skill has helped me in my current position, as I can more easily identify opportunities to expand and explore services on campus.

Conclusion

If a new graduate is anything like me, one of the first questions he or she will have will be, "Where do I start?" My advice would be for supervisors to stay alert to opportunities, including positions they may not have considered in the past. By taking a position as a staff member in a large academic library, I developed and learned skills that were different from my peers who were not given the same opportunities during their first few years out of library school. These skills included extensive reference experience, the ability to look at the big picture and recognize new trends, and the development of a service record that has opened doors and provided opportunities to work with people on projects that most new librarians do not get to experience.

As I look back at how my career has evolved from a customer service clerk at the public library to an associate professor at a large research library, I have realized that I have been successful due to the opportunities provided me by having a supportive supervisor and library administrators who understood the importance of encouraging all employees to become active in shared governance and professional library organizations. All library employees, regardless of position, must be encouraged to become active in local and national organizations as well as supported to become involved with library and campus committees. This is the exact type of support I received from my supervisor, Robyn Huff-Eibl, and Dean Carla Stoffle at the University of Arizona Libraries, and was the single most influential reason I stayed in a staff position for as long as I did. Not only did I develop practical skills that have proven beneficial in my current position, but I have also laid the foundation of an impressive service record, which will support my hopes of receiving tenure in the future.

Further reading

Brin, Beth, and Elissa Cochran. 1994. "Access and Ownership in the Academic Environment: One Library's Progress Report." *Journal of Academic Librarianship* 20, no. 4 (September): 207–212.

Gamble, Lynne E. 1989. "University Service: New Implications for Academic Librarians." *Journal of Academic Librarianship* 14, no. 6 (January): 344–347.

Horenstein, Bonnie. 1993. "Job Satisfaction of Academic Librarians: An Examination of the Relationships Between Satisfaction, Faculty Status, and Participation." *College & Research Libraries* 54, no. 3 (May): 255–269.

Kovel-Jarboe, Patricia. 1996. "Quality Improvement: A Strategy for Planned Organizational Change." *Library Trends* 44, no. 3 (Winter): 605–630.

Kozsely, Marianne Gabriella. 1991. *Support Staff Input in Academic Library Decision Making.* Master's thesis, Kent State University.

Lubans, John, and Heather Gordon. 1994. "From Quick Start Teams to Home Teams: The Duke TQM Experience." In *Total Quality Management in Academic Libraries: Initial Implementation Efforts. Proceedings from the International Conference on TQM and Academic Libraries*, edited by Laura Rounds and Michael Matthews, 123–130. Washington, DC, April 20–22.

McKinzie, Steve. 2000. "Twenty-Five Years of Collegial Management: The Dickinson College Model of Revolving Leadership and Holistic Librarianship." *Library Philosophy and Practice* 2, no. 2 (Spring). Available: www.uidaho.edu/~mbolin/lppv2n2.htm (accessed July 15, 2008).

Sheble, Mary Ann, and Debra W. Hill. 1994. "Academic Library Committees: Their Role in Participative Management." *College & Research Libraries* 55, no. 6 (November): 511–526.

Stephens, Annabel K. 1989. "Staff Involvement and the Public Library Planning Process." *Public Libraries* 28, no. 3 (May/June): 175–181.

von Dran, Gisela M. 1993. "Empowerment—A Strategy for Change." *Journal of Library Administration* 18, no. 3/4: 3–18.

CHAPTER 9

campus connections: building a library and campus leader

Alanna Aiko Moore

Developing relationships and building community can benefit an individual librarian and also contribute to the success of the library. As a new librarian 18 months out of graduate school, I had one professional position in Chicago under my belt when I accepted a position at the University of California at San Diego. While moving to a sunny climate on the west coast was definitely part of my dream job, I was overwhelmed with learning the intricacies of a position with wildly different duties and responsibilities and navigating my way around a university campus that was much larger and more intimidating than anything I had encountered in the past.

Succeeding in my position as the Sociology, Ethnic Studies, and Gender Studies Librarian would require me to build strong relationships with faculty and students in three different academic departments who were accustomed to working with the previous librarian, who had been in the position for more than ten years. In addition, I would need to learn about the campus and its culture as a whole in order to become familiar with the students; to identify the best tools and resources to serve them; and to develop connections with potential allies who could support the mission of the library.

My supervisors at the University of California, San Diego, recognized the importance of building relationships and developing connections with my departments across campus both for the departments' benefit as well as my own. They invited me to consult with them often, offered tools and concrete suggestions to assist me with my outreach efforts, and were receptive to my ideas and plans. Building faculty relationships and campus connections increased my knowledge of the specific needs of each academic department, allowed me to gain familiarity with different campus organizations and units, and developed my leadership and outreach

105

skills through interactions with various "movers and shakers" on campus. My network of personal relationships simultaneously increased the visibility of the library throughout the university campus and provided me with support and assistance from outside the library.

This chapter discusses how my involvement with three academic departments and campus organizations developed my leadership skills and raised the visibility of the library. I outline a process for building campus connections and offer suggestions on how managers can help their staff build community by cultivating relationships and conducting outreach to different organizations and students. Although I speak from my experience as an academic librarian, the methods discussed in this chapter are easily reproduced for all other types of libraries. The creation of a supportive campus community helped me succeed on a personal level and grow as a professional, and positioned the library as a visible and viable partner in campus activities.

Community, connections, and relationships

I am a second-career librarian. Prior to entering graduate school, I worked for 11 years as a community organizer with local groups and coalitions on issues of social justice. Community organizing is about building relationships and bringing together many different people and voices that are directly impacted by an issue or problem. Community organizing works to develop collective solutions and personal relationships while addressing the concerns of a community.

I decided in 2002 to leave the nonprofit sector and to pursue an advanced degree in library and information science. Working with underserved populations, I saw firsthand the importance of equal access to information and resources and how this access could build power and create change. I wanted to continue to work on social justice issues, and a career in librarianship seemed a strong match for my values and ideals. It would allow me to continue to serve people and to create positive changes in society.

In my new career as a librarian, I continue to practice the principles of community organizing and have applied them as I developed relationships and built connections at the University of California, San Diego. As a librarian, it is vital to build and strengthen connections with people who have an interest in the library and the services that it provides. As a former grassroots organizer, I have a deep commitment to building these connections, developing community from the ground up, and fostering a climate of respect and trust. I believe this is the key to building lasting relationships with strong allies. Relationships take time to build, and all parties must invest in getting to know one another, to share, and to take risks. A relationship developed with respect can change a service transaction into something transformative and empowering. The "asking" and "serving" take on a different tone. Library relationships based on the principles of community organizing encourage public participation and allow all members of a community—including the library and members of the UC San Diego campus—to actively engage in the process of creating solutions.

As a community organizer, I learned to listen to the people with whom I was working in coalition. In my role as a librarian, it is equally important that I listen closely to the library needs of the campus community and am responsive to the issues that are brought up. When I initially meet with students, staff, and faculty one-on-one at UC San Diego, I have the rare opportunity to hear honest opinions about the library and the services we provide. I make time to listen since opportunities to receive candid and critical feedback from the people we serve is rare. Listening to feedback from students, staff, and faculty developed my knowledge of the university, campus-wide programs and services, and enhanced my leadership skills.

Journeys away from the library

For many librarians—especially new librarians who are struggling to learn the duties and responsibilities of their positions—it can be intimidating to leave the comfort of the library. However, in order for librarians to be truly successful, they must build connections outside of the library. This is true for all types of librarians—public, academic, school, and special. In my case, this meant stepping outside the Social Science and Humanities Library building and traversing the campus to meet with students, faculty, and staff in academic departments, campus organizations, and student groups. My previous position as a general reference and instruction librarian had not prepared me for this level of outreach, and I admit that I was initially incredibly overwhelmed.

Supervisors can assist the librarian with this task by helping him or her to navigate an often complex landscape. I was encouraged to tackle my learning curve head-on: my supervisors and I met often in the first few months to create a plan of action. In order to assist me in navigating my new position and building connections outside the library, we decided to map out the different "players" at the University of California, San Diego, and then plotted a course that would guide me to outreach success.

> ☑ **QUICK TIP**
> Give new librarians a chance to understand their surroundings. Laying out key players in both the library and the larger community or institution can help them make connections between library services and users.

Actually, we plotted several separate courses, and in the end delineated three distinct routes. The first route was the path of service to the primary library community served by an institution. In my position, this route would be a gradual journey on which I would build relationships with the students, staff, and faculty from the academic departments of Sociology, Ethnic Studies, and Gender Studies. The second route entailed building a solid thoroughfare to different campus groups and organizations. At the university, this included student organizations, campus community centers, and a wide variety of units and campus departments. The final route was (and still is) the most important to me: creating a straight line to other people on campus who could offer moral support and advice. This route was about establishing relationships and building community for oneself. Assist your staff in creating this route by having them ask themselves questions such as, "What kind of community do I need to build in order to achieve personal happiness and professional success?"

Having a plan helped me to overcome my initial anxiety, and I began the task of building connections with people who work outside the library. Faithfully following all three routes helped create my own map, navigate the landscape, and discover successful campus connections and leadership opportunities. By encouraging librarians to meet with stakeholders and develop relationships outside the library, employers will increase the profile of the library and build collaborative partnerships with organizations and individuals outside the library—no matter the type of library. In addition, your organization will exponentially increase the impact of the library as an institution and its programs across the board.

> ☑ QUICK TIP
>
> Building the profile of the new librarians serves the dual purpose of increasing the new librarian's profile and the library's profile within the community. It can also help build loyalty within new staff as you show them the value and pride you feel in having them on your team.

First route: serving the library community

Encourage your staff to start small by concentrating on taking that first step outside the safety and domain of the library. Focus on the first route—a path to building relationships with the primary library community usually served. In my case, I met with my supervisors and we discussed each of my academic departments—Sociology, Ethnic Studies, and Gender Studies. For each department, we listed the chair, faculty who had previous contact with the library, and significant graduate students. Whenever it was possible, my supervisors provided background information on each person and their history and experiences with the library.

The next step was developing an outreach plan. My supervisors suggested that I begin by writing e-mails to the faculty members in each department. In these e-mails, I introduced myself, told them a bit about my background, and offered to teach library instruction classes and to purchase materials for their research or teaching. My supervisors stressed that follow-up to these initial e-mails was very important and proposed that one follow-up strategy was requesting appointments with the chair of each of the departments. I had never met with the chair of an academic department, so together we developed a script with library talking points and included a request to attend quarterly faculty meetings. The talking points were invaluable when I met with the departmental chairs a few weeks later; they assisted me in providing facts and concrete information about the library, which secured permission for me to attend faculty meetings. At my

> ☑ QUICK TIP
>
> Practice scripts and talking points with new staff to ensure all members of the library are on the same page in explaining services and features of the library.

first faculty meeting, I delivered a presentation that highlighted new library resources and tools, offered my instruction and research services, and answered many questions from curious faculty.

The introductory e-mails and my attendance at the faculty meetings led to name and face recognition on campus. When I was outside the library, I often ran into faculty who remembered my presence at meetings. Individual faculty and graduate students began to call and e-mail to make one-on-one appointments, discuss their research interests, and schedule instruction sessions. I drew on the concept of community—the things we shared and had in common—in building these relationships.

The guidance and support that I received from my supervisors enabled me to hit the ground running in the first few months of my position. They realized the importance of sharing institutional knowledge and were able to get me up to speed quickly by discussing the history of my position, the key players in each department, relationships that had been developed with the past incumbent, and overarching student and faculty beliefs and assumptions about the library. Their belief in early and frequent staff development increased my skills, boosted my confidence, laid the groundwork for meaningful relationships with several faculty members, and established concrete connections with all three departments.

Second route: know the larger community

The second route I followed in my journey to establish connections and build relationships led me to different campus groups and organizations. At the university, these groups included student organizations, campus community centers, and a wide variety of units and campus departments. Although I was eager to begin outreach to the larger campus community in order to build synergy between the library and the rest of campus, I was unsure which groups would be most appropriate. Once again, I turned to my supervisors, this time taking them a list of campus organizations for possible outreach efforts. Together, we decided that I would begin building connections and relationships with the three Campus Community Centers—the Women's Center, the Cross-Cultural Center, and the Lesbian Gay Bisexual Transgender Resource Center. One of the reasons that we decided to work with the Campus Community Centers was because we knew that many of the materials in my subject areas of Sociology, Ethnic Studies, and Gender Studies would be of interest to them due to the interdisciplinary nature of their missions. Each center also has its own library, and in order to provide as diverse a collection as possible, we wanted to ensure that the library and the centers were not duplicating book purchases.

In order to begin discussion on ways we could collaborate, I set up a meeting with the directors of all three centers. At the meeting, I introduced myself and shared information about the resources and materials that directly pertained to the centers—monographs, serials, and databases that addressed issues of gender, women, and family for the Women's Center; diversity, culture, and race for the Cross-Cultural Center; and sexuality, gender identity, and politics for the Lesbian Gay Bisexual Transgender Resource Center. The talking points about the library that my supervisors and I had developed for faculty meetings also proved to be very useful in these meetings. The educational resources were of great interest to the directors, who were unfamiliar with many of the library's holdings. We also discussed opportunities for collaboration, such as cosponsoring speakers, film screenings, and a campus-wide joint book club.

In the weeks that followed the meeting, I was invited to participate as a library representative in orientation events during the first month of the academic quarter. My supervisors were supportive in granting me work time to attend these outreach events and felt it was important to reach out to these traditionally underserved groups. I accepted invitations to represent the library at the Cross-Cultural Center's "Block Party" and the Lesbian Gay Bisexual Transgender Resource Center's "QCamp"—the orientation for incoming LGBT students and allies. At both events, I distributed general library materials, such as brochures, newsletters, and bookmarks. I also transported books and materials that were specific to the needs of the students, staff, and faculty attending each event. For example, at QCamp I brought books that addressed gender identity and sexual orientation, including unexpected items like *The Whole Lesbian Sex Book* and *The Best Gay Asian Erotica*. At the Cross-Cultural Center Block Party, I displayed *The Encyclopedia of Rap and Hip Hop Culture* and *Voicing Chicana Feminisms: Young Women Speak Out on Sexuality and Identity*.

> ☑ QUICK TIP
>
> Get them out of the library! Sending a fresh new face out into the community—and even counting that time as work time—can help get the library reintroduced to the community. Provide staff with materials to make sure users become aware of both the services and materials that the library provides.

Attendees were thrilled to see library resources for specific audiences and how these materials supported students from underrepresented and marginalized communities. Many students remarked that it was refreshing to see the library represented at places and venues where it traditionally was not visible, and empowering to see "the edgy, current books we had at hand." A library presence at these events made the library accessible and shattered the perception that the library is only a physical place where you go to receive a service. From these outreach events and others like them, the way that individual faculty, staff, and students viewed and thought about the library and librarians began to shift and be transformed.

I made many contacts at the two events. I met the entire staff of both organizations, and also networked with stakeholders who were attending the events or were sitting at tables adjacent to me. Over time, the initial connections I had made at these two events deepened into relationships. When I ran into staff of the centers around campus, I inquired about their work and they asked if there were new developments in the library. I was added to the invitation list for the centers' fund-raisers and private events. I was encouraged to think about opportunities to collaborate with the library and the wider campus community, and began to recognize these opportunities when they were presented. Managers should encourage their staff to think big and to look for affinity and commonality with other people and organizations not in their immediate environment. These efforts will help develop a wider net of connections outside the library.

Relationships with the Women's Center, the Cross-Cultural Center, and the Lesbian Gay Bisexual Transgender Resource Center libraries increased my ability to serve and support the students, staff, and faculty that each center serves while also reaching the wider campus outside the physical building of the library. These relationships and building of community eventually led to my appointment to the Lesbian Gay Bisexual Transgender Resource Center's Advisory Board.

One of the key elements to the success of outreach is constant support and encouragement. I was given both by my supervisors as I pursued relationships with the centers. I was empowered to make decisions on my own and to conduct outreach in a manner that felt comfortable to me. Through these outreach activities and relationships, I began to develop my leadership skills and build a library presence in unpredictable venues.

Third route: building community for self

The final route is the most important: creating relationships and building community for oneself. In librarianship, it can be very easy to focus on the needs of others and to put one's self last. Librarians need to build community to have meaningful connections with others and feel engaged and present in the work that they do. It is important that managers support individual community building for each individual employee's health and well-being. Supervisors can help to build community within the library by sponsoring events that allow employees to build relationships and practice self-care in a non-work setting. The University of California, San Diego, Libraries does this by offering free yoga classes to all employees twice a week in a private conference room in the main library.

For librarians from underrepresented groups, it is essential to build community with other people who share commonalities around issues of race, gender, sexual orientation, and other identities. Many times, it is necessary to build this community with people outside the library. As a queer librarian of color, it was important to build community with people of color and the queer community. I joined the UCSD LGBT Staff and Faculty Association and got involved in planning activities and programs. I also began attending monthly People of Color Support Lunches for faculty and staff of color. Through the LGBT Faculty and Staff Association and the People of Color Support Lunches I met and befriended university employees from a variety of backgrounds who shared similar identities. Having this type of campus support made my own work more relevant. It also broke the isolation I was feeling as one of the few librarians on staff who was both queer and multiracial.

> ☑ QUICK TIP
>
> Create or promote opportunities for new librarians to build social connections with other staff from the library or the larger institution.

As a manager or supervisor, you want your employees to practice self-care and be present in the workplace. Managers can support this by modeling personal community building and offering support to librarians by encouraging each and every one of them to build community for themselves. Furthermore, by acknowledging that librarians from underrepresented groups need additional support, relationships, and connections, supervisors play a crucial role in contributing to the success of their employees. Supporting librarians from underrepresented groups in the creation of community increases retention rates and decreases their isolation, which lessens the chance that they will look for employment elsewhere. This in turn aids in the recruitment of new librarians from underrepresented groups who feel welcome when they see a diverse library staff from a variety of cultures, ethnicities, and backgrounds present in the workplace.

At the University of California, San Diego, my supervisors acknowledged my need to connect with other people around issues of race and sexual orientation and gave me time and encouragement to create the space that I needed. Supporting the building of community for individual self reflects well on the library as an institution, since through individual involvement, the presence of the library is developed, made visible, and accessible.

Three roads, one destination

Learning to navigate the university campus and following the three routes steered me toward success in building connections with people who work outside the library. Community organizers often talk about "assessing the community." Assessing the community entails getting to know the community that you will be working in, the history of the issues, and the people involved. Librarians who assess the community and work to build connections meet individuals who may have the power or resources to help the library succeed; develop personal relationships with these individuals; and build community between the library and the people who use it. In my interactions and conversations, I gained an outside perspective on what the library was doing well as well as feedback on areas in which the library could improve. This acted as an informal survey and assessment of our services and programs. In addition to being well-connected to the outside community, I was also able to represent the library as an institution, and the commitment of our organization to issues affecting the wider community of the university.

By encouraging librarians to meet with stakeholders and develop relationships outside the library, you will increase the profile of the library and build collaborative partnerships with outside organizations and individuals—regardless of library type. In addition, your organization will exponentially increase the impact of the library as an institution and its programs across the board.

Flexibility and freedom

Constructing three solid paths that led to strong relationships and campus connections depended on my ability to attend meetings and be present at events. My supervisors have been incredibly generous about giving librarians a flexible schedule, which allowed me to attend outreach events at the Campus Community Centers; meetings for the Lesbian Gay Bisexual Transgender Resource Center's Advisory Board; and other campus-wide committee meetings. As a manager, you may be reluctant to grant a flexible schedule and time off to attend campus-wide meetings, but the rewards are well worth it. Librarians bring back so much to the library—in my case, campus contacts, new skills, increased leadership, and additional exposure for the library.

Moreover, my supervisors gave me ample freedom in my endeavors to create connections and relationships with my academic departments, campus organizations, and for myself. I was given the space and time to pilot projects and float ideas, and the freedom to make mistakes. This was a huge gift; instead of being told in detail how to accomplish a task, I was granted the freedom to experiment and create my own methods and systems. This freedom to explore and make mistakes developed my ability to solve problems and strengthened my decision-making skills. Most important, my freedom to learn and grow came with constant and consistent support. My supervisors have an open-door policy and are constantly available to bounce ideas off of and to ask for feedback and advice. They both have hectic schedules and tight daily agendas, but they always make time for my questions and focus their undivided attention on me when we meet.

Funding and training

My success in my first year on the job was due in large part to the investment that my supervisors made in my professional development. To my great fortune, my supervisors provided both funding and paid time off to attend trainings and conferences. The conferences provided learning and networking opportunities, such as the American Library Association (ALA) Annual and Midwinter conferences and the Association of College and Research Libraries (ACRL) conference.

Other staff development opportunities were more specialized. My academic departments require many library instruction sessions each quarter, so my supervisors encouraged me to attend the LOEX (Library Orientation Exchange) conference to strengthen my instruction skills. Recognizing a need to deepen my understanding of information literacy, my supervisors also took the lead in encouraging me to apply for and attend the ACRL's Immersion Program, an intensive five-day residential institute on the best practices in library instruction. I learned about information literacy, practical techniques to make my instruction more interactive, and methods for assessment. When I returned to campus, they suggested that I present what I had learned at a Lunch and Learn for the librarians and staff so that everyone could benefit from my experience. They also worked with me to immediately incorporate the new teaching techniques into my curriculum.

My supervisors continued to support me in building community for myself. When I expressed an interest in attending conferences and trainings that addressed race and diversity issues in librarianship, funding was provided. I attended the five-day Minnesota Institute for Early Career Librarians from Traditionally Underrepresented Groups, the California Academic and Research Librarians Diversity in Academic Libraries conference, and the Joint

> ☑ QUICK TIP
> As much as your new librarians can learn from looking out—toward collaboration—they can also learn from looking in. Encourage and support opportunities for library conference participation and push your new staff to share their findings on campus collaboration and learn from others with similar experiences.

Exhibit 9.1. Million-dollar investment

When I hired my first librarian I was told, "You just made a million-dollar investment—support it well." The million-dollar investment is calculated when you consider the cost to recruit, including the time of the 20-plus staff involved in a recruitment, the cost of flying the candidates to the campus, housing and feeding them during their stay, relocating the chosen candidates, paying their salary and benefits, and training them and developing their skills so they can do the job. After a few librarians, I learned that supporting a million-dollar investment takes many forms.

> Alanna Aiko Moore, the twentieth librarian I've hired in my career as department head, is a good case in point. Alanna arrived at the University of California, San Diego (UC San Diego) as a second-career librarian. She had a lot of experience in her previous profession but was relatively new to the profession of librarianship. From the beginning, it was obvious she had the drive, enthusiasm, and commitment to perform well. The goal was to provide her the support she would need to do her job and allow her to develop and grow.

As I've learned over the span of 20-plus new hires, support comes in many different ways. For some librarians, it's beginning steps. This may be their first professional position in an institution that requires professional activities. They may have moved from a small college to a large university. They may not have had interactions with faculty. Support can run the gamut—everything from teaching how to navigate academic department politics to how to navigate around campus. For mid-career librarians it may be the need to develop the higher-level aspects of their position or devote themselves to personal research interests. Support may take the form of developing new skills, learning new technology, or increasing their expertise in their academic specialty. For others, it's a matter of moving from line librarian to a management position and developing a new suite of skills in that area. Despite the level or position or future aspirations, leadership development becomes a critical part of the process. Leadership is one of the most important skills needed by librarians, whatever their position. Whether they are leading a team of colleagues, a national committee, or a unit in the library, being able to lead, and lead effectively, is a critical skill.

> In the beginning of Alanna's tenure at UC San Diego, I worked closely with her to discover her strengths and style. This is an individualized process; every librarian is different, with different skills, experiences, and strengths. From there we worked together to identify ways in which she could support her position, areas needed to develop, and areas for professional growth and development. Alanna didn't need much persuading to get involved and continue her development and education, but rather gentle reminders to pace herself and select her activities judiciously. As a librarian new to UC San Diego, Alanna quickly established her qualifications by informing the academic departments she served that she had arrived, what her credentials were, and what she had to offer them. Locally, she volunteered for several campus committees, where she established her credentials by actively participating in the work of the committees, volunteering to support the direction of the committees, and serving the committees in a professional manner.

(cont'd.)

Exhibit 9.1. Million-dollar investment *(continued)*

At UC San Diego, a combination of professional development and education, university service, and research or other creative work is expected of every librarian. The library is committed to supporting this level of activity with a generous development budget (currently $2,200 per librarian per year), a substantial training budget, support for administrative travel, time to participate in training and conferences, and support from supervisors and Library Administration to guide and mentor as needed. In addition, the Librarians Association of the University of California (LAUC), of which every UC librarian is a member, provides opportunities to participate in a statewide association and has grant funding available to support research. Informally, support takes many other forms, including encouragement, assistance in identifying conferences, guidance on setting priorities, and belief in the librarian.

> In professional activities outside UC San Diego, Alanna was recognized as a leader. From her role as a Spectrum Scholar to serving as chair of the Spectrum Leadership Institute Planning Committee, from a session moderator to a presenter, and from writing student papers to publishing peer-reviewed articles, Alanna developed her role as a leader in the profession. Alanna has only been at UC San Diego for two years, but it is already evident that she is a true leader.

As the profession prepares for the next round of recruitments, expected in a few years as the next wave of librarians retires, the profession will be looking for leaders to guide us into the future. These leaders must be able to adapt to a changing environment, embrace the diversity of the profession and those we serve, and continue to encourage and develop the next generation of leaders. Our role, as both supervisors and colleagues, is to invest in librarians with encouragement, support, and funding so they can grow and develop. With rising stars, such as Alanna Aiko Moore, our future is secure.

Tammy Nickelson Dearie
Department Head, Social Sciences & Humanities Library
University of California, San Diego

Conference of Librarians of Color. At these conferences and training sessions, I continued to build relationships and made connections with other librarians of color across the nation, several of whom I have collaborated with on articles and presentations. I also learned new strategies for building diverse workforces and gained knowledge of pedagogies incorporating critical race theories. These accomplishments were made possible because my employers believed that investing in my staff development early and frequently would develop my leadership skills and build a knowledge base that I could share with the library and entire campus community.

Transferable skills

An area that new librarians often overlook is the ability to put your past skills to work immediately at your new job—what experts refer to as transferable skills. I was fortunate in that my supervisors strongly believed that the skills learned in my past employment should be validated and translated into the work that I did in my current position as a librarian.

First, they encouraged me to create a list of transferable skills. In my position as a community organizer, I had conducted countless trainings and workshops. My supervisors pointed out that these years of instructional experience would be relevant in my new position as a librarian, as I already was comfortable and skilled in public speaking, presentations, and creating curriculum. In addition, as a former community organizer, I had more than ten years of experience conducting outreach to constituents and building relationships with people in order to create social change. This expertise involved working with diverse groups of individuals from a variety of racial, ethnic, and socioeconomic backgrounds. My comfort with talking and listening to constituents and experience working with diverse populations was recognized as a strength by my supervisors, who suggested that I use this knowledge as I began building my three roads to outreach. Their recognition of my proficiency and ability in instruction and outreach boosted my confidence and made it easier to pursue campus and community relationships.

> ☑ QUICK TIP
>
> Conduct an inventory of transferable skills with your new staff member. Use their résumé or application to supplement their list of skills with other skills they would have.

Managers should also assist a new librarian in conducting a "self-inventory." Encourage your employee to take an honest look at himself or herself. Ask the employee to write down how he or she views himself or herself, and explain that this exercise can help construct an idea of how other people see him or her. Assist by helping the individual brainstorm the specific skills that he or she brings to the profession, to identify attributes that best describe behavior or skills, how he or she contributes to the department, and how he or she plays a leadership role.

Conclusion

The benefits of developing relationships and building community are numerous. Having the skills and ability to do this allows a librarian to listen and be responsive, bring out diverse voices to add to the discussion of ideas, and create collective solutions that reflect the wishes and needs of the people that we serve. Supervisors can be supportive in many small ways that have an incredible impact. By creating connections outside the library, librarians are able to visualize new ways to support and serve students, staff, and faculty and change the campus climate.

Further reading

Kraemer, E. W., D. J. Keyse, and S. V. Lombardo. 2003. "Beyond These Walls: Building a Library Outreach Program at Oakland University." *The Reference Librarian*, no. 82: 5–17.

Kuchi, T., et al. 2004. "Librarians Without Borders: Reaching Out to Students at a Campus Center." *Reference & User Services Quarterly* 43, no. 4 (Summer): 310–317.

Mehra, B., and D. Braquet. 2007. "Library and Information Science Professionals as Community Action Researchers in an Academic Setting: Top Ten Directions to Further Institutional Change for People of Diverse Sexual Orientations and Gender Identities." *Library Trends* 56, no. 2: 542–565.

Norlin, E. 2001. "University Goes Back to Basics to Reach Minority Students." *American Libraries* 32, no. 7 (August): 60–62.

Norlin, E., and P. Morris. 1999. "Developing Proactive Partnerships: Minority Cultural Centers." *The Reference Librarian*, no. 67/68: 147–166.

Tag, S., et al. 2005. "Creating Connections: Library Instruction Across Campus." *Research Strategies* 20, no. 4: 226–241.

Walter, S. 2005. "Moving Beyond Collections: Academic Library Outreach to Multicultural Student Centers." *Reference Services Review* 33, no. 4: 438–445.

Part II

out of the library

CHAPTER 10

leadership training programs and institutes: models for learning to lead

Mark A. Puente

I n my library career thus far, I have been fortunate to take part in two competitive and nationally recognized leadership programs for librarians. My experience with both the Spectrum Scholar Leadership Institute and the Minnesota Institute for Early Career Librarians has been nothing less than transformative. Through describing the curricula involved in both of these programs and by giving an overview of the other major institutes that are available to librarians, I hope to convey the significant impact that programs such as these can make on the career and job satisfaction of job participants. Having the opportunity to build leadership skills in a setting designed for that purpose with a group of likeminded people can be inspirational and move an individual to a new plateau in his or her professional development.

The Minnesota Institute for Early-Career Librarians

In July 2006, a group of 24 young and new-to-the-profession librarians convened in Minneapolis for a weeklong institute for emerging leaders working in academic libraries. I was selected to participate in the Minnesota Institute for Early Career Librarians from Underrepresented Groups (MIECL), a leadership training program that was founded in 1998 by two of the University of Minnesota (UM) Libraries' chief administrators, Linda DeBeau-Melting and Peggy Johnson. The pair conceived the idea as a result of their experiences mentoring and working with UM resident librarians from ethnic minorities. According to the MIECL Web site, only 12 percent of academic librarians are from ethnic groups that are historically underrepresented in the field of librarianship. Many of the young librarians with whom DeBeau-Melting and Johnson worked faced similar challenges of perceived isolation and the lack of a peer network in a work environment that remains ethnically homogenous and that consists of a rapidly aging workforce.

The MIECL has been offered every other year since 1998 and is populated by a group of 24 attendees, all within the first three years of their professional careers. Admission to the institute is by a competitive application process. According to the MIECL Web site, the institute has a dual focus: to [combine] "training in leadership and organizational behavior with developing a practical skill set in key areas for professional librarians" (University of Minnesota Libraries, accessed 2008). Initially the MIECL consisted of both academic and public librarians but, after the inaugural effort, the institute planners realized that the two groups have divergent needs and decided to focus the weeklong training program on academic librarianship. Recognizing the additional challenges associated with retention and tenure processes facing many librarians in this group, DeBeau-Melting and Johnson revised the curriculum to include workshops and sessions that deal with these issues.

As participants in the MIECL, we attended seminars on topics such as grant writing, research and scholarly communication, library assessment, and instructional design. Many faculty members from the Minnesota Libraries contributed their time to foster our talents and interests and to aid in the coordination of important social events held during the course of the week. In addition, local, regional, and national educators and trainers are engaged to facilitate the program and to provide training and skill development for the residents of the institute.

I was accepted into the MIECL after my first year of professional library experience with the University of Tennessee's (UT) Minority Residency Program. From the onset of my employment at UT, I was encouraged, along with my fellow residents, to take on leadership responsibilities within the library organization, the university, and the Knoxville community. Moreover, my colleagues and I were encouraged to become active in professional organizations within the library and information profession, and to seek out opportunities for professional development and training.

My experience with the MIECL may have been somewhat unique in that I attended with both of my residency program cohorts and recognized several familiar faces from my library school and from committee work with ALA. However, among the participants, we shared so many commonalities that new relationships and friendships were quickly forged. The group of selected attendees was diverse ethnically and in gender, and included early-career librarians working in public services, archives, systems and technology, and technical services positions, among others. Although we all shared diverse backgrounds, our work spanned every major area of academic library responsibilities.

The key 2006 Institute facilitators were Kathryn Deiss and DeEtta Jones, themselves respected authorities in library leadership, organizational and cultural competency, and communication theory. Our daily schedule was filled with seminars and training programs aimed at developing practical skills such as grant writing, library assessment, decision making, active listening and mediation, and various other topics. An academic approach was taken in the discussion of less tangible concepts such as organizational culture and change, and cross-cultural competency building.

The facilitators presented real-life examples of leaders and administrators in academic librarianship who have been instrumental in shaping the policy and practice of the industry. Weighted equally in the training were structured sessions and small group discussions geared toward self-assessment and discovery about individual strengths and leadership potential with the goal of creating strategies for realizing that potential and creating a personal vision for one's career path. This blend of teaching methods, excellent presenters, and hands-on discussion and planning combined to construct a powerful institute experience. As a group, my MIECL cohort examined literature and engaged in often lively discussions about issues critical to the future of academic libraries. The sessions involved many interactive exercises aimed at developing skills and competencies, which we could take back to our home institutions and professional organizations. These were skills we could utilize as we engaged in tasks such as conflict management and decision-making processes.

An unanticipated benefit for most all of my institute colleagues has been the establishment of a professional network of peers on whom we now depend for input and advice as many of us navigate through retention, publication and tenure processes, position changes, and many other phenomena that accompany careers in academic librarianship. Beyond the program curriculum, MIECL afforded us ample time to socialize with one another, share experiences about our respective institutions, and commiserate about many of the challenges we face as new academic librarians from underrepresented groups.

> ☑ QUICK TIP
> Building a network of colleagues is as crucial as the leadership programming offered at institutes.

Many from the 2006 MIECL were involved with various committees at their institutions or had accepted leadership positions in professional organizations prior to the institute. This fact may make gauging the effect of the MIECL on our respective careers and on leadership roles we've assumed since attending the institute quite onerous. In a recent article, Florence Mason and Louella Wetherbee, themselves library leadership-training experts, assert that measuring the efficacy of leadership and development programs such as the MIECL is challenging due to the lack of longitudinal studies on institute participants, or ones employing a control group to compare leadership roles and achievements. Moreover, they contend that the subjectivity involved in defining a "leadership skill" creates difficulty in devising studies that will "yield stable and valid results" (Mason and Wetherbee, 2004: 212).

> ☑ QUICK TIP
> Sending a group of colleagues to an institute at the same time can be a way to multiply the impact of any institute, leadership workshop, or program.

Nevertheless, the competencies built and the insight gained from the MIECL experience are felt strongly by me and my colleagues from the institute. The effects of this experience upon career progressions or on leadership opportunities pursued or realized may not be seen for years to come. In the short term, however, I have observed several of my fellow MIECL attendees making significant career transitions within the profession, taking on leadership positions in groups such as ALA or the Association of College and Research Libraries (ACRL), and being accepted into other professional or leadership development programs, such as the fledgling Emerging Leaders program of the ALA. No doubt, the experience for me was especially potent due to the fact that all three minority residents from the University of Tennessee (UT) attended the institute together. We were able to return to UT invigorated and refreshed with new aptitude and information to apply as a group as well as individually.

To summarize the benefits of MIECL, I can say quite honestly that, having recently transitioned to a new position, I utilized many of the skills that I learned at the MIECL during my job search and in my final deliberations about career options. Also, I benefited greatly from the input of my MIECL peers, and from the objective and sagacious advice offered by one of the institute's facilitators who helped guide me throughout my job search. The support network created as a result of this program is at least as significant as the practical tools and competencies that one gains from the experience. However, it was a combination of the people and the programming that brought home to me that institutes such as these can make a real and lasting influence on one's career.

The Spectrum Leadership Institute

During my library school work, I had the opportunity to take part in another leadership program, one which combines a leadership institute experience in the context of a long lasting relationship with the program. In the summer of 2007, the American Library Association celebrated the tenth anniversary of the Spectrum Scholars program, a scholarship program that has had a significant and visible effect on the face of librarianship. Spectrum began as a three-year initiative with the original intent of providing scholarship funding for 50 scholars annually from traditionally underrepresented ethnic groups. Specifically, the program seeks to support students of American Indian/Alaska Native, Asian, Black/African-American, Hispanic/Latino, or Native Hawaiian or other Pacific Island heritage or ethnicity in their pursuit of a degree and career in librarianship or information science. With a subsequent commitment from ALA Council, a developing endowment, and additional recent funding from the Institute of Museum and Library Services, the program has expanded so that, in 2007, more than 60 master's level scholarships and ten doctoral fellowships have been awarded. To date, the Spectrum Scholarship Program has supported more than 400 library and information school students in the form of a one-time $5,000 scholarship—with support totaling over two million dollars. In addition to this generous funding, the scholarship program pays for the students' ALA membership during their scholarship year and fully supports their attendance at an annual leadership conference, the Spectrum Leadership Institute (SLI), which is held in conjunction with the ALA annual meeting.

I was fortunate to be a recipient of a Spectrum Scholarship in the summer of 2003. My SLI experience was unique in that it was attended by Scholars from the previous academic year as well. (The 2002 SLI, scheduled to take place in Toronto,

Canada, had been canceled due to concerns over the outbreak of SARS in that region.) In addition to the financial support provided by the scholarship program to attend the institute, the University of Arizona's Knowledge River program provided an additional stipend to cover my expenses associated with attending the annual ALA conference. As with the MIECL and other leadership programs, the Spectrum Scholar Leadership Institute takes a practical approach to skill building and self-discovery in order to impart the basic principles needed for Scholars to become leaders in their field and stewards of the Spectrum Scholarship Program.

The SLI introduced me to many concepts about professional organizations, their committee structures, how they function, and what groups such as ALA can provide to support my career. The SLI affords the Scholars training and professional development as well as the opportunity to network with one another and with the presenters and clinicians at the institute. Those who serve on panels or who present on the myriad topics are seasoned or emerging leaders in the profession from every type of library and information organization. For many students or recent graduates of library and information science programs, walking into the institute is the first time they realize that they are part of a larger community of scholars as, frequently, there may be only one or two Spectrum Scholars in any given library science program. The SLI serves as a forum for scholars to communicate with one another, build community, and broaden the definition of diversity so that it extends beyond the ethnic and cultural diversity with which it has become synonymous.

The curriculum for the institute varies each year but focuses on programs, lectures, and workshops that seek to connect the scholarship cohort with practitioners who have made significant contributions to policy, theory, and practice in librarianship. For example, one component of the 2007 institute, held in Arlington, Virginia, was a "break-out" session during which four former Spectrum scholars who either had, were beginning, or were in the midst of completing their PhDs shared with institute attendees their experiences along this path. The presenters shared the motivations behind their decisions to pursue doctoral degrees and were candid about the challenges and rewards that accompanied that decision. On the schedule for the 2006 institute held in New Orleans was a lively and interactive panel program titled, "You're hired! Mock Interviews." The session was coordinated much like a game show in which two teams, consisting of current and past Spectrum Scholars, were presented with interview questions by a panel of guests and were required to devise, extemporaneously, appropriate responses to the questions, with critiques and advice following. Each year, the curriculum changes and adapts to new areas of interest and excitement.

> ☑ **QUICK TIP**
> Leadership in scholarship is a crucial skill that can be developed with a specific focus on research and presentation skills.

During my time at the 2003 institute, one of the most memorable parts was the opportunity to witness Scholars making formal presentations to the larger group. Prior to the SLI, a "call for papers" was made to the Spectrum Scholars listserv, thus emulating the procedure for a conference or convention of a professional organization. Three informative presentations were chosen (approximating the competitive process, as well) and were very well-received. This opportunity afforded me and the other participants the chance to participate in the scholarly presentation process in a welcoming environment and proved to be one of the highlights of our institute experience.

One unique characteristic of the SLI is that the curriculum is modified annually with the hopes of bringing to the fore critical issues related to the city or region in which the institute is being held. For example, the New Orleans Institute featured a compelling presentation given by representatives from the Common Grounds Collective, a community-initiated volunteer organization that provides relief, medical care, supplies, and aid in the reconstruction efforts to affected regions since the devastating hurricanes that hit the Gulf Coast in 2005. The presentation served to raise the collective consciousness of the scholarship class and, as well, presented each participant with the opportunity to become involved with the reconstruction effort. Indeed, the Scholars exemplified great initiative by taking up a collection and making a donation to the organization prior to the end of the institute.

The SLI is spearheaded by ALA's Gwendolyn Prellwitz, program director for Spectrum Scholarship, whose unwavering support and relentless work on behalf of the effort has been key to the program's success. Prellwitz works to extend the benefits of the institute for participants for years by involving Scholars in the Spectrum Scholarship Special Interest Group (SSIG), whose charge it is to plan Spectrum events on the national and local level and to increase the visibility of Scholars throughout the country. Participating in this interest group is yet another opportunity for leadership experience. In addition, Prellwitz guides a cadre of volunteers, comprised of many former Scholars and program supporters, in the planning and execution of the annual SLI. Former scholars are most visible in the event's closing ceremonies, a graduation of sorts, and the official transition of the institute participants from scholars to alumna. The sense of community that one experiences from this event is quite palpable. It has been my own experience that relationships are forged through the institute experience that continue for years afterward.

> ☑ QUICK TIP
> Collaborating to help create future versions of the institute can help participants build long-lasting relationships and cement their leadership skills.

Overall, the benefits of the institute for me were significant. The experience helped instill in me a desire to contribute to the library and information profession at large and to effect change in attitude and organizational culture in the workplace. The skills garnered from the institute experience have facilitated discovery about my personal strengths and limitations as a leader and manager. The SLI is much like other leadership training institutes in that it attempts to address the concept of leadership both within the context of one's involvement in professional organizations and as it applies to one's professional goals and aspirations. Perhaps the only limitation in this regard is that, because the institute curriculum is geared toward students and new professionals, much of the programming must address the challenges associated with the job search and the process of discernment about one's career direction. Nevertheless, the SLI presented as clear and broad a picture as possible about the importance of Spectrum Scholars taking on leadership roles in their careers and organizations. In addition, the success of the Spectrum Scholarship leadership program is evident from the number of alumni actively engaged in professional and community organizations and from those serving in managerial capacities on a professional level.

Luckily, there is strength in numbers, and the Scholars were, and continue to be, support for one another and a source of information about many dimensions of our careers and lives. The combination of experiences from Spectrum and from MIECL left an indelible impression on me and has helped guide me to an appropriate and comfortable place within the organizations with which I am involved and at the institutions where I've worked.

Survey of literature and leadership programs

The MIECL and Spectrum programs are two very different but successful models for providing leadership training for students or early-career librarians from ethnic and racial minorities who are underrepresented in the field. Academic institutions, professional organizations, public library systems, and state and regional library associations throughout this country and abroad have established and developed a plethora of leadership training programs for librarians in every stage of their careers and for virtually every type of librarian.

I will give an overview of a handful of these leadership programs, hoping that managers can understand the types of programs that are available and help their librarians to take advantage of them. Many types of programs are out there, centered at the state, national, and international levels. By describing the programs, I hope to convey not only my enthusiasm for the benefits that can be gained through attending institutes, but also some of the unique features that their designers have chosen to feature. Even if many of the institutes listed in the following sections are not appropriate for librarians in your institution, you may be able to adopt some of their features. In other words, some of the institute experience may be replicated through having speakers, programming, and initiatives in place within a library, bringing the experiences back home for every staff member in the library.

National leadership programs for early-career librarians

Initiated in 2007, ALA's Emerging Leaders program offers the opportunity for young or new-to-the-profession librarians (within five years of receiving their library or information science degree) to gain a glimpse of the inner workings of an organization as large as ALA. The group of roughly 120 librarians engages in a "virtual project" on which they collaborate with three or four other Emerging Leaders over the course of six months. The program, founded by ALA president Leslie Burger, convened its second class in 2008 with plans to continue. The focus here is unique in that it is designed to give the participants a glimpse of the inner workings of a large professional organization such as ALA. The Emerging Leaders program is also one of the few that accepts any type of information professional into the program with no geographical constrictions or restrictions about the type of library where participants work. Although it is clear that elements of the program are still being developed and refined, it offers the opportunity for the selected participants to meet and network with peers and engage in formal and informal discussions on a host of topics.

In one of the institutes targeted toward early-career public librarians, Infopeople, with a grant from the California Library Association, developed the Eureka! Leadership Program, based on a similar leadership program targeted toward midcareer public librarians (see more information about the Executive Leadership Institute later in this chapter). The first Eureka! Leadership Institute, held in 2008, was designed for early-career public librarians with "leadership potential" (Infopeople, accessed 2008). The facilitators for this program are Becky Schreiber and John Shannon, content strategists and consultants who have worked with public library and university systems as well as state and national library networks to establish leadership training programs. The pair also facilitated the Snowbird Institute and many other leadership training programs.

A program cosponsored by the National Library of Medicine (NLM) and the Association of Academic Health Sciences Libraries (AAHSL) in cooperation with ARL's Office of Leadership and Management Services serves librarians in the academic health sciences. The NLM/AAHSL Leadership Fellows program is focused on preparing emerging leaders for health science librarianship. The curriculum includes introducing participants to leadership theory and practical tools for helping to guide change within one's library and connecting professionals through mentoring and networking opportunities. One of the striking facets of the mentor relationship is that mentors are directors of academic health sciences libraries, and the fellows visit their mentor's home library for two weeks as part of the yearlong program. Participation is throughout the year and involves in-person leadership institutes, attendance at Association of American Medical Colleges (AAMC) annual meetings, a mentor/fellow match, Web-based course work, and a two-week site visit to the mentor's home library.

Leadership development programs available at the state level

Numerous state library associations sponsor leadership development programs for their constituents, with many providing opportunities for paraprofessionals or library and information science students as well. Naturally, providing leadership training on a state or regional level may present an opportunity to individuals employed by organizations with limited resources and/or more strict staff development policies. A few of the state programs available for library leadership development include ones in Ohio, Texas, and Illinois.

The Library Leadership Ohio (LLO) is one example of a program that accepts professional librarians with two total years of experience, as many as two applicants pursuing the Master of Library or Information Science degree, and up to three candidates with four to ten years of paraprofessional experience working in libraries. LLO was facilitated by John Shannon and Becky Schreiber, who started the Eureka! program described earlier.

Similarly, the Texas Library Association sponsors a weeklong retreat and subsequent two-year development program called Tall Texans. This program is open to degreed and non-degreed library professionals and information science "practitioners" with greater than five years of experience in the field.

The Ohio and Texas programs are not anomalous in their acceptance of non-degreed or paraprofessionals into their leadership training. In fact, a cursory review of state and regional library leadership training programs seems to indicate that the policy is predominant among those sponsoring organizations, particularly for those programs focusing on early to midcareer information professionals. The need to include paraprofessionals in leadership training with degreed information professionals should be apparent since the two groups work in tandem and must collaborate with each other on a daily basis. In my view, it is critical to include this sector of the workforce in leadership training as, so often, all types of challenges require that paraprofessionals assume increased responsibilities in our organizations.

Synergy is the Illinois Library Leadership Initiative established in 2002 by Illinois State Librarian Jean Wilkins. An interesting inside look at this training was published in 2004 by Carolyn Sheehy, who explains the genesis and theory of the initiative and discusses the results of an evaluative study on the program. Although the training is open to all types of librarians in all stages of their careers, this study focuses on the effect of the program on academic librarians and draws implications for the future of leadership in academic librarianship in Illinois. Sheehy posits that Synergy may be an exemplary model for other states to adopt.

Library leadership development programs at the international level

Two leadership programs that offer leadership training for international librarianship are worth mentioning. The Bertlesmann Foundation in Germany sponsors a leadership training program for librarians employed in major public libraries in larger metropolitan areas. The Mortenson Center at the University of Illinois, Urbana-Champaign, has sponsored leadership development institutes for international librarians since 2004. Funded by a grant from the IMLS, and in partnership with the Illinois State Library, the program has been attended by Illinois librarians as well as librarians from throughout Canada, Latin America, and Africa. The intent of the program was to establish a model that could be implemented by other organizations in the United States and abroad.

Perhaps the greatest challenge to approaching leadership training from an international perspective is establishing curricula that are relevant to a broad audience with great diversity in languages, collections, and modes of operations and funding. How this type of leadership training will evolve is yet to be seen, but the need for it is critical given the phenomenon of globalization and challenges and opportunities that await the global information market.

Leadership development programs for mid- and senior-career professionals

At the other end of the spectrum from leadership training programs for early and midcareer librarians and information professionals are those geared toward individuals who are already engaged in significant leadership capacities or whose experience and expertise make them poised for imminent assumption of such roles. Beyond the leadership "institute" model, a doctoral program in Managerial Leadership in Information Professions has been established recently at Simmons College in Boston through a generous IMLS grant. This academic program uses a hybrid approach of on-site workshops and distance-learning courses and is designed to accommodate professionals already engaged in managerial or administrative posts in the industry. This approach may help mitigate the adjustments necessary for working professionals to pursue this endeavor and mirrors the trends in LIS education and course delivery. The Simmons program is patterned after the National Center for Health Care Leadership Competency plan (NCHL), which utilizes competency-based learning theory to guide its curriculum and training.

Perhaps the most enduring leadership training institute sponsored by an academic institution is the UCLA Senior Fellows Program. Established in 1982, this three-week, intensive residency program is geared toward library directors or executive managers poised to lead major research libraries. Held biennially, the fellows program utilizes case studies, group discussion, guest lectures, and time for private research to educate the participants on topics related to practice and theory of leadership in research libraries. A weeklong immersion program on the opposite coast, the ACRL/Harvard Leadership Institute for Academic Librarians, was established in 1990 at Harvard University in conjunction with ACRL. Entry into the program is restricted to "those with significant administrative responsibility in an institution of higher education, and who show high promise for making a significant contribution in the future" (ACRL, accessed 2008). The development program offers participants the opportunity to reassess their leadership styles and to establish a new vision and new goals for their libraries and institutions. Programs such as these serve the library and information profession well as they challenge those already engaged in leadership roles and high-level administration in libraries to take an objective look at their effectiveness as leaders while simultaneously revisiting the theoretical foundations that shape their vision.

An excellent comparison between the ACRL/Harvard program and the Frye Leadership Institute in Atlanta is offered by Dan Gjelten and Teresa Fishel, who discuss the structure, content, and objectives of the respective programs, and reflect upon the "personal transformations" that were experienced as a result of attending both institutes (Gjelten and Fishel, 2006). The Frye Leadership Institute, also for mid- to upper-level academic library administrators and directors, is a two-week leadership training program that is open to information technologists, academic faculty, and administrators interested in the changing landscape of information technology. Gjelten and Fishel underscore the fact that the Frye Institute imparts a macro perspective for library and information professionals particularly about how the libraries support the strategic priorities of the institution at large. The institute also requires attendees to identify a specific project for consideration during their training, on which they commit to working for a year following the experience. This requirement creates a system of accountability for the participant, encouraging the translation from theory into practice as well as ensuring that the principles learned from the institute experience are kept at the forefront of thought beyond the initial resident workshop.

The Association of Research Libraries sponsors a leadership development program for midcareer librarians from underrepresented groups called the ARL Leadership and Career Development Program (LCDP). Since 1997, the LCDP has trained four cohorts in topics related to "strategic issues that are shaping the future of research libraries" (ARL Diversity Initiatives, accessed 2008). The goal of the program is to develop awareness and competencies to better prepare academic librarians from minority groups for leadership roles in research libraries. This 18-month program, in its second curricular iteration, consists of several major components. The program includes two multiday leadership institutes and opening and closing ceremonies held in conjunction with the ALA's midwinter and annual meetings. Participants establish a mentor relationship with a "career coach," often the director of an ARL library or a manager or administrator identified as having similar professional and research interests as the program fellow. The participants schedule a visit to the career coach's institution. Finally, participants are guided in identifying and developing an area of scholarly inquiry related to the summary of strategic directions for ARL, 2005–2009.

ARL also sponsors an executive leadership training program called the Research Library Leadership Fellows Program (RLLF). Currently in its second year, this program is geared toward senior-level managers in research libraries but is not limited to participation by ethnic minorities. ARL has been lauded for sponsoring several leadership training programs for academic librarians and library and information science students and deserves special mention as a longtime leader in offering a menu of leadership and management programs. ARL, through its Office of Leadership and Management Services (OMLS), has been providing leadership activities for academic libraries for more than 25 years and has had the longest and most consistent record of promoting leadership training and skills-building training in the profession. Thousands of librarians, primarily from academic institutions, have benefited from one or more of the OMLS programs, services, publications, consultations, or training workshops offered over the years.

A similar requirement is a critical component of a leadership program established by the Urban Libraries Council (ULC). Currently funded with support from IMLS and other entities, the ten-month Executive Leadership Institute (ELI) is focused on public librarianship and takes a contextual, active-learning approach to skill-building and problem-solving. The program was developed for midcareer executives or administrators with extensive project and budget management experience. Institute fellows identify a critical, real-time challenge facing their organization or community and work with their ELI sponsor to formulate strategies to address the "leadership

---

Exhibit 10.1. Interview with Anthony D. Smith

In 2007, Anthony D. Smith, Director of Digital Libraries for the University of Miami, was selected to be part of the fifth cohort of program fellows for the ARL Leadership and Career Development Program. For Smith there was no real strategic agenda when he applied, but the benefits derived from participation in the program have proven worthwhile for him personally as well as professionally. I spoke with him shortly after his return from the program, and here is what he had to say:

> In my mind, the greatest reward that comes from my participation is the development of a national network of peers. This is a group of professionals for which I have a tremendous level of respect, with a similar career perspective. We have a similar perspective because we are all at equivalent points in our professional careers and because we all represent minority groups and face similar challenges within the working culture.

The first of the leadership institutes for Smith was hosted by the University of Nebraska, (UN) Lincoln, in April 2007. When asked what about the four-day experience left the most lasting impression on his mind, Smith commented that it was the warmth and level of involvement exemplified in the actions of Joan Giesecke, Dean of the Libraries at UN.

> Joan spent a considerable amount of time with the group sharing her career experiences. She provided a thorough tour of the libraries which included Systems, Special Collections and Digital Production, in addition to other operational areas. Joan concluded day four with a fun, interactive session on library development and donor relations. The session involved role-playing by the fellows and served as a very nice conclusion to our four long days of hard work. I believe this sort of interaction is invaluable and adds considerably to the richness of the LCDP program.

The comments by Smith demonstrate the level of commitment that is required of the institutions hosting the leadership institutes to ensure success of the program for its participants.

---

challenge" (Urban Libraries Council, accessed 2008). Like the Frye Institute, this facet of the training adds longevity to the program as it requires the commitment of the librarian to work on the leadership challenge for two days a week over the course of the institute, guided by professional coaches. For the trainee the result, in theory, is an identifiable, perhaps tangible outcome whereby a problem or crisis is solved, a policy initiated, or a program implemented.

It should be noted that this by no means represents a comprehensive literature survey on the topic, nor does it present an exhaustive list of leadership training programs in librarianship. Many other programs exist or are more sporadically offered depending on funding sources and other considerations. The intent of this survey is to present an overview of the literature and programs that are extant, which have proven longevity, and which may have made a significant contribution to the practice and theory of leadership in the library and information profession. Furthermore, the programs and literature surveyed reflect initiatives that, consistently, have graduated participants sometime during the past three decades. Many more leadership training programs exist or are currently in development.

Keys to a successful leadership institute experience

Although sometimes leadership programs themselves are subsidized by the sponsoring organization, additional support is often necessary from library institutions that may have to provide librarians or students with the scheduling latitude and funding to attend faraway programs. Adequate leave time is key to having a successful experience and may have to be granted to the employee. In addition, employees need additional support for attending the program and follow-up meetings at conferences if that is part of the program.

The success of these institutes (my experience at the MIECL as a typical example) is incumbent upon the practitioner to be fully engaged and participate actively in assigned readings, exercises, and discussions prior to and during the program. However, without the support of the administration and mentors at the participant's home institution (in my case UT Knoxville), the experience will not be as rewarding or, for many, even possible. The application process often requires written recommendations from the directors (university librarians or deans) for attendees. Financial support from the home institution is highly desirable in the form of reimbursement for travel and board associated with institute attendance, thus alleviating any extraneous financial burden from the experience. The participant, no doubt, will invest a great deal of time and energy outside of the daily work schedule to this process. To support them, ample administrative leave time should be granted, if possible, so that earned vacation or other personal leave need not be expended. Needless to say, any time an academic professional takes away from the office will, most likely, result in backlogs and additional pressures upon the return home. These are considerations that must be factored into the equation when considering applying for this training.

Quantifying the impact of leadership institutes

I believe that my experience with the Minnesota Institute and the Spectrum Leadership Institute is not singular, but something that is common among all the participants of programs such as these. From personal experience, it seems that leadership institutes do an excellent job of motivating participants to become more active in organizations both inside and outside of the profession. The networks formed at these institutes are what I rely upon to maintain that momentum as my career progresses. Apart from self-reports, though, it is a challenge to measure quantitatively the effects of a weeklong or even yearlong program on the career trajectory and leadership skills of the attendees. Several studies have been done that attempt to measure the impact or even just relate experiences in a qualitative sense. I would like to outline the results of four of these articles here, demonstrating that mine was not a singular experience, but something that has been shared by others and measurable by at least some rubrics.

C. Allen Nichols offers a self-report of the skills he acquired when he chronicles his experience at three leadership training institutes in a 2002 article from *Library Journal*. Allen asserts that the aggregate experience of having attended the Library Leadership Ohio, the Snowbird Institute, and the Medina County leadership programs helped him to develop a "polished vision for [his] involvement in the profession" (Nichols, 2002: 40). He indicates that he and his confreres, graduates of the 1993 Ohio Library Leadership (LLO) program, more or less took over the leadership of the Ohio Library Association (OLA) after the experience. Many graduates of the LLO remain active in the state organization in addition to serving in high-profile posts in professional organizations within and beyond librarianship.

Although assuming the entire leadership of the state library association is a remarkable example, I have witnessed a similar phenomenon occurring with the graduates of the leadership institutes in which I have taken part; many of the same faces and names are appearing on committee rosters and establishing themselves at least as participants, and often leaders, within organizational groups and governing bodies of professional organizations. Although informal, this appears to serve as evidence of the success of these programs.

In a more quantitative way, Kay Barney studied the results of one specific institute on career satisfaction and career path of its attendees and found significant positive impact. Patterned after the Snowbird Institute, the Aurora Leadership Institute (ALI) focuses on midcareer librarians (those with five to ten years of professional experience) in Australia and New Zealand. Barney conducted a study of the 2003 Aurora class, in which she attempted to measure the perceived satisfaction with the training program by the attendees as well as the impact of the institute on their careers. Interestingly, Barney emphasizes the exigencies in library leadership development in light of the projections for retirement in the profession within the next decade. Her article reinforces that building leadership skills for the individual is crucial not just to that person's success, but to the success of our profession.

As previously discussed, quantifying the success of leadership training institutes is very difficult as there have been few systematic, evaluative research studies on the topic. Drs. Teresa Neeley and Mark Winston conducted a study of graduates of the Snowbird Institute that was held annually from 1990 to 1998 in Colorado. The research project focused on academic librarians who had less than five years of professional experience by the time they attended the institute, a requirement for entry into the program. Of the survey respondents, 40 percent indicated that they were still in the same professional positions since attending the institute and thus attributed little effect of the experience on their overall career progressions (Neely and Winston, 1999). The researchers did note, however, that self-evaluations seemed to indicate increased activity in other areas, such as publications and presentations. For neophyte academic librarians employed in tenure-track positions, having components of training that address the process of and, perhaps, dispel some of the myths about the publication process would be of tremendous help. Although it appears impossible to quantify the effects of leadership training on one's career trajectory, other measures, specifically scholarship, did weigh in on the positive and measurable outcomes of institute attendance.

Dr. Jana Varlejs of Rutgers University conducted a similar assessment of those who participated in the New Jersey Academy of Library Leadership (NJALL) from 2002 to 2006, 2005 excepted. According to this study, a majority of graduates of the program credited the experience with raising their expectations for anticipated career progressions, or to the development of emotional or professional competencies that have enabled them to take on leadership roles in their jobs, in professional organizations, or in civic, religious, and similar types of organizations (Varlejs, 2007).

Last, regarding the corpus of literature on the benefits of leadership training programs, in the summer of 2007, in conjunction with the IFLA World Congress, a satellite conference was held on the topic of leadership in the information world. The proceedings of the event are forthcoming but will include important papers on the topic of leadership training programs in a variety of contexts and will contain further consideration of some of the programs mentioned here. Karen Downing from the University of Michigan and several others treat the topic of leadership training programs for librarians from underrepresented groups. Tom Forest presents a paper on the topic of public librarian leadership training in Great Britain. Marilyn Gell Mason and Rachel Van Noord, both from WebJunction, discuss leadership training opportunities available through e-learning; self-paced and mediated modules delivered entirely on the World Wide Web. The WebJunction Web site also hosts a discussion board that contains several threads regarding leadership training programs. If, as with higher education, leadership training opportunities on the Internet become ubiquitous, it will be interesting to see the manner in which those programs are evaluated and studied and how online training will fit into the broader context over an extended period of time.

Conclusion

My experiences with the Spectrum and Minnesota Institutes and the long list of programs described here are but a few of the leadership training programs for those in the library and information science profession. The focus of these institutes is to develop and encourage the leadership potential of information professionals, sometimes from ethnically underrepresented groups, and numerous opportunities exist for almost every type of librarian, in almost any geographic region, and at any stage of one's career. Much of the literature indicates that these programs have had a positive effect on the participants. In self-reports, graduates of these institutes say they have benefited from these experiences by acquiring new skills, knowledge, and insight that has proven helpful in their careers and as they pursue and accept leadership roles in professional organizations. Much of the difficulty in ascertaining the efficacy of these training programs is due to the subjectivity involved in defining leadership skills, and few longitudinal studies have been conducted on this topic. Nevertheless, a correlation seems to exist between participation in leadership training programs and the pursuit and acceptance of leadership posts, and participation in presentations and publications.

This has certainly been my experience. The observation that has been articulated less often in the literature (again largely because this is almost impossible to gauge) is that there appears to be a sense of the creation of best practices for this type of training. It is evident from the similarities in curricula surveyed—indeed from the rosters of facilitators at many of these institutes (often featuring the same names)— that programs are feeding into one another and being patterned after models that are perceived as being highly successful. Moreover, it is evident from the survey of leadership programs in existence today that practical, outcomes-driven components are integral parts of training and aid in measuring overall success.

It will be interesting to see how curricula change as the constituency changes and as more professionals who are younger and who may have different learning styles and

---

Exhibit 10.2. Web sites of leadership institutes

For more information about the programs described here, the following Web sites should be helpful:

ACRL/Harvard Leadership Institute for Academic Librarians:
www.ala.org/ala/acrl/acrlevents/leadershipinstitute.cfm

ALA Emerging Leaders:
http://wikis.ala.org/emergingleaders/

ALA Spectrum:
www.ala.org/ala/diversity/spectrum

ARL Leadership & Career Development Program:
www.arl.org/diversity/lcdp/index.shtml

ARL Research Library Leaders Fellows Program:
www.arl.org/leadership/rllf/index.shtml

Eureka! Leadership Institute:
www.infopeople.org/eureka

Library Leadership Ohio:
www.neo-rls.org/llohio/llohio.htm

Minnesota Institute for Early Career Librarians:
www.lib.umn.edu/sed/institute/index.html

Mortensen Center for International Library Programs:
www.library.uiuc.edu/mortensen/

Senior Fellows at UCLA:
http://is.gseis.ucla.edu/seniorfellows/index.htm

Synergy: The Illinois Library Leadership Initiative 2007;
www.cyberdriveillinois.com/departments/library/whats_new/synergy2007_ann
.html

Texas Accelerated Library Leaders: Tall Texans:
www.txla.org/groups/talltex/tallldi.html

ULC's Executive Leadership Institute:
www.urbanlibraries.org

varying competencies participate in these programs. This is especially interesting in regard to technical expertise and human resource management. Again, my experience with these institutes has been nothing less than transformative. I look forward to the next opportunity to develop my skills further, to assess how well I've applied the knowledge I've acquired, and to revisit my personal and professional goals.

References

ACRL. *Harvard Leadership Institute for Academic Librarians.* Available: www.ala.org/ala/acrl/acrlevents/leadershipinstitute.cfm (accessed September 4, 2008).

ARL Diversity Initiatives. *Leadership & Career Development Program.* Available: www.arl.org/diversity/lcdp/index.shtml (accessed July 27, 2008).

Gjelten, Dan, and Teresa Fishel. 2006. "Developing Leaders and Transforming Libraries." *College & Research Libraries News* 67, no. 7 (July/August): 409–412.

Infopeople. *Eureka! Leadership Institute.* Available: www.infopeople.org/eureka/ (accessed July 27, 2008).

Mason, Florence M., and Louella V. Wetherbee. 2004. "Learning to Lead: An Analysis of Current Training Programs for Library Leadership." *Library Trends* 53, no. 1: 187–217.

Neely, Teresa Y., and Mark D. Winston. 1999. "Snowbird Leadership Institute: Leadership Development in the Profession." *College and Research Libraries* 60, no. 5: 412–425.

Nichols, C. Allen. 2002. "Leaders: Born or Bred? Confessions from a Leadership Training Junkie." *Library Journal* 27, no. 13 (August 15): 38–40.

University of Minnesota Libraries. *Minnesota Institute for Early Career Librarians.* Available: www.lib.umn.edu/sed/institute/index.html (accessed July 27, 2008).

Urban Libraries Council. *ULC's Executive Leadership Institute Guidelines for Selecting Fellows, Sponsors and Projects.* Available: www.urbanlibraries.org/participationguidelines.html (accessed July 27, 2008).

Varlejs, Jana. 2007. "The New Jersey Academy of Library Leadership: What Impact Has It Had? In *Continuing Professional Development: Pathways to Library Leadership in the Library and Information World,* edited by Ann Ritchie and Clare Walker, 183–198. Munich: K.G. Saur.

tilling fresh ground: cultivating minority librarians for library leadership through programs and initiatives

Tamika Barnes McCollough
Iyanna Sims

L ibrarians are multifaceted professionals who perform numerous varied roles. We traditionally are organizers and disseminators of information—gatekeepers who ensure information seekers have access to good and valid information for research or informed decision making. However, with the changing landscape of librarianship we have significantly gone beyond our traditional role. We have now become business professionals, lawyers, and database managers. Librarians have found themselves in the role of price negotiators who acquire electronic resources, lawyers who review and modify contracts, and database managers who maintain, update, and, in some cases, enhance knowledge databases such as online catalogs. In addition, to meet the ever-growing virtual-information need of consumers, we have become Web developers providing Web 2.0 services that enhance patrons' library experience with RSS feeds, blogs, and podcasting.

As if this wasn't a long enough repertoire, we dare suggest that librarians can add yet another role to an already extensive list. What more could we possibly be doing in the field of librarianship, you may ask? Believe it or not, librarians can be likened to an agricultural farmer. Yes, that's right, farmers! Characteristic of a profession that constantly adapts to changes efficiently and effectively, librarians, like farmers, have begun to till fresh ground of early-career librarians in a response to the change in age and ethnic demographics in the profession. According to the Diversity Counts report from offices within the American Library Association (ALA), African Americans and Latinos are seeing a decrease in the number of credentialed librarians under the age of 45 (ALA Office of Diversity and ALA Office of Research and Statistics, 2007). Librarians in leadership have responded to these figures by developing programs and initiatives to begin to raise strong minority library leadership. These efforts are cultivating librarians from the beginning of their academic training to early-career endeavors.

The soil: minority-based initiatives and programs

Several programs have been put into place to help develop minority librarians or librarians at minority institutions. In this context, the term *minority* is defined as a person or institution that primarily serves American Indian/Alaska Native, Asian, Black/African American, Hispanic/Latino, or Native Hawaiian/Other Pacific Islander. These programs range from academic initiatives aimed to get minorities interested in the field to professional initiatives that are developed to retain and develop the leaders of the future. Table 11.1 shows just a few examples of these types of programs.

This is just a very brief synopsis of each program. Visiting each of the Web sites given in Table 11.1 can help provide more detailed information about the components or how to apply, or contact information. However, you will find in this chapter engaging primary accounts of two librarians at North Carolina A&T State University's F. D. Bluford Library who have taken advantage of these avenues to prepare for leadership. The personal accounts shared give detailed descriptions of each program and the benefits of involvement. Tamika Barnes McCollough, current head of the Environmental Protection Agency Research Triangle Park Library, shares a personal account of the Spectrum Program. Iyanna Sims, Electronic Resources Librarian at North Carolina A&T State University, provides an account of the Historically Black Colleges and Universities (HBCUs) Library Alliance Leadership Institute and Exchange Program.

The growth of a seed, part I: Tamika's story

My story begins in 1995 as a paraprofessional in the acquisitions department at North Carolina State University (NCSU) Libraries. At the time, I thought my purpose for working there was to figure out what my career path would be. I had no idea that I would work at that library for more than two years before I would discover what I really wanted to do. I had thought it would somehow be associated with the medical field since I was a biology major. As the two years quickly turned into four, I discovered that my career was staring me in the face every day. The recruitment from my supervisors and colleagues began early on. Surprisingly, many of the paraprofessionals I worked with also suggested that I become a librarian. My first thought was "What exactly does being a librarian mean, and why would I want to do that?" I put the thought out of my mind and just focused on learning and doing my job.

Soon I became involved with the staff association, not because I thought it would benefit me, but because a colleague in my department pushed me into it. My

Table 11.1. Minority-based programs and initiatives

Name	Intended Audience	Link for Further Information	Money/Experience
Spectrum Program: Established in 1997	Library School Student	www.ala.org/ala/ diversity/spectrum/ spectrum.htm	$5,000 scholarship, 3-day leadership and mentorship component
Association of Research Libraries (ARL) Initiative to Recruit a Diverse Workforce	Library School Student	www.arl.org/ diversity/init/index .shtml	$5,000 per academic year with a possibility of renewal and a 3-day leadership and mentorship component
Minnesota Institute for Early Career Librarians: Established in 1998	Early Career	www.lib.umn.edu/ sed/institute/index .html	7-day leadership component
ARL Leadership and Career Development Program (LCDP): Established in 1997	Midcareer	www.arl.org/diversity/ lcdp/	18-month leadership program
HBCU (Historically Black Colleges and Universities) Library Alliance Leadership Program	Early Career	www.hbculibraries .org/html/leadership .html	5-day leadership program with additional days the following year to present results of project
HBCU (Historically Black Colleges and Universities) Library Alliance Exchange Program	Early Career	www.hbculibraries .org/html/exchange- program.html	2-week exchange program

involvement in the staff association greatly contributed to my professional development. That organization made me get out of my comfort zone in acquisitions and do more than just go to work, do my job, and then leave. The involvement made me interact with people in different departments and, indirectly, educated me about activities that took place outside of my world in acquisitions. I had to quickly learn the best ways to communicate and collaborate with people in different departments and at various levels throughout the library when planning and promoting events.

At the time, I wasn't sure what I wanted to do for the rest of my life or even the next five years. I started to listen more to my supervisors about becoming a librarian. I started to observe what librarians were doing and began my investigation. Before I began looking at programs, I had no idea what getting a master's in librarianship would entail. So while looking, I also questioned individuals who were attending school and those who already had their degrees. I decided the best fit for my personal situation would be to attend North Carolina Central University (NCCU) School of Library and Information Sciences located in Durham.

After I began the program in August 1997, I heard about an initiative to recruit minority librarians to the field. At the time, I did not even look into it. I mistakenly considered it too much work while I was busy with a full-time job and school. I am extremely grateful that several people corrected my shortsightedness at the time, people who believed in me and wanted to help me. One particular instance involved Nancy Gibbs, who came to my desk with a copy of the information to tell me that I should look into it. Of course, because she took the time to bring it to my attention, I took the time to read it.

The information she gave me was about the Spectrum Initiative. The Spectrum Initiative was going to award 50 students $5,000 to assist with educational needs and a leadership institute. I was fortunate that I was working for a university and one of my benefits was the opportunity to take a class in the fall and spring semester, with the tuition waived. This was a fantastic benefit, but I wanted to take classes straight through and finish as quickly as possible. Since I had to give up my part-time employment when I began school, I was not sure how I would pay for additional classes without having to take out student loans. Needless to say, the $5,000 caught my attention. I applied and felt extremely fortunate that my references were supportive. I also encouraged and nagged Jamal Cromity, who worked with me at the library and also attended classes at NCCU, to apply. In addition to wanting a friend alongside me, I wanted someone who I thought deserved the opportunity to participate. I consider myself lucky that a supervisor took the time to realize potential that I did not see in myself at the time.

☑ QUICK TIP
Keep in mind that family and personal support systems are especially important in the lives of those in the early parts of their career.

I still remember the feeling I had when Lillian Lewis called me at work one afternoon and told me that I was one of the 50 chosen to receive this scholarship. It was hard not to scream; I had to quickly remember that I was in a business setting. That day began a professional journey that I hope I will never forget. The best part is that my co-worker and friend Jamal also was selected. I was ecstatic and knew that this would be a great opportunity, but did not realize at the time just how great. As a new initiative for ALA, we were asked to attend the annual conference that year in Washington, DC. It was not a part of our award, but they wanted faces associated with the names and this initiative when they made the announcement at the annual business meeting. Through the generosity of NCSU Libraries and the library school, I was able to attend my first annual conference and begin my service to Spectrum. This was a new experience for me, so I took my own support system and had my mother go along with me. In addition to her being my support, it also gave my mother a glimpse inside the profession; she was able to tackle the exhibits and go to a reception with me. Once I received the first installment of the scholarship in the fall semester, it gave me comfort to know that my classes were paid for and now I could use my personal money to invest in my first personal computer. I was able to work on my assignments from home, which was an unexpected benefit and a great feeling.

In June 1999, I attended my three-day leadership institute, which is part of the award. The institute took place prior to the annual conference in New Orleans. To be honest, I was not sure what to expect. The award included travel, meals, and accommodations for those three days. All I knew is that we'd be introduced to numerous people and that they would speak to us about the program. The days were full of cultural awareness and appreciation, interaction with the leaders in the field, inspiring speakers detailing practical skills needed to be a leader, and opportunities to meet and network with ALA members who held top positions. Listening to the library leaders, I learned that *advocacy* was a term that I needed to become comfortable with. Looking back, I realize that having a chance to talk with a person such as E. J. Josey, who has made a mark in library history, is amazing.

> ☑ QUICK TIP
> Advocacy within an organization–even proving your own value–is just as important as advocacy outside of the library walls.

We heard from inspirational speakers such as Eugenie Prime, who taught us that no matter where you work you have to be successful at making management realize your value. This is a lesson that I have kept in the forefront of my mind as I have moved to new positions and grown in the profession. Meeting with leaders in ALA, such as the executive director and the president, gave us dedicated time to hear about what paths they took to get to the leadership roles they were currently serving. Few librarians have had the opportunity to meet these leaders and ask questions in such a small setting.

As I have talked to new librarians over the years, I realize more and more how lucky the Spectrum Scholars are to have these experiences and how it helps us feel that we have made the right decision to work in this field. Librarians have a variety of jobs and professional opportunities from which to choose. The fact that I got to meet several historic figures and seasoned librarians and had the benefit of their willingness to share their wisdom was priceless. As a supervisor you may have librarians who, like me, can make more sense of the history, trends, and challenges of the profession by hearing the stories of the people who lived and worked through those experiences. How can you re-create such an experience for your staff? One way to achieve this goal is to provide opportunities for your staff to attend local or national meetings. Just remember that these

> ☑ QUICK TIP
> Hearing from leaders and innovative thinkers in the field can rejuvenate librarians and provide creative fodder for new projects. Supporting attendance at local and national conferences and inviting speakers to come to the library are two ways to accomplish this goal.

meetings can seem overwhelming for a new person, so try to make sure that you introduce the new librarians to people in your network or have them tag along with you to meetings. This will help the new librarian out tremendously because he or she will have someone that can answer questions as they arise. Another way to help your new librarians learn more about this profession is to invite speakers to visit and talk to your staff. It is likely that someone local, who is volunteering for a professional organization at the state or national level, would enjoy sharing his or her experiences.

The part of the institute, and any other leadership training since, that was unique for me during that time, was the fact that culture was intertwined with the leadership curriculum. So many messages were given out during those days that at times it was difficult to digest everything. Many realized for the first time that even though they worked in a library at which they were the only minority, they were not alone in this journey. We now had a family of scholars that we could call on that covered a wide spectrum of age, gender, years of experience, and ethnicity.

Another aspect of my particular institute was a mentorship program. Every Spectrum Scholar was assigned a mentor. The goal of the mentor-mentee relationship was to provide the mentee with a professional that was available for questions and that would help the mentee set goals for his or her career after the institute. In addition to the person I was assigned to, I also found my own mentors during that time. I found people who were in positions that I aspired to be in or had leadership qualities that I admired. Approaches to mentoring vary, and many articles in the literature address establishing mentoring programs for those supervisors who may be interested in giving their new librarians this type of experience. Personally, it has worked out better for me to select my mentor versus having one assigned to me, both out in the field and within the organizations I have worked. One example of a mentoring program within a library is the program at F. D. Bluford Library. After a new librarian has been working at the library for about one year, he or she is given names of tenured librarians who are willing to be mentors. The new librarian has the opportunity to select the person based on their identified career needs and goals. I feel that this approach works for several reasons. Waiting until the librarian has been in his or her position for about a year helps the person become acclimated to the environment. The new librarian then has a chance to meet and work with several of the people that will be on the mentor list. This gives the new librarian a chance to choose the type of mentor they feel they need.

My co-writer of this chapter and I both chose as our mentor Euthena Newman, Division Head of the Technical and Automated Services Division of North Carolina's A&T State University's Bluford Library, but for different reasons. Iyanna chose her because Newman used to do the work that she was currently doing. I chose her because she was in technical services and I was in public services and I figured I

> ☑ **QUICK TIP**
> Mentoring programs that allow mentees to select their mentors, rather than having someone assigned to them, can, and should, be established.

would get a better understanding of the library as a whole that way. Plus, she was at a level in the organization I was trying to achieve in the future.

Each of the components of the institute exceeded my expectations. As great as the monetary award and the leadership institute were, the advantages of being a Spectrum Scholar continued even after those three intense days of 7:30 a.m. breakfast with a speaker, lunch with a speaker, and evening receptions with ALA leaders. I was able to take a leadership role with planning future institutes, apply the lessons I learned to my day-to-day activities at work, and build my network.

I am grateful that since my institute in 1999, at least part of the planning committee for the institute included some past scholars. Now the entire planning committee is made up of scholars and the tireless efforts of the staff in ALA's Office of Diversity. This model of having past scholars participate meant I was able to immediately put some skills that we learned during our institute into action and have a welcoming environment to develop existing ones. This also gave me the perfect opportunity to volunteer my time and give back to a program that was important to me. It was my goal to make sure that future scholars benefited from the institute as much as I had, if not more. Through the support (i.e., time, travel funds, encouragement, etc.) of my employers over the years, I have been able to serve Spectrum in many capacities for five out of the seven institutes that have taken place since my own.

My personal involvement with Spectrum ranges from being behind the scenes, participating on panels, and even helping plan Spectrum's tenth anniversary celebration activities. I have been asked to speak about my professional experiences, the benefits of networking, and how to become a leader within a professional organization. Spectrum has given scholars a venue to learn and apply planning and presenting skills within the safe environment of the institute. One of the most rewarding experiences was celebrating ten years of Spectrum. My involvement with this major milestone was organizing a luncheon with Sonia Alcantara (2004 Scholar) and Shannon

> ☑ QUICK TIP
> Learning to present in a safe or controlled environment can be an excellent launching point for more professional speaking and scholarship engagements.

Jones (2001 Scholar). This was a major undertaking because we were no longer just planning an event for 50 to70 scholars like we had in the past; we were planning an event for hundreds of people attending ALA. We had our share of anxious nights until the day the event was over, but throughout it all, we had an excellent support system. We called on and had the help from many scholars from and supporters of Spectrum. I never knew it would be so hard to keep an event running smoothly and on time. However, the event featuring a keynote by world-renowned poet and activist, Nikki Giovanni; remarks by Arizona Representative Raúl M. Grijalva and Spectrum Champions and Past ALA Presidents Carla Hayden and Betty Turock; and a beautiful performance by national recording artist and librarian Tracy Worth (2001 Scholar), all hosted by San Diego County Library Director José Aponte, was unforgettable and well worth all of the work involved.

To add to the list of applied leadership skills, I have been in charge of planning a Professional Options Fair (POF). The POF is a venue at which the scholars have a chance to interact with professional librarians that represent divisions throughout ALA (e.g., Library Division and Management Association, Reference and User Services Association, and Association of College & Research Libraries), a variety of professional organizations (e.g., Medical Library Association, Special Libraries Association, and American Association of Law Libraries), post-graduate residencies and types of positions held such as reference, library professor, cataloging, and children's services, just to name a few. Usually, two hours are dedicated to this event and scholars are encouraged to visit with as many of the professionals as possible to expand their knowledge about the numerous responsibilities and activities of librarians. Many scholars have left the event reassured they have made the right career choice, while others leave with a new perspective because they had no clue that their possibilities were endless. Spectrum has given the scholars an opportunity to give back in many ways, including planning events. This skill can be easily transferred to other conference-planning events and even locally. Within your own organizations, library events always need to be planned. Supervisors can have one of the new librarians be responsible for an annual social event or for planning a reception for a program.

> **☑ QUICK TIP**
> Ask new librarians to get involved with event planning in order to build leadership skills.

So what are some practical skills or information I learned and how have I applied it to my professional experiences? One of the most important messages I picked up is that this is a profession in which you should always be learning or adding new tools to your personal toolbox. One way I did this was to attend the Minnesota Institute for Early Career Librarians. This adventure allowed me to choose a mentor within my organization with whom I could discuss our assigned articles and set initial goals for myself before attending. Afterward, I had a chance to share my experiences and worked with my mentor to apply what I learned to the organization.

My second lesson is the value of being able to communicate and motivate. This sounded so simple initially until I had to not just work on a committee, but lead several people that lived throughout the country. This is when I got to put into practice all the techniques that I was taught, such as delegating specific tasks, establishing workable deadlines, and showing appreciation for a job well-done. I have not only used this skill (hopefully successfully) with committees within professional associations but also teams I had to lead within my library and even as a department head at North Carolina A&T State University. Take a chance and allow a new librarian to lead an established committee. If they are not ready to take that leap of faith, try making them the lead of a special project or giving them a certain task that a committee needs to accomplish, such as distributing or analyzing the results of a survey.

> **☑ QUICK TIP**
> Give new librarians a special project or an important committee to chair to help build their leadership skills and confidence.

Another critical lesson was learning to be comfortable speaking in front of people. For those who are reading this and know me, you may find this hard to believe, but I do not like speaking in front of large groups. Of course, during library school I had to stand up in front of the class and give a report, but by then I had formed a relationship with the group and felt comfortable. I was able to work on the public-speaking fear by being involved with Spectrum and having the chance to introduce speakers, lead small-group discussions, and participate on panels. Most recently, I participated on a panel with Scholars from various years and we discussed what we learned from our individual

☑ **QUICK TIP**
Encourage early-career librarians to present, present, present.

institutes and the importance of staying involved with Spectrum. I'm not saying I do not still get nervous, but I have learned to prepare myself and I am now more comfortable. I gave a speech to more than 200 people when I decided to run for a position on the SLA Board of Directors, have taught countless students, faculty, and staff about library resources and services, and teach at two area library schools. The anxiety of public speaking can be conquered. The best way to start getting over the public-speaking fear is to practice. As a manager, encourage your new librarians to speak and to speak often. You can have them give a report during a library faculty meeting about a project they completed or have them submit a proposal and present at a conference with you. This will show the new librarian how to successfully prepare and give him or her the opportunity to have a support system throughout the process the first time they present.

The last highlight I want to discuss is networking to build your professional contacts. In an attempt to stay connected with Spectrum and the Minnesota Institute participants, I established a strong e-mail communication and stayed up-to-date on listservs established for both groups. Participating in these programs has given me an instant network of hundreds of librarians that have some shared experiences. Although it was not mandatory for us to be on the listservs, I felt that not participating was not an option for me. If you are supervising someone new, I would suggest that you determine what listservs or blogs that deal with the profession as a whole or job function will benefit the new employee most and encourage them to sign up. With the ability to

☑ **QUICK TIP**
Help employees identify the listservs and blogs that will help them build a network and learn more about the issues in their job and career.

use RSS feeds you can even limit the amount of e-mails one receives. Set up a time to discuss what the new librarian has learned or may want to implement in the library. In addition to the established networks, I try to stay active in the profession, keep up with former students I have taught, and keep business cards of people I meet at conferences or workshops. I personally believe that to keep building your network you have to stay active. Being active or giving back to the profession can be done in many ways, including writing about your experiences, presenting your research at a conference, or volunteering to be a guest speaker at a local library school. These types of experiences will expose you to so many people both in person and virtually. New librarians may be overwhelmed by learning their new responsibilities, so managers may need to remind them about the importance of professional organizations. This may involve taking the time to send them e-mails or speak to them about upcoming events.

I know that everyone does not teach, but if you meet LIS students at a workshop, conference, or while you are guest speaking, give them your business card and keep the lines of communication open. By periodically checking in with a past student of mine and hearing about his experiences, I did not hesitate to go to work at North Carolina A&T State University. His day-to-day experiences gave me more insight than what I would have absorbed from visiting during the interview. If you collect business cards from people at workshops and conferences as I do, make a note on the back about where you met and any interesting information about them such as need for interns or people to help with a research project, or interest in committee work, etc. Building my network is not just about how each person I meet can help me, but also about how I may be able to connect friends and professional colleagues together. Through my networks, I have been able to suggest speakers, and connect people with internships or jobs and even leadership opportunities.

Ten years ago, I would never have foreseen this path, but it has been a great journey so far and I have learned some valuable skills that I feel have enhanced my career. The administration at both North Carolina State University and North Carolina A&T State University were extremely supportive in my efforts to stay involved in a program that was important to me personally and professionally.

The growth of a seed, part II: Iyanna's story

After graduating from college, I accepted my first real eight-to-five job as a paraprofessional at North Carolina A&T State University's F. D. Bluford Library. Like so many, I didn't know the intricate details of the operation of a library. My knowledge of the intricacies only consisted of checking out books and the nice lady who helped me find good resources for my research paper during my undergraduate studies. I started the job with the mind-set of the position being the perfect pit stop until I professionally found myself. Little did I know, destiny was busy at work. I did not know that I would fall so deeply for libraries. My view of libraries and librarians changed dramatically. I no longer saw the library as a place books were stored and librarians as merely those people who could magically find a hidden book.

I enjoyed every facet of librarianship and soon knew that this was the direction that I wanted my career to take. I had finally found myself professionally. Simultaneous to this epiphany, I, along with other paraprofessionals, was constantly encouraged to attend library school to become a professional librarian. The encouragement seemed to be repeated as a daily mantra as my supervisor at the time shared with me information on scholarships and library school program offerings. After two years, I decided to take my career to the next level and attend library school to become a professional librarian.

Unfortunately, during library school, I did not take advantage of the initiatives and programs that were offered at the student level (such as the Spectrum Program).

I was working full- and part-time and did not think that I could take on any more responsibility. Although I did not take advantage of these opportunities while I was a student, I was fortunate enough to expand my practical knowledge and experience from library-assistant jobs in law libraries and a television-tape library. Also, an internship at a law library in my last semester of graduate school proved to be very beneficial as I was able to observe different levels of leadership and gain some sense of direction. Although these practical experiences were wonderful and provided much insight, in hindsight, I am quite sure taking advantage of programs and initiatives such as the Spectrum Program would have enhanced my academic career a great deal.

However, early-career librarians who missed out on similar opportunities as well, take heart! My story will show you that all hope is not lost. Early-career minority librarians can take advantage of plenty of professional opportunities while they are working. In addition to the aforementioned ARL Leadership and Career Development Program, many other local programs exist. An example is the Texas Library Association TALL Texans Leadership Development Institute, the primary focus of which includes, but is not limited to, an emphasis on fostering cultural diversity in library leadership with a target audience of practicing librarians. The key is to seek out these opportunities and to seize the moment when it presents itself. This was definitely the case for me.

In my second year of being a professional librarian, opportunity knocked and I eagerly opened the door. Waltrene Canada, dean of the Bluford Library, called me to her office and sat me down. She explained to me that North Carolina A&T State University was chosen to participate in a pilot leadership institute after having been involved in the initial planning for the HBCU Alliance, and in the grant-writing process, and asked if I would like to participate in the role of mentee. I jumped at the opportunity. I was not disappointed; it proved to be more beneficial than I could ever expect.

The HBCU Library Alliance leadership pilot institute

The HBCU Library Alliance is a consortium that supports the collaboration of information professionals dedicated to providing an array of resources designed to strengthen Historically Black Colleges and Universities (HBCU) and their constituents (HBCU Library Alliance Institute, 2006). In keeping with the organizational mission of promoting excellence in library leadership, alliance leaders developed a leadership institute. Before implementing the planned institute, a pilot was developed in 2005 "to test the tools, methodology and case studies of leadership; assess institutional environmental scan and strategic plans; assess leadership styles; and develop mentoring and coaching skills," as eloquently described in the Alliance's leadership institute grant proposal to the Mellon Foundation.

I was among the 18 participants (nine seasoned librarians and nine potential leaders) who were charged to critically evaluate the program and its contents. It was an extensive week of workshops that stimulated extensive discussions on strategic library leadership. Topics ranged from creating a strategic plan to the use of tools such as the Myers-Briggs Type Indicator (MBTI) for effective leadership. Even though I was there in the capacity of critiquing the value and usefulness of information presented, I was also there as a student. In most cases, I felt more like an apprentice soaking in all of the information from the workshops and the wisdom of the seasoned librarians that surrounded me. I probably gained more applicable information than gave constructive criticism. Hopefully, they did not get too much of the short stick, as I did share my humble opinions on the structure and content of the institute in the evaluation form. The workshops listed below are a sampling of the type of invaluable information imparted to the Institute participants:

The strategically focused organization

This workshop delved into the world of strategic planning, including defining and explaining the important role of strategic thinking and planning play in strategic management. As a part of this workshop, factors such as environmental scans, analyzing stakeholders, and characteristics of a strong mission and value statement were discussed in great detail. Such an approach to strategic planning was very beneficial to me as a new librarian. It gave me a clearer picture of creating a strategic plan from the beginning to end. Furthermore, it was invaluable to see the characteristics of an effective and achievable plan. This type of conversation is undoubtedly important for current leaders to communicate to future leaders to ensure the development of successful strategic plans that will continue to foster the growth and advancement of libraries.

Vision-driven leadership

The vision-driven leadership workshop was geared toward enhancing leadership effectiveness through psychological type. The session emphasized the concept of knowing oneself and understanding others to develop strong relationships. In order to achieve this, leaders must not only be conscious of the personalities of those around them, but also their own emotional intelligence. In fact, as learned from attending the Institute, Daniel Goleman, author of *Emotional Intelligence*, states leadership success is directly related to emotional intelligence (Goleman, 1995). Being able to recognize one's own and others' is key to effectively motivate and manage ourselves and others. Emotional intelligence skills not only motivate and inspire others, but create positive work climates. This indicates the usefulness of tools such as the Myers-Briggs and Emotional IQ tests in effective leadership, and actually shows psychological assessments can go beyond indicating the sanity of personnel.

Transformation and transition

The transformation and transition component of the Institute was devoted to ideas related to leading transitions and managing change. For a leader to be successful in approaching change, one must create effective strategies to respond to changes in the environment and profession, which includes performing an honest evaluation to identify and address resistance factors. To say exposure to such information was very timely is an understatement. As a new member of a profession that has undergone much transformation with more on the horizon, the insight from the dialog was extremely useful. I gained knowledge in how to effectively manage change and transformation as I prepared for a leadership role in an ever-changing profession. I felt even more equipped.

These sessions were very enlightening as well as validating. First, I gained a better understanding of the delicate balancing act library leaders face when planning for the future of the library organization. Library leaders must develop mission, values, and goals that not only support the university or college, but also support the important functions of the library including services, information literacy, and library technology. Equally important, as a new librarian, the workshops showed the importance of motivating people to support your vision and plan for the organization, and the best way to motivate people is to understand them. Needless to say, the workshop discussing the use of personality tools like the MBTI and emotional intelligence testing was extremely eye-opening for a potential leader.

I had not realized the *serious* usefulness of such instruments for effective staffing and committee/task force organization. The wise facilitators of the workshops explained how analyzing such data can assist leaders in the development of committees and task forces.

> ☑ QUICK TIP
> Using tools, such as the MBTI, that help identify the strengths and proclivities of employees can help develop healthy, positive community dynamics within the work team.

This is due to individuals' known strengths being heightened and different personalities working in harmony to create a work environment in which everyone is not only comfortable, but confident in their professional skin. For instance, as best said by the Myers-Briggs Foundation, "a thinking preference provides an impersonal analysis of the situation, while a feeling preference provides a look at the personal and human consequences of an action" (Myers-Briggs Personality Type, n.d.). Therefore, leaders can use this tool to gain perspective from various viewpoints, and all employees feel valued. This was a very interesting and validating workshop for a potential leader who is a self-confessed people person, and believes that a happy and productive staff is one that feels they are valued for their contribution and play an integral role in the growth of the organization. While this is my personal managerial philosophy, several examples in both library and business literature can attest to the correlation between high morale and high productivity. An article written in *Virginia Libraries* by Dan Connole (2000) shows the success and ways of implementing staff morale. The ever-popular FISH! Philosophy shows what happens when leadership encourages a positive work environment: "creativity, inspiration, and innovation" (Learning, 2007). Library managers should read for themselves and encourage new librarians to read this type of material on a long-existing aspect of leadership, improving staff morale. A plan is only as great as the people who carry it out, and being informed of different ways of encouraging staff to buy in and execute a plan is crucial.

Other workshops, such as communicating and listening effectively, were also offered and served as a nice refresher. Such standard workshops are always practical and reiterate important skills that can be used at any career level. Just as important and an extremely beneficial addendum to the workshops were the breakout sessions. These sessions were geared for further discussion and hypothetical applications of the principles discussed in the workshops. For me, the breakout sessions provided a moment to sit at the feet of the seasoned library leaders. I was able to converse with and learn from the knowledge of the directors and deans of the HBCU institutions in the breakout sessions. The leaders shared in detail their experiences related to the workshops. It was a chance to observe leader-orientated thought processes as we examined case studies that explored topics such as budgetary concerns and personnel challenges. The breakout sessions, along with hypothetical applications of lessons learned, group activities, and journaling, kept the institute engaging and fresh.

I saw and approached the Leadership Institute Pilot as a fertile training ground. Each workshop was an excellent model that could be used on a smaller scale in one's own library or as an informative track at a professional organization conference at the local level. Library managers should look for opportunities to encourage dialog for new librarians to discuss ideas such as strategic planning and implementing tools that can be used to rethink and reshape leadership. Perhaps if there is a professional development committee in place at the library, the committee can be charged with establishing mini-workshops or seminars that encourage conversation on topics such as strategic planning and managing change and transformation. These workshops, such as the ones at the Institute, can provide immediate application by analyzing case studies, developing creative group activities (such as grouping personality types together to see their approach to a particular situation), and role-playing, and even encourage reflective journals (all done at the leadership institute). To take these discussions a step further, library managers should be encouraged to propose stronger leadership and management tracks at local conferences. Leaders of today can begin doing their part to train leaders of tomorrow by using conferences as a training ground by becoming proactive in submitting proposal ideas that relate to library leadership.

> ☑ QUICK TIP
>
> Use professional development committees within the library to establish forums for big-picture discussions on topics such as introducing transformative change and encouraging risk-taking and innovation.

More soil: the exchange program

Involvement in the HBCU Library Alliance (HBCULA) Leadership Institute yielded yet another leadership training opportunity. Another component of the Leadership Program is an exchange program between HBCULA libraries and the Association of Southeastern Research Libraries (ASERL). The exchange program was developed to provide HBCU librarians with an opportunity to address a specific issue of strategic importance to their libraries with the assistance and expertise of ASERL library leaders (HBCU Library Alliance Institute, 2006). As I grow in my career, I am more convinced that the role of constantly changing library technology is a strategic issue in any library. I also see the importance of librarians continuing to emerge as technological leaders and integrating new technologies in delivering optimum services to the greater community. When I read the announcement of the exchange program, I knew this program would be a great avenue for dialog with other libraries in this area. I applied with much support and encouragement from my administration and colleagues.

With my fingers crossed, I anxiously waited for session two of the Leadership Institute, where the five chosen exchange participants would be announced. During the summer of 2006, I was chosen along with four other associate-level librarians from HBCU libraries to participate in a two-week exchange program. I was paired with Wake Forest University's Z. Reynolds Smith Library in Winston-Salem, North Carolina. Although this library was close—approximately 45 minutes from my own library—despite popular belief I was not disappointed. I was elated because Z. Reynolds Smith Library is known to be a library forging toward the technological future. Lynn Sutton, Wake Forest Library Director and a kind and innovative leader, phrased it best in her quote for an *American Libraries* article: "We share the same intensity in meeting user needs" (Burger and Lewis, 2007: 36).

For two weeks, I was able to engage in extensive dialog with all of the team members at the library: Collection Management, Information Services, Technology, Technical and Access Services, and Special Collections and Archives. Visiting each team allowed me to see the use of various types of technology being incorporated in work flow and providing services. For instance, Z. Reynolds Smith was using Perl script to enhance features in their library automation system. The Archives team was using a digital resource management system to program metadata for their digital collection. Seeing such applications gave me inspiration for my own library. Like many leaders I have observed, I was open to the inspiration and was moved to action. In fact, as soon as I returned to my own library I used techniques taught in an impromptu advanced cascading style sheet class given by the Web services librarian to revamp our library's intranet page.

Spending extensive time with each team allowed me to see different management styles and approaches. I had an opportunity to join preliminary meetings regarding implementation of software applications and laying the groundwork for a collaborative digital project. Although my participation in the planning usually begins in the implementation stage, in some cases I have been a part of the beginning process of a few technological projects in my library, such as redesigning the library's Web site. Sitting in on these meetings at Z. Reynolds Smith Library, I saw a visible thread of commonality. We all have the same challenges, concerns, and questions to answer when beginning a new project. As a leader in training, I saw the incredible value of open communication and conversation with other libraries in achieving goals and missions.

The advantages of being in close proximity to my host institution exceeded beyond the convenience of light packing. Since we were close, Z. Reynolds Smith and F. D. Bluford libraries had an opportunity for in-person collaboration. We shared ideas on the development and implementation of an archival picture identification project. We have discussed coming together to identify other opportunities of collaboration when scheduling permits. The exchange experience was not only conducive for leadership training, but has encouraged information sharing by building a bridge between libraries that are only 45 minutes apart with the same goal of providing excellent information services.

An exchange program is a worthwhile venture for library managers to research for replication at the local level. Library administration can forge partnerships with nearby libraries to have new librarians shadow a department of interest for a few hours or maybe a day. Creating these types of partnerships is also advantageous, as leaders begin to think of creative ways of enhancing library services and even collaboration on grants and other special projects. If library management wants to test the waters first, it can be done departmentally.

> ☑ QUICK TIP
> Cross-training helps not only with staffing shortages, but with interpersonal relations and a holistic vision of the library's work.

Doing an "exchange" departmentally not only exposes new librarians to the details that contribute to the bigger picture, but also enables cross-training for the unfortunate times of personnel shortage.

Spreading roots: lessons and applications

Both programs, the HBCU Library Alliance Leadership Institute Pilot and its component the Exchange Program, were great leadership training resources. From these two programs combined, I learned various thoughts and practices of leadership. I have mentioned several "take-aways" in my previous discussion of the programs, but to highlight, I have tons of mental and written notes for when it is my time to lead. I have notes on creative and effective approaches to budgeting, personnel practices, and planning based on my conversations and networking with participants of the Leadership Institute. Now, some of these notes I haven't yet been able to put into effect, as I have not had my opportunity to fully lead, but when I do, I will be better prepared to confidently embrace the challenge due to these training opportunities.

I have, though, been able to apply some things that I have learned in my current position. Having served as chair on a couple of in-house committees, I have been able to do an informal assessment of committee members' characteristic traits. Based on my mere observations, since I never could find an appropriate time or lead way into administering the MBTI during meetings, I tried to encourage fellow members and assign tasks according to their strengths. I am quite sure I could have been more successful if I had had hard quantitative data, but hopefully the committee members felt a sense of value and contribution.

Since I have been having such a positive early-career experience, I have also given back by using one of the best methods around. I have become a mouthpiece for programs such as the ones of which I have been able to take advantage. For example, during the HBCU Library Alliance annual meeting, I strongly encouraged a couple of my colleagues to take advantage of the Exchange Program if possible. I have become a promoter of researching professional programs that provide leadership training and even seeking out organizations where library leadership training can be done informally through mentoring or just watching seasoned library leaders in action.

Tips on becoming a farming librarian

After reading our experiences, you may be wondering how you can be a part of such programs and initiatives: How can I give back to the younger librarians seeking to fulfill a leadership role in the profession? What can I do at my own library to cultivate librarians for library leaderships? In the following paragraphs, you will not find a definitive answer to all of these questions and others you may have, but you will find a list of suggested tips to begin to plant your own harvest of library leaders based on our experiences and observations.

Survey the land: research

Have you had the chance to research opportunities available for library school students, early-career librarians, or even midcareer librarians? For our purposes, we have only listed programs whose targeted audience is minority librarians. However, plenty of programs cater to any type and career-level librarian. Being informed of the opportunities that are available in the land of librarianship, you will know what training tools are applicable for the seeds in your library. Once you are informed, others are informed. You can share the good news of leadership training that is available and effective. You will be leading others to lead.

Find perfect seeds for the harvest: observe

Observe closely the seeds around you. Hidden talent that can be beneficial to librarianship abounds. It may be hidden in the shy paraprofessional who enjoys Web development on the side or the eager young librarian who has great ideas. Dean Waltrene Canada can attest to being observant to the seeds around you. She states, "Iyanna was chosen because of her receptiveness and willingness to learn in order to further develop her leadership potential" (personal communication, October 1, 2007). If you are in tune to the strengths and interests of your staff, you will likely find someone who would be willing to follow in your professional footsteps.

Water the harvest: encourage and support

Once you have recognized great potential, simply encourage and support. We both were encouraged by administration to become and stay involved in the Spectrum Program and the HBCU Library Alliance Leadership Institute. Administration at both North Carolina State University Libraries and North Carolina A&T State University's F. D. Bluford Library not only encouraged us to attend library school, but continued to support us in our early-career stage. Both libraries did so by allowing flexibility to participate in these programs. F. D. Bluford Library administration allotted Tamika time to travel to meetings and permitted Iyanna to take a two-week leave of absence to participate in the Exchange program. Such actions not only show unyielding support, but emphasize the commitment to leadership training.

Don't be afraid to work the land: get involved

All leadership training opportunities might not be feasible for everyone. Do not let this discourage or intimidate you. Allow it to be a moment of creative expression. Start seeking different avenues of leadership training. Think of larger-scale activities you can do on a smaller scale. If the university can't afford for your library to participate in certain workshops due to financial and staffing constraints, host your own in-house workshops, in-person or virtually, which discuss certain aspects of leadership. Others can definitely learn from your experience. Also, seek out moments of collaboration with other libraries. You might not be eligible to apply for the HBCU Library Alliance Leadership Institute Exchange program, but exchange programs can be done locally with other libraries who are interested in training leaders or even departmentally within the library itself.

Quick note on becoming a growing seed

Early-career librarians: Allow yourself to be a seed. Start looking for mentors in your library if no formal mentoring program is established. Begin to look for mentors and training opportunities in professional organizations and roundtables to which you may belong. Talking one-on-one with a seasoned library leader is invaluable leadership training. Remember, we librarians are great and open resources!

Exhibit 11.1. A word from our mentor

According to Nankivell and Schoolbred (1996), there are six types of reasons for mentoring: managing, networking, coaching, acclimatizing, reducing professional isolation, and promotion (p. 5). The mentoring program at F. D. Bluford Library, North Carolina A&T State University, started in 1999, focusing on all these six reasons for mentoring, but places emphasis on coaching in preparation for professional advancement and promotion.

Senior faculty at Bluford Library is paired with one or more junior faculty to provide guidance and support as they move up the career ladder. Encouragement and support in the area of job performance, research, and service becomes the focus. The result of the mentoring program at Bluford Library has resulted in more professional involvement of the library faculty through presentations at local and national conferences, promotions and the awarding of tenure, and publications.

The relationship formed between the mentor and mentee becomes almost symbiotic in that the mentor benefits as much as the mentee.

Euthena Newman
Head, Technical and Automated Services
Professional Mentor to Tamika and Iyanna

Source: Nankivell, C., Shoolbred, M. (1996). *Mentoring in Library and Information Services: An Approach to Staff Support*, British Library and Research and Innovation report 10, British Library Research.

Conclusion

Hopefully, we have inspired libraries to till fresh ground. Maybe we will spark discussion among the profession of creating creative leadership training programs and initiatives that can be done locally within the library and nationally, in the profession as a whole. Both library administration and early-career librarians can take heart in our examples that the profession's concerted effort to concentrate on emerging leadership is producing a great harvest.

Further reading

Edward, E. G. 2007. *Leadership Basics for Librarians and Information Professionals.* Lanham, MD: The Scarecrow Press.

Giesecke, J. 2001. *Practical Strategies for Library Managers.* Chicago: American Library Association.

Hart, C., L. Lewis, E. McClenney, V. Perry, I. Sims, and A. Webber. 2007. "The HBCU Library Alliance: Developing Leadership." *Virginia Libraries* 53, no. 4: 16–20. Retrieved July 8, 2008, from Library Lit & Info Full Text database.

Johnson, P. 2007. Retaining and Advancing Librarians of Color. *College & Research Libraries* 68(5): 405–417. Retrieved July 8, 2008, from Library Lit & Info Full Text database.

Kim, K., Chiu Ming-Hsin., S. Sin, and L. Robbins. 2007. "Recruiting a Diverse Workforce for Academic/Research Librarianship: Career Decisions of Subject Specialists and Librarians of Color." *College & Research Libraries* 68, no. 6: 533–552. Retrieved July 8, 2008, from Library Lit & Info Full Text database.

Neely, T., and L. Peterson. 2007. "Achieving Racial and Ethnic Diversity Among Academic and Research Librarians: The Recruitment, Retention, and Advancement of Librarians of Color—A White Paper." *College & Research Libraries News* 68, no. 9: 562–565. Retrieved July 8, 2008, from Library Lit & Info Full Text database.

Rossiter, P. H. 2007. *Making a Difference: Leadership and Academic Libraries.* Westport, CT: Greenwood Publishing.

Stone, A. 2007. "Spectrum Turns 10." *American Libraries* 38, no. 2: 42–43. Retrieved July 8, 2008, from Library Lit & Info Full Text database.

References

Academic Research Libraries. 2007. Available: www.arl.org/diversity/lcdp/ (accessed September 2007).

ALA Office of Diversity and ALA Office of Research and Statistics. 2007. *Diversity Counts.* Chicago, IL: American Library Association.

American Library Association Spectrum Initiative. 2007. Available: www.ala.org/ala/diversity/spectrum/spectrum.htm (accessed September 20, 2007).

ARL Initiative to Recruit a Diverse Workforce. 2007. Available: www.arl.org/diversity/init/index.shtml (accessed September 2007).

Burger, John, and Lillian Lewis. 2007. "Each One Teach One." *American Libraries* (February): 34–36.

Connole, Dan. 2000. "Building Staff Morale." *Virginia Libraries* 46, no. 4: 13–15.

Goleman, Daniel. 1995. *Emotional Intelligence.* New York: Bantam Books.

HBCU Library Alliance Institute. 2006. Available: www.hbculibraries.org/index.html (accessed September 20, 2007).

Learning, Charthouse. 2007. *FISH! Philosophy.* Available: www.charthouse.com/content.aspx?name=home2 (accessed December 18, 2007).

Myers-Briggs Personality Type. Available: www.myersbriggs.org/my-mbti-personality-type/my-mbti-results/learning-about-your-mbti.asp (accessed October 2007).

networking as staff development:
introductions, invitations, and associations

Miguel A. Figueroa

Benefits to the individual and the organization

Is networking a tool for the individual, or is it something that can benefit the organization and the individual simultaneously? My first job out of library school—working for Neal-Schuman Publishers, Inc.—required of me something that was never part of my LIS curriculum: networking. I needed to develop and make use of personal contacts because a certain measure of my success with Neal-Schuman would be how well I was able to connect with the professional community. What I did not initially realize, however, was that networking would be a measure of success, not only on a yearly evaluation, but also in developing as a leader. By networking I increased my knowledge of the profession, developed leadership skills through memberships in professional associations, and increased my productivity with a cadre of mentors and peers.

To my great fortune, my supervisors at Neal-Schuman realized both the importance and the challenge of successful networking. They provided a formalized process to get me off to a strong start and offered the support that would ensure my efforts were successful.

This chapter explores how networking can serve as a tool for both individual professional development and organizational growth. It outlines a process for building a new professional's network and examines how managers can easily help their staff members in this task.

Networking and staff development

As much as staff development can happen on the job and in the library, a tremendous opportunity for growth exists outside of the library. Whether at a conference, attending a local continuing-education course, talking with colleagues, or working on committees, employees have numerous opportunities to learn about their jobs, even when they are away from the workplace. More important, in these opportunities away from the job, they have tremendous potential for building a network that will continue to supply them with best practices, ideas, and a knowledge base that they can continually consult. While doing this, the employee improves the visibility of the organization and feeds back new knowledge to the staff.

Consider networking in the library world as "six degrees of library science." Perhaps only six degrees exist between one librarian and the next great idea, solution, or strategy that can be incorporated into the institution. By encouraging employees to venture out into the library world, build networks, and develop ties to other professionals, your institution can learn and harness the power of great ideas. Double, triple, or even quadruple the number of people working on your big-idea projects, the number of voices in a discussion.

Networking can also be a supplement to training. All supervisors invest heavily in training their staff, especially new staff. However, as much time as they would like to be devoted to training, supervisory needs can simply get in the way. A well-developed network can fill in day-to-day training needs (reference search strategies, programming ideas, lesson plans) or help staff get started on the right foot with new projects (organizational assessments, publicity campaigns, etc.) A diverse network can supplement for a consultancy in large and small tasks alike. In these ways, the network serves both the individual and the organization.

As much as the library can benefit from an employee's use of a network, it can also benefit from participation in networks. If the network can help increase the profile of an individual, it can also help increase the prestige of an institution. By encouraging the best and brightest of your employees to network, you can demonstrate the quality of your institution's staff and its programs. The threat, of course, is that by putting the best and brightest out there, they may be lured away by another institution. However, if done correctly, encouraging individuals to network and supporting their efforts will send a strong message to both the employee and other professionals that your institution supports professional growth.

The process

It *is* possible to just let networking happen. It is a process and act that most of us don't think about. Many of my best network partners were found in times when I wasn't consciously networking. However, if my supervisors had not put networking on my mind and created a formalized structure for performing and process for evaluating, I would never have been so successful or so ambitious.

Each manager can consider how involved in networking he or she wants the staff to be and how much he or she feels it can benefit the organization. You can choose to make networking a primary goal or a bonus on top of all of the other skills you are trying to impart to your new staff. What will be important, and what these simple practices will help you do, is to put networking on the radar of your new staff.

Conduct an initial inventory

Before you can really build a network, you should take a moment to survey the landscape. New librarians, whether new to the profession or new to your institution, will likely walk through the door with the start of a network already in place. They may or may not be aware of what they have already built through library school, internships, or their previous employment. You can take an easy step toward building a network by inventorying who they know on day one.

Ask new employees who they know. By asking such questions, employers can gain valuable insights into the type of employee they have just hired. I recall listing a mix of seasoned librarians, educators, and LIS classmates with focused interests. I would hope that this mix indicated to my employers that I was someone who was interested in both the practice and the theory behind the profession. My list also reflected a diversity of areas—public, academic, and school libraries; archives and museums; children's services, reference, and instruction—that should have led my employers to believe that I was interested in learning about the full breadth of librarianship rather than specializing in a specific area.

Asking an employee to list who they know may also be a first step toward having them recognize the network they've already unconsciously formed. Although many library school students make a practice of collecting business cards throughout library school, the concept of a larger network may still be foreign. For me, listing my contacts and really taking the time to think about what each one knew, how they related to my own professional development, and how I might utilize this band of contacts in my future role within this organization greatly helped me in transforming what were simply business cards and handshakes into something more helpful and real in the workplace.

> ☑ **QUICK TIP**
> Listen for not only names, but also institutions and job titles. Networking is about making connections, and both the place someone works and the job that they do can provide an inroad.

Of equal importance may be to examine the different levels of network contacts within an individual's list. In my case, the process included separating out those of my former classmates whom I might call upon on a daily or weekly basis from those instructors and professors who might be available for guidance on a monthly or quarterly basis. Finally, I might call upon those individuals who I had only met in passing solely for a specialized need. I considered this last group of people acquaintances to whom I would have to explain how I knew them. By going through the process, new professionals can begin to understand both how their network currently works and how it might be enhanced and further developed within their new position.

As a supervisor, you can provide feedback throughout this inventory. Encourage new staff to value both the names that you know (the big names of professors or library leaders) and the names that no one knows (their fellow students or young friends in the profession). New librarians should be encouraged to talk through each of their contacts and share the value of each individual they know. Some on the list may just be stepping into the profession, but they will eventually grow in expertise and value within your network.

By inventorying the current list of contacts, you might instill in the new employee a sense of value. Those handshakes and business cards aren't just "take-aways." They are invaluable entrees into a wealth of knowledge. They are to be considered, thought about, and valued. This exercise might also make clear to your employee that you are the type of employer who will not only invest in networking time, but whom also truly *values* networking time. In other words, your employees are not simply sent on throw-away trips. They are sent on working visits to conferences, meetings, etc. Instilling this process of reflection may be the first step toward showing your employee the integral role networking will play in his or her professional life.

> ☑ QUICK TIP
> There's no real evaluation of a network or its members. Encourage new staff to list all contacts and to associate value or potential to them. Although one name may not seem like a "somebody" at the time, they may become a very valuable contact for your new staff as both grow and develop.

Supplement the inventory

Inventorying contacts should also be an exercise for the employer. As the names are put forth, supervisors can begin to make connections for the new employee and for himself or herself. I recall that as I listed my contacts, my supervisors nodded and chimed in with notes of recognition, stories, or observations. They commented on job titles or asked me more about a particular place of employment. The listing was an opportunity for my supervisors to tell me more about mutual acquaintances—their connection with my organization, their potential helpfulness in my pursuits, and even more about their history and contributions to the profession. They also took note of the names with which they were unfamiliar. They noted who my closest contacts were and asked how frequently I spoke with them. One of the lasting impressions my supervisors made on me was the value they put into every name on the list.

> ☑ QUICK TIP
> Be an active partner during the inventory. Make connections, suggest additional contacts, and take notes.

Although I didn't realize it at the time, in the coming months some names from my initial role call would play an important part in my job duties. My supervisors would come in with a project and suggest I contact X or Y that I had mentioned in those first few weeks. They mentioned not only the names they were familiar with, but also the names that were new to them from that first inventory. Apparently they, too, had taken note of the names I listed and had made connections between who I knew and what I might be doing. They kept my list in their minds and recognized names as they read through the professional news or came across articles or interviews with some of the list members. My inventory was not simply an exercise in establishing my own network; it was an opportunity for them to expand their network through me.

Finally, one of the key elements of discussing whom an individual knows is to also begin discussing whom they *should* know. Within my report of those professionals I had already met, my supervisors began to list the names of other people I should meet. Making connections between one set of individuals and another is a very effective way of encouraging new professionals to reach out and meet more people. As I listed individuals and their interests or specialties, my supervisors made connections to the wider profession. By simply gauging my interests and the interests of those I knew, my employers were already working to make enhancements and additions to my network of professional contacts. The knowledge base was already growing without my even having gone to actual networking events.

Gauge professional interests

For many new professionals, the question "What are you interested in?" can be answered with a simple "Everything." Employers may believe, however, that the same question was answered by the new professional's résumé. For both the employee to narrow his or her area of interest and for the employer to develop a better sense of where the employee has been and where he or she wants to go, opening up the question for greater discussion is worthwhile.

Organizational affiliations

In determining interests, one of the first areas my employer asked me to describe was my involvement in professional organizations. Opening up the conversation to involvement in professional organizations is an easy way to gauge what large or narrow areas of interest an employee may have. Discovering involvement in the Special Libraries Association (SLA) for a newly hired public librarian may be as revealing as discovering involvement in the Medical Library Association (MLA) for a newly hired law librarian. The associations do not match. This may be the result of changed interests from library school to the working profession or of lingering interests in a different area of librarianship. Mass involvement—memberships in SLA, ALA, MLA, etc.—may be the result of an unfocused tenure in library school or may be indicative of an individual interested in the profession and ready for involvement in associations. Moving toward more focused questions of specific involvement may prove even more revealing. Many new professionals may have only limited involvement, such as participation in student organizations or attending a local meeting. Involvement in sections or roundtables may reveal a more focused interest and perhaps a closer affiliation to that particular area of

> ☑ **QUICK TIP**
> Encourage association involvement and make sure it is appropriate to the job being done.

librarianship. Reasoning behind involvement—joining SLA for its Information Technology Section, for example—may clarify what may seemingly be missed connections.

Ultimately the goal of this discussion is both to gauge the interests of the new hire and to begin to impress upon him or her new opportunities to network based upon specific interests. One of the best ways my employers enhanced this conversation about associations was to explain each of the associations and to reference their own involvement within these organizations. Gaining an insider perspective and understanding how a professional integrates each of these organizations into their day-to-day lives can demonstrate both the usefulness and the potential limits of each. Simultaneous to the discussion of the supervisor's involvement should be an explanation of how the supervisor might help the individual to further his or her involvement in the particular association. In my case, both of my supervisors had been extensively involved in several organizations. In addition to detailing their own experiences, they took the opportunity to begin brainstorming my own future involvement. This included dropping names of people I should meet; admitting areas where they weren't as involved and suggesting names of people who might help me further my involvement; and refocusing my interests to new organizations, sections, or roundtables that might better suit my new responsibilities as an employee.

Job growth

Beyond the discussion of associations should be a larger discussion of the new professional's specific career goals. In my mind, this focus was epitomized by my employer's simple question, "What do you want to be doing in five years?" For a new employee, this could be a significant challenge and may not be a question to include in the first week. The question should be acceptable after some time on the job, once the employee has experienced the organization and seen the various roles occupied by its employees. The challenge to the employee is to make connections between what one is currently doing and how one can grow from that into new opportunities. The discussion can be revealing regarding how new employees see the direction of their development. Do they seek more opportunities for supervision or more chances at project management? Are they interested in changing the direction of the organization? Can they point to a specific job title or staff member and say they want that role?

This discussion should help managers and new librarians hone in on the type of people that should populate the new professional's network. In an ideal situation, the manager might suggest names for possible mentorship. This may also be an opportunity to simply list people to watch or to try to talk with at conferences or other meetings. The idea here is to develop a list of people to model and learn from.

The employer might also go further and help the employee make connections between how networking might help him or her progress toward these goals. Certainly one does not want to encourage a new employee to network out of the organization and into a new job, but perhaps the employer can suggest networking within organizations to gain experience in committees or managing projects. Opportunities for subject specialization may exist through involvement in outside professional organizations. The more you can demonstrate the effectiveness of networking and the ways in which you will support networking to achieve the employee's end goals, the more likely the employee is to invest in this process.

Exhibit 12.1. Three library associations with new member opportunities

American Library Association (ALA): www.ala.org
The oldest and largest library association in the world, ALA promotes the highest quality library and information services and public access to information and offers professional services and publications to members.

For new professionals, ALA's New Members Roundtable (NMRT) offers guidance through what can sometimes be an overwhelming association. NMRT's committees offer opportunities for new members to grow their association committee experience, and a liaison committee connects NMRT members with experienced ALA leaders (www.ala.org/ala/nmrt/nmrt.htm).

ALA's committee intern program is also an excellent opportunity for new professionals to learn the ropes of the organization (www.ala.org/ala/ourassociation/committees/otld/otldcmteminutes/internguidelines.htm).

The Special Library Association (SLA): www.sla.org
Founded in 1909, this international association represents the interests of thousands of information professionals in more than 80 countries worldwide. Special librarians are information resource experts who collect, analyze, evaluate, package, and disseminate information to facilitate accurate decision making in corporate, academic, and government settings.

At every annual conference, SLA hosts a First-Timers and Fellows Connect session where new members and first-time attendees mingle with established members and learn how to make the most of their conference experience.

Medical Library Association (MLA): www.mlanet.org/
The Medical Library Association (MLA) provides more than 4,000 health sciences information professionals with educational opportunities, a knowledge base of health information research, and promotion of the importance of quality information for improved health to the health care community and the public.

MLA offers a mentoring program for both new and mid-career librarians. Mentors volunteer and interested librarians can search MLA's mentor program for specific details including state, institution, and expertise (www.mlanet.org/mentor/mentor_search.php).

Like SLA, MLA offers an opportunity for new members and established professionals to meet at the annual conference. MLA's Colleague Connection pairs partners ahead of the conference and allows the two to work out their own meetings and schedules.

Make introductions
Perhaps one of the most difficult things for new professionals to do is to start a conversation with an experienced professional. Despite the openness and general cooperative nature of our profession, it is nonetheless a tough task to walk into a room and start a conversation from nothing.

Working from the supplemented list of contacts, an employer can take the lead in making introductions, starting with his or her own inner circle of friends and colleagues and working toward more distant and removed contacts. Making introductions allows employers the opportunity to shape the new professional's networking experience—putting him or her in touch with the right people from whom he or she can learn and grow. It is also an opportunity to put the institution out into the larger network of librarians.

At Neal-Schuman it was easy to get started with introductions. We had numerous authors and collaborators from whom I could learn, and numerous opportunities to meet and greet them (conferences, local meetings, etc.). What became clear, however, was that no matter whom we were meeting, the introductions tended to follow the same format. A standard brief introduction always included where I went to library school, for whom I previously worked, etc. Usually someone would mention why I was hired—skills, experience, education, etc. That would be followed with how I was expected to grow within the company. In retrospect, these last two elements of the conversation served my employers very well. It allowed them an opportunity to demonstrate the quality of their recruits and it made clear to others that this new hire was not only going somewhere, but he or she was going somewhere within this particular organization.

> ☑ QUICK TIP
> Create a standard introduction or story that you can share with new network contacts. Highlight specific characteristics, details, or experiences of your new employee that can spark conversation.

The role of my supervisor in these early introductions was to break the ice—give both myself and my new acquaintance several opportunities to talk. It was also an opportunity for my employer to help shape the conversation and make sure that I would be able to take something from the conversation that was not only valuable to myself, but also to the institution. Mentioning what I would be in charge of or how I was expected to grow within the company might encourage the new contact to remember these points, and offer advice or even support when problems were encountered. An example of one such introduction follows:

> Miguel Figueroa just came to us from the University of Arizona's Knowledge River Program. He has a history in retail and we are hoping he can bring that sales experience to our marketing efforts. Miguel will be in charge of recruiting new authors and developing proposals, so if you have any interesting ideas or possible names he should seek out, let him know.

To get me started, my supervisors often worked through their own library colleagues and personal friends. Trusting a colleague with the development of an employee shouldn't be problematic. If anything, it is networking in action—utilizing the pool of trusted colleagues to help accomplish professional goals. It is integral that my employers clearly indicated to their colleagues what they were asking.

After a few months, my supervisor invited a friendly colleague who was involved in a particular organization to help me get oriented to the association. My supervisor explained my role, explained how he felt I was ideally suited for the particular organization, and laid out the type of inroads I needed to make in the association.

Over the next few months, this colleague invited me to local association meetings, worked through crowds, and made introductions. Throughout the process, a standard line was utilized—who I am, who I work for, my role in that institution, and the directions in which I was headed. By utilizing a trusted colleague outside the organization, my employers could still ensure that the purpose of my networking was clear. I was not networking for a new job; I was networking as a new representative of an established institution.

Arranging meetings

After introductions, the next logical step is meetings. One-on-one meetings are excellent opportunities for development, especially if the other party is more experienced or knowledgeable. At Neal-Schuman, lunch meetings were a regular part of business. Lunch meetings gave us the opportunity to meet with new and repeat authors and try to engage them in a new project. They were incredibly important, providing opportunities for both business and personal development. Executing a meeting correctly, however, didn't happen naturally. It took significant preparation and practice.

As a manager, you should want your new employees to make the most of meetings. New employees, however, may not be initially adept at making meetings meaningful. They may need practice and guidance. At Neal-Schuman, my first months included many opportunities for practice as I mirrored my supervisor through the process. This involved everything from being included in the invitation e-mails (back-and-forth exchanges including an introductory e-mail, scheduling back and forth, etc.) to planning the day before the event. My managers encouraged me to do a little research for conversation starters and to know more about the guest. I was asked to compile materials to take to the meeting—proposals, articles, outlines, etc. Managers can also ease new employees into the process by setting up and accompanying the employee on a few dry runs. My first few meetings were safe affairs with established authors with preexisting relationships with Neal-Schuman. My supervisor took the lead and let me interject as I felt comfortable. It allowed me to be a part of the meeting, but from a safe position.

Finally, after each meeting, whether attended independently or while still under the wing of an experienced supervisor, managers should encourage their employees to share their experiences. Push the employee to list the key take-aways. Going further to report about the

> ☑ **QUICK TIP**
> Provide safe opportunities for learning how to conduct a networking meeting. Use your own colleagues or other staff members to show the new employee the ropes.

meeting might also be useful and help make the interaction more memorable. Key topics to review are decisions reached, names mentioned, offers made, and major topics discussed. Putting this in writing will also allow employees to review the results of the meeting at a later time and ensure that any actionable items are followed through.

Navigating outings

As an extension of the mirroring technique for conducting meetings and of the process of making introductions, supervisors may also want to take an active role in navigating outings. By this, I mean chaperoning the first few excursions to association meetings or local events.

One of the key tasks that needed to happen before my departure for a conference or meeting was a meeting with my supervisor to talk about my purpose. It may sound like micromanagement in theory, but in practice, it proved to be a very powerful tool for my supervisors and a comforting tactic for myself as the new professional. Quite simply, my supervisor asked me what my purpose of going to the meeting was. Sometimes it was tied to a key area of my job description, and sometimes it wasn't. What was important was that my supervisor, from his vantage point, could make connections I may not have thought of. Specifically, he could mention upcoming projects at our own company that might benefit from my attendance. He could also make sense of names and speakers and give me ice-breakers for conversations. When departing for longer trips to conferences, my supervisor looked over the conference program to highlight key meetings and sessions that I may have overlooked. It was clear that my supervisor was actively involved in my development. He wanted me to succeed as much as I did. He showed a genuine interest in what I was doing and demonstrated some key opportunities on which I could capitalize.

> ☑ QUICK TIP
>
> Take an active interest not only in what conference or meetings your new employees are attending, but also what they are doing at those meetings. Preplan, shadow, and debrief meetings to maximize value.

When my supervisor attended meetings with me, the opportunity for development and growth increased. The on-site process can be more than simply introducing new employees to other meeting attendees. Here the point may be to tackle some of the more complex situations that arise at professional meetings.

Many managers take on the exhibit hall as an exercise in staff development. Managers take new employees through exhibit halls to introduce the library-vendor relationship. New employees are taught how to ask questions, make product recommendations, invite training or follow-up calls, and even price out products.

Another important outing to navigate is the reception, which is usually hosted by either a vendor or high-ranking members of the association. It is often difficult for new employees to make the most of receptions. Too often they get caught in a corner having a drink, not finding anyone to talk with, and then leaving. Walking a new librarian through a reception and showing him or her how to make inroads into conversations, how to identify key contacts (look for ribbons, keep an eye on name tags, etc.), and how to present themselves can help prevent lost opportunities.

In addition to knowing how to talk to people at a reception, new employees may need to know what can be discussed at a reception. Although it is appropriate to exchange business cards at a reception, it may not be appropriate to exchange an article for review or comment.

Organizing and securing networks

With all of the effort being put into networking, it is important to ensure a method is in place for organizing the new employee's network. For many, this is as simple as putting a rubber band around a stack of cards. For others it involves following up with an e-mail. And still others will go the extra step to make their networks more easily acceptable and ready to utilize.

As I've written before, my supervisors asked me to follow up on meetings with individuals and to recap the key take-aways from each meeting. They also encouraged me to take a moment and follow up with those I had met. A simple e-mail will often work to reinforce an introduction and to build a long lasting relationship. Once I knew this was expected of me, I took greater care in meeting individuals and noting on business cards where I had met the person and what we had talked about. This made following up with an e-mail easier and more personalized. If the case required, I could also follow up with actionable items or requests for another meeting.

Utilizing tools such as Microsoft Outlook's contacts function or even a simple spreadsheet can help make contacts more manageable. Importing not only contact information, but also some memos or notes about the meeting, will help the contact become more accessible when needed. In my more ambitious moments, I created tables with contacts listed by areas of expertise or interest. This was particularly useful in my job as I looked for possible authors, but it also proved useful when people asked me for advice or when I needed a program speaker or other presenter. I found that those in my network were flattered to be thought of and also to know that someone had taken an interest in them and had really taken note of their interests.

Last, a great lesson learned from my supervisor was to never view a network or relationship as static. One should periodically touch base with these individuals, even when no help is required. By simply dropping a random note or e-mail, colleagues will be reminded of their relationship to you and will be ready for the time when something actually is needed. Also, new employees should not focus only on collecting new network members; they should also try to be included in others' networks. Touching base with those in the network will help remind others of the employee's interest and involvement. They will become something more permanent and real in the profession.

Embracing networks

One of the most meaningful and rewarding experiences for your new employee may be the moment when you embrace their newly formed network. My supervisors did this in simple but numerous ways.

At conferences and meetings, my supervisors took time to not only introduce me to who they knew, but to also meet the young people in my burgeoning network. It may seem a simple act, but for both me and my colleagues, it demonstrated my organization's value for networks and for professionals of all levels. My colleagues walked away feeling validated from meeting my supervisors and knowing that I worked in an environment that truly valued me. One of the more surprising things my supervisors did was follow up on my introductions by asking more questions about each person. They showed a genuine interest and remembered job titles, places of employment, and even interests. It was a firsthand demonstration of how to network effectively, and it was a reminder of how I should be using my own network.

> ☑ QUICK TIP
> Find easy ways to engage your new employee's network, especially if they haven't been very engaging with the group in a while.

Once you have reached out to your new employee's burgeoning network, you can also begin encouraging him or her to use it. For my supervisors, this was done in both formal and informal ways. Often, we would come across a topic of discussion that could benefit from additional opinions. In those moments, my supervisors turned to me and asked me to send out feeler messages to my colleagues and friends in the profession. My supervisors were really helping me to understand opportunities for using a network and encouraging me to invest time in it. At other times, my supervisors would ask for three names of specific contacts who could help review a project or offer feedback on a specific initiative. It was in these instances that my supervisors helped reinforce the value of knowing my contacts and connecting specializations and interests to names and faces. What was an unexpected benefit for me was that in contacting these network members and seeking out their opinions, my profile grew. The contacts recognized that I was someone with whom they could actively network. They knew they could call upon me. Many felt honored to be asked for their opinion and developed a connection with my organization. Ultimately, as the profile of my network grew in the eyes of my supervisors, so too did my own profile in the eyes of my network members.

Conclusion

Networking can be as active or passive a process as you decide. With some initial work and some minor maintenance, you can help your new staff become active networkers. Through a simple process of inventorying your new employees' networks, providing shadowing opportunities for staff to learn networking skills, and encouraging follow-up, you can create a culture in which networking is seen as a necessary and integrated part of your work environment. Most important, as your new staff network, they will build not only the essential communication skills required of networking, but they will tap into a community of professionals who can supplement their education and practice in numerous ways. Networking is not only a staff development opportunity; it is also a tool for professional development.

Further reading

Kram, Kathy E., and Lynn A. Isabella. 1985. "Mentoring Alternatives: The Role of Peer Relationships in Career Development." *The Academy of Management Journal* 28, no. 1 (March): 110–132. Available: /www.jstor.org/stable/256064 (accessed July 1, 2008).

Nierenberg, Andrea. 2002. "Tips on Encouraging Positive Networking Tactics." *Employment Relations Today* 29, no. 1 (April): 27–31.

Peters, Tom. 2007. "The Brand Called You." *Fast Company* (December 18). Available: www.fastcompany.com/magazine/10/brandyou.html (accessed July 1, 2008).

Ross, Catherine Sheldrick, and Patricia Dewdney. 1998. *Communicating Professionally: A How-To-Do-It Manual for Librarians*, Second Edition. New York: Neal-Schuman Publishers.

Wright, Cheryl A., and Scott D. Wright. 1987. "The Role of Mentors in the Career Development of Young Professionals." *Family Relations* 36, no. 2 (April): 204–208.

CHAPTER 13

staff development through association conferences and meetings; or, the developing of a Latino librarian

Ida Z. daRoza

Throughout my career as a library technician, I have been fortunate to have administrators who have been generous in allowing me to attend professional development opportunities in the field of library science. These opportunities have greatly contributed to making me the enthusiastic librarian that I am today. My participation in conferences has created not only a change in attitude, but also a change in stature and professionalism. This chapter discusses how I became more involved in local and national associations, attending conferences and meetings, and how my direct supervisors created a culture that supported my professional development.

Why conferences?

Library staff of all levels can benefit from the opportunity to attend association meetings, workshops, and conferences. It may not always be easy for libraries to provide this opportunity. Along with larger funding limitations are the day-to-day obstacles of running a library, and so the library needs to remain staffed with both frontline employees and higher-level managers. In short, everyone cannot be gone all at once.

As challenging as it may be to find time to send staff away to conferences, managers will see definite benefits. Among the many benefits for both the individual and the organization are the following:

- Finding mentorship from other professionals in the field
- Learning about the many types of local, state, and national associations
- Becoming an active part of the library profession
- Listening and learning from leaders in the profession
- Joining association listservs for interaction with others between meetings
- Becoming eligible to receive, read, and write for association magazines and newsletters
- Helping define the type of librarian and specialty one may want to follow
- Keeping current with new ideas, concepts, and technologies
- Feeling good that your library is investing in your professional development
- Learning communication skills through interaction with others and public speaking
- Promoting the library and its services to others in the profession

Even though we live in a 2.0 world where we can learn, meet, and socialize without meeting in person, it is necessary and beneficial to meet other professionals face-to-face. As evidence, even the most active bloggers go to conferences to meet other bloggers in person. They put faces to names and delve beyond one-line comments. They create a dialog. It happens throughout conferences, in small hallway meetings and in large, filled auditoriums. Seeing people one-on-one fills an important need of affiliation.

Building interest—and comfort

Library staff will have varying levels of interest in going to association functions. Some may be more reticent than others, not finding it appealing to be among a crowd of people at an association meeting. Others may see conference involvement as additional time committed to an already demanding work schedule. It is ultimately up to the manager to help build an environment of interest and comfort in conference participation. Among the simple facts they can stress is that we are in a "people" profession and need to find ways to be comfortable with meeting and providing service to people. Associations provide a great opportunity to practice our social skills.

> ☑ QUICK TIP
> Stress the social nature of our profession. Librarians need to become comfortable with social situations—and associations can help in that process.

It did take me time to develop a comfort level in an environment in which everyone knows one another, and even more time to actually feel like a part of the group. Managers can help new staff by encouraging them to take advantage of the numerous networking opportunities available at conferences. Explore options for new attendees, such as shadowing programs or new-member roundtables, or even by offering to escort new staff through their first few receptions. ALA offers a New Members Roundtable (NMRT) first-timers' orientation and party. Here more senior association members offer advice to new and first-time conference-goers in an environment in which novice conference-goers can mingle with one another. Discovering a mix of opportunities for new staff to shadow close associates and to break out on their own is ideal. Creating cliques and social crutches may actually discourage the networking that really needs to happen at conferences. Encouraging a mix ensures that at both the current conference and at future conferences, someone will be there to offer a level of comfort.

> ☑ QUICK TIP
> Create opportunities for first-time conference attendees to socialize with colleagues and time to break out on their own.

After attending several conferences, I now thrive in association environments because I know I am in a room of like minds and interests. Now, I enjoy meeting people, and do not hesitate to walk around, introducing myself to everyone. To help expand my comfort at conferences, I arrive equipped with the essential tools. My friends tease me that I am like a magician who shoots out playing cards from his sleeve, but instead of playing cards, I am armed with business cards. At every conference I have attended, I have found that extending my hand and a business card is an ice-breaker and is met with warm reciprocation. It is an easy way to build comfort and familiarity in an unfamiliar room.

Building benefits—before they even leave

A manager can increase the benefit of conference attendance for both the individual and the institution by asking the attendee to submit a written report or presentation to the rest of the staff. Create opportunities and reasons for the attendee to stay engaged with the meeting or conference. Creating this accountability demonstrates to the employee the serious nature—and investment—of conference attendance. Every institution for which I have worked has asked me for this kind of feedback, and I have found that it has helped me to encapsulate what I learned before I forget. Moreover, my enthusiastic reports have proven to my managers that attending meetings is important and meaningful to me, and this has sometimes encouraged others to attend future events. Ultimately, conference attendance should work for the benefit of both the institution and the individual. Creating opportunities for individuals to report back brings the knowledge of the conference to all institutional staff and provides a growth opportunity for the individual.

Getting started locally

Supervisors can take the first steps toward association and conference involvement by looking into their own backyard. Librarians meet in communities large and small. By looking into your own backyard, you can identify small, local meetings that can be attended at a low cost and with little time demands on you or your staff. Taking the extra step and inviting a new staff member along to a meeting you are already attending is an easy and effective way to build involvement.

ARLIS: local introductions to local leadership

My first experience with associations began when I was a library technician at the Academy of Art University Library in San Francisco. The director who hired me was very involved in the Art Libraries Society of North America, Northern California Chapter (ARLIS NC). I was fortunate to have her encouragement as she suggested that I might enjoy attending the ARLIS NC meeting.

I will never forget that first meeting on April 12, 2001. Through the arrangement of an ARLIS member who was also the art curator of the Harry W. and Mary Margaret Anderson Art Collection, the meeting included a private tour through the offices and home of one of the largest private collectors of abstract American art. It was amazing to walk through the home in which the Andersons lived and see the spaces where they enjoyed this famous art.

Over the course of my early involvement with ARLIS, I became strongly influenced by the membership. I quickly benefited by meeting other art librarians and catalogers who shared common issues in our particular field of art librarianship. In discussing the day-to-day issues of art libraries and the broader context of the profession, I became more knowledgeable and more passionate about my work. Ultimately, it was these personal connections made at ARLIS that convinced me to get my master's degree in library science.

Over the next four years I worked full-time, went to school, and continued to enjoy going to ARLIS NC meetings. In addition to the education and networking, the meetings provided me special VIP access to the leading San Francisco museums, galleries, and art colleges. While pushing my educational reach, ARLIS also challenged me to become a leader. Committed participation led to my becoming increasingly involved with the association and eventually being asked to run for vice-chair/chair of the ARLIS Northern California chapter. My experience as vice-chair helped me understand how library associations work within the profession. I observed the practical skills of leading meetings, creating an agenda, and working with committees. Ultimately, all of these wonderful opportunities happened to me all thanks to a forward-thinking supervisor who introduced me to association participation.

> ☑ QUICK TIP
> Bring new staff into leadership positions. Find ways they can support your leadership efforts or go the extra step to nominate new staff for appropriate leadership positions of their own.

Finding local opportunities

You can find local associations in many ways. One of the easiest is by checking the Web site of the closest school of library science. They usually have on their Web sites contact information of local, state, and national association information.

My alma mater, San Jose State University School of Library & Information Science (SLIS) has great Web links to conferences and associations (http://slisweb.sjsu.edu/resources/conferences/lisconferences.php) of both local and national significance (see Exhibit 13.1).

Most national association Web sites connect users to local chapters or divisions. Finding and attending a local chapter meeting before going to the national level can save money and time. By getting a taste of what the local level is engaged in, you can

---

Exhibit 13.1. Web sites of conferences and associations

AALL (American Association of Law Libraries): www.aallnet.org

AASL (American Association of School Librarians) National: www.ala.org/aasl

ALA (American Library Association) Annual: www.ala.org

ALISE (Association for Library and Information Science Education): www.alise.org

ARMA International Competency Development Project: www.arma.org

ARLIS/NA (Art Libraries Society of North America): www.arlisna.org/

ASIS&T (American Society for Information Science and Technology): www.asis.org

ASCD (Association for Supervision and Curriculum Development): www.ascd.org

BCALA (Black Caucus of the American Library Association): www.bcala.org/

CALA (Chinese American Librarians Association): www.cala-web.org

COLT (Council on Library/Media Technicians): www.colt.ucr.edu/

IFLA (International Federation of Library Associations): www.ifla.org

ISKO (International Society for Knowledge Organization): www.isko.org

JCDL (Joint Conference on Digital Libraries): www.jcdl.org

PLA (Public Library Association): www.ala.org/ala/pla/pla.cfm

REFORMA (National Association to Promote Library and Information Services to Latinos and the Spanish-Speaking): www.reforma.org/who.html

SAA (Society of American Archivists): www.archivists.org

SALALM (Seminar on the Acquisition of Latin American Library Materials): www.salalm.org

SLA (Special Libraries Association): www.sla.org

---

sense what the national experience might be. Local involvement may also prove easier and less time-intensive than national involvement. For new staff members who are especially interested in building networks and possible mentor relationships, working at the local level with individuals who can be easily accessed via phone or in person may work better.

Moving up: national associations

My local ARLIS chapter was not the only significant association in my professional development. I started my participation on the national level slowly. I was fortunate to get a sneak peak at the big leagues in June 2001. The American Library Association (ALA) had its annual conference in San Francisco at the Moscone Center two blocks away from the Academy of Art Library, where I worked. The ALA conference was huge and overwhelming. I remember looking at all the acronyms in the brochure and feeling extremely confused. The conference halls of the Moscone Center were filled with 1,600 vendors whose products were strange and new to me.

The saving factor that made this huge conference manageable was my involvement in the Council on Library/Media Technicians (COLT) conference concurrent with the ALA conference. Our library subscribed to the COLT magazine, a magazine dedicated to library issues and concerns of library support staff. Through this magazine, I learned that COLT was having a concurrent conference for library support staff with many of the same speakers that were presenting at the ALA conference.

☑ QUICK TIP

Look for focused conferences within conferences. These focused tracks might make an overwhelming conference more manageable.

I was able to get the financial support of my administration to attend one day of the COLT ALA conference. I picked a day that featured cataloger Gene Kinally of the Library of Congress. Having seen his posts on the AUTOCAT listserv, I felt I was getting a chance to meet not only a cataloging superstar, but also someone with whom I was slightly familiar. I remember dressing up in my best suit that morning, wanting to make a good first impression. After listening attentively through the presentation, I stayed after and asked him numerous questions. I led with a quick introduction, mentioned that I recognized his name from the listserv, and pointed out that I was new to conferences. I asked him what his job at the Library of Congress was like, how many items he cataloged, and even some specific cataloging questions. He was very kind and answered every one of my questions. This conference inspired me with more wonder, respect, and curiosity about the library profession.

I walked away from this experience at a national conference with tips I have used for future conferences—lessons that can be shared by supervisors with new staff before any conference:

- *Do some research on the speakers before attending*. This can be as simple as identifying the name and making the connection to postings on a listserv. The more extensive the research, the more likely it will prove useful.
- *Ask the speakers appropriate questions based on your research and the speaker's message*. Also, make sure to put your questions in the context of your experience. Making it clear that you are a new professional can go far in making experienced librarians interested in talking with you. It might also help them gauge the completeness of their answers.
- *Dress professionally*. You are representing yourself and your library, and it is a sign of respect for the speaker.

Finding community in associations and conferences

In 2002, I applied for a Spectrum Scholarship from the American Library Association Office for Diversity to help pay for my master's degree in library science. Along with a group of 28 others in 2003, I became a Spectrum Scholar. As part of the scholarship, I was invited to attend a three-day institute sponsored by the ALA Diversity Office designed to help scholars get direction and advice in their beginning careers. The institute is held each year before the ALA annual conference.

At the Spectrum Leadership Institute, I listened to motivational speeches given by library leaders Camila Alire, Carla Hayden, Patti Montiel Overall, Tracie D. Hall, and many others. It was also at the Spectrum Institute that I discovered for the first time the value my bilingual skills could provide to librarianship.

Becoming a Spectrum Scholar and becoming involved with the American Library Association Office for Diversity provided me with numerous mentors who encouraged me in different ways from the ways the art librarians had. These librarians of color helped my self-esteem and gave me a sense of pride I hadn't had before in being a bilingual librarian of color.

I learned the importance of increasing the ranks of diverse librarians, especially as the minority and bilingual populations keep growing nationally. I learned how the shortage of librarians of color prevented many of these populations from gaining full access to services. Most important, however, I learned how I could find community within an association.

> ☑ QUICK TIP
> Seek out opportunities to meet with not only librarians with similar skill sets, but also social circumstances. Nearly all associations provide focused forums, which bring together librarians with shared ethnicities or social values.

Utilizing your community

After receiving the Spectrum Scholarship and attending the Spectrum Institute, I completed my graduate education at San Jose State University in 2005. Having experienced a new community at the Spectrum Institute during ALA, I felt strongly that my place in the field of librarianship should be in bilingual service. One of my fellow Spectrum Scholars, Pete Villaseñor, introduced me to REFORMA's Northern California Chapter, Bibliotecas Para la Gente (BPLG). I became friends and colleagues with other Latino librarians through the local BPLG chapter and instead of touring art museums, as I had with the local ARLIS NC chapter, I began visiting libraries focused on the underserved, usually impoverished, Spanish-speaking communities in San Francisco, Oakland, and San Jose. My involvement in associations had once again opened me to new knowledge and moved me in new directions. I found the places at which I needed to be working.

Despite gaining awareness for the need for bilingual librarians in the Bay Area, I was still working in a library position in which I did not have the opportunity to use my Spanish or help the Spanish-speaking population. Aside from the occasional request to translate for Spanish-speaking users and staff, I was not doing what I was called to do.

The final push came when I went to ALA's conference in New Orleans in 2006. There, at a Spectrum reunion dinner with colleagues, I talked about my desire to be doing something more meaningful with my Spanish. I had finally found a place to talk about the challenge of being happy in my current professional position, but being called to do more.

At that dinner, I was lucky enough to be seated next to Luiz H. Mendes, who encouraged me to reach outside my comfort zone. Tracie Hall also challenged me:

Change jobs, even if you are afraid. Do it, she said. Do it with fear. Stop just talking the talk and start walking the walk. Others also shared experiences of their own risk-taking, including moving across the country to work with underserved communities. After that conference I gained a newfound sense of motivation to look for a job for which I could use my bilingual abilities.

This was an important lesson in my conference-going experience. It challenged me to find a core circle of colleagues and to open up to them with trust. This experience moved me in a new direction, but it could just as easily have encouraged me to take on a new project, to resolve an existing conflict, or to flesh out a new program. The face-to-face elements of conferences and associations eventually lead to a colleague-to-colleague relationship that is necessary for growth and development.

Inspired by the conference and meetings with the other Spectrum Scholars, I did leave the comfort zone. Just two months after the conference, I left my job and went to work for a public library system. I interviewed and was hired by the San Mateo County Library System just 30 miles south of San Francisco. I believe I sincerely showed them in my interview that I wanted to contribute to their goal of helping their diverse communities. I was offered and took a challenging job as a cataloger of materials in multiple languages. I was also asked to serve as a member of the system-wide Spanish Services Committee with representatives from all 12 branches. I feel fortunate that even working as a cataloger, I have had the chance to participate in library policies and programs for the Spanish-speaking community through being on my library's Spanish Services Committee.

While serving on this committee, I watched the San Mateo County Library Web site enhance its English and Spanish version, which distinguishes it from other library catalog Web sites. Designed by two of my Latino colleagues, Cristobal Miranda and Robert Esparza, it took first place in the American Library Association's 2007 Swap and Shop Best of Show Competition for Best Web Site within our budget range. I am proud to work at a library that has made moves to provide bilingual access to the library catalog.

Giving back to associations

After a few months of working for the San Mateo County Library System, I received a phone call from the American Library Association Office for Diversity, which awards the Spectrum Scholarships. I was informed that the 2007 ALA conference in Washington, DC, would be the ten-year anniversary of the Spectrum Initiative, which created the Spectrum Scholarship. The office was planning several featured programs and asked if I would participate as a speaker at one session. My Spectrum experience—and in many ways my association experience—had come full circle. I had moved from novice participant to active presenter.

I was asked to speak on a panel titled "Ten Years Later—Where Are They Now? Spectrum Scholars Shining in the Field." The panel brought together four Spectrum Scholars, each representing a different area of library service: public, academic, school, and administration.

I immediately said yes to the speaking invitation, although I did not tell them that I had a major fear of public speaking. I started taking speech classes with a private coach and worked and practiced my speech for four months.

I was really pleased to be able to give something back for the ALA department that had given me so much. I was also thrilled to find out that Tracie Hall, Assistant Dean, GSLIS, Dominican University, and Luiz H. Mendes, Electronic Resources Librarian, California State University, would be my fellow panel presenters. Both had been so influential in helping me make my decision at the previous year's annual conference to move to public librarianship.

After delivering my presentation for the Spectrum program at the 2007 Conference in Washington, DC, I was able to reflect on my experiences over six years, growing from a timid first-time attendee of a concurrent conference, to an engaged participant with a network of colleagues, and now speaking at the annual conference. I am still in awe that all of this has happened. I know that it was not by luck or merely by my own doing; it was facilitated by the encouragement of supervisors who recognized the importance of involvement.

Creating opportunities: cross-association involvement

Throughout my association experiences, I have tried to maintain involvement across associations. It is a challenge to commit staff time to multiple circles, but it can prove useful when unlikely circles merge and create new opportunities.

Although I had taken on a leadership position in CLA's Access, Collections and Technical Services Section (ACTSS), I still tried to find time for other groups and organizations. I never stopped attending the bimonthly local REFORMA BPLG chapter meetings. I still stayed in contact with my Spectrum colleagues and found time to work within my system with the Spanish Committee.

A month before my first CLA conference as vice-president/president-elect of ACTSS, I received a phone call from my Spectrum and REFORMA colleague, Peter Villaseñor. Peter was now the president of the REFORMA BPLG Northern California chapter. He now found himself scrambling to find someone to fill in for a canceled presenter for an upcoming panel at the CLA conference. He turned to me to take the missing place. I agreed and found myself

> ☑ QUICK TIP
> New staff should never let go of their contacts from previous associations. The opportunity for collaboration across associations or networks always exists. Even creating opportunities for staff to talk with one another about their association involvement can inspire new opportunities.

faced with the challenge of preparing to participate in a presentation titled "If you invite them, they will come . . . *Y ahora que?* Teens in the library." With the help of my speech coach Sharon Bower, who had helped me with my ALA DC speech preparation, and my experiences with bilingual programming for the San Mateo County Library System as a part of the Spanish Committee during the year, I was able to find my way.

This unique and valuable opportunity could have happened only with my continued involvement in multiple associations. And valuable it was; I shared the San Mateo County Library System's salsa dancing program from Spanish Heritage month. It was an excellent opportunity to promote the library's accomplishments in reaching out to the Latino community and to learn from other libraries with similar programs.

To make sure that my speech presented the library system correctly, I took the extra step of touching base with the assistant director. When I speak at a library conference, I need to be aware that I represent not only an association, but the library system for which I work. Before presenting at the CLA conference, I discussed my upcoming presentations with the Assistant Director of the San Mateo County Library, Anne-Marie Despain, and reviewed the PowerPoint slides and various templates that I was planning to use in my presentation. This not only helped me represent the library appropriately, it also gave me another point of view to review my work and offer advice and information to make it stronger.

> ☑ **QUICK TIP**
> Keep informed about staff involvement in associations. Encourage staff members to talk with you about their involvement to ensure that the library is represented appropriately.

A look back

As I flew back from Long Beach after attending the 2007 California Library Association annual conference, I thought with amazement that it was only a few years ago that I was in library school and going to the CLA conferences at the student rate, or trying to borrow friends' badges to get in to just look in on librarians' meetings. It was amazing to me that in the past four days I had gone to meetings at which I met people who I had seen quoted in textbooks, made a presentation, and was also elected as a state association officer. I thought to myself, *How did I get here?*

I know that I would still be on the outskirts if it were not for the supervisors, administrators, and mentors who have invested in me and not only allowed me to participate in associations, but introduced them to me. I learned to be an active librarian from these association programs where I met kind, likeminded librarians giving a voice and effecting positive changes in the field of library science.

I am also lucky to have an understanding husband who, not being a librarian, helps support my work in librarianship and time away at conferences. I am still a tadpole in the library pool of things but I feel I owe a great deal to the associations and administrators who have helped me financially and with mentorship to participate. I will do my best to pay them back in service to the library profession and in my work, as long as I am able. It truly is a circle of service, and I am proud to find myself somewhere in it.

Further reading

Alire, C. A., and J. Ayala. 2007. *Serving Latino Communities: A How-To-Do-It Manual for Librarians*, Second Edition. New York: Neal-Schuman Publishers.

American Library Association. 1972. *ALA Handbook of Organization.* Chicago: American Library Association.

American Library Association. 2000. *Membership Best Practices: Recruitment, Retention, Recognition, Rewards.* Chicago: American Library Association.

Guereña, S. 2000. *Library Services to Latinos: An Anthology.* Jefferson, NC: McFarland.

Pavon, A.-E., and D. Borrego. 2003. *25 Latino Craft Projects: Celebrating Culture in Your Library.* Chicago: American Library Association.

professional service on national library committees: developing the skills to lead

Georgie L. Donovan

W hen I first started my job as Special Assistant to the Dean at the University of Arizona Libraries, the associate dean, Janice Simmons-Welburn, was extremely busy with her responsibilities serving as the chair of the nominating committee for the Association of the College & Research Libraries (ACRL). ACRL is the arm of the American Library Association (ALA) focused on academic and research librarians who work in community colleges, two- and four-year institutions, large research and university libraries, and other academic settings. Janice was heavily involved in ACRL, but also in other divisions of ALA such as Library Administration and Management Association (LAMA) and Reference and User Services Association (RUSA). In one of our rare "down" moments, she talked to me about ACRL. "I think it's a wonderful association—and the ACRL conference is the very best conference that's out there. I have met so many lifelong friends through ACRL." Janice had had a full career of working in many different areas of librarianship, and, as a longtime library leader, had attended dozens of conferences on higher education, librarianship, and technology. Her words stuck with me.

She talked about ACRL as the place where one could come together with other academic librarians and make social connections that would stretch into relationships spanning the years, relationships that would broaden one's mind about the possibilities of librarianship. ACRL has a strong strategic plan with far-reaching goals related to advocating for libraries, facilitating the research and publication process, and improving teaching and learning as well as assessment of learning outcomes on campus. However, the intangible and possibly best part of working with ACRL (as with any library professional organization) is building relationships with colleagues in other libraries around the country and beyond.

These relationships help us understand what challenges other libraries face and what innovative solutions they are proposing to deal with them. It helps us expand our minds about the various types of leadership, organizations, services, and policies in the greater world of libraries. We get to know not just that a library has developed a new diversity outreach program, but what it's like for a person on the ground implementing that program and what are her daily challenges and frustrations. We gain the wisdom of friends in other libraries to help us through difficult times in our own institution when it's impolitic to complain to co-workers. Moreover, as a group of librarians across the country working together on a common project, we can accomplish great things. We can advocate for legislation, develop standards and tools that will help librarians in every library, plan and host conferences and professional education opportunities, and raise the quality of work life for library professionals. When Janice talked to me about ACRL, she touched on all of these qualities, and her sincerity sparked in me the desire to get involved.

That first committee appointment

Soon after I started working at University of Arizona, I submitted my volunteer form for ACRL, open minded about where I might be assigned. I ended up working on the Roundtables Sub-Committee for the ACRL National Conference to be held in Minneapolis in 2005. This committee involved a requirement to attend every ALA midwinter and annual meeting including a four-hour work committee meeting during the conference. I would also need to attend the ACRL National Conference to help out with the roundtables and, of course, see the fruits of our labor through to the end. Between conferences, I would need to:

1. help get the word out so that librarians would submit a proposal to lead a roundtable;
2. review the submitted proposals and make recommendations about which ones had the most potential;
3. come to a consensus decision with the other committee members about which proposals would be chosen as roundtables; and
4. help develop guidelines for the librarians leading roundtables so they could produce stimulating discussion during their sessions.

The work was great fun. My committee had ten librarians from around the country, some with long careers in libraries (associate deans and department heads) and some like me who had recently entered the field. We created a few innovative features of the roundtable process. Roundtables are one type of program featured at the ACRL National Conference. One or two librarians lead a small discussion group on a specific topic; for example, "How are you implementing chat reference?" or "How can you raise money for a new library building?" or "What kinds of services

are out there for international students?" During the allotted time period, a group of
conference attendees who probably have never met will come together for an hour
and discuss the topic, with the program leader posing interesting questions and
keeping the ball rolling.

My committee worked to select the best proposals and assigned each topic a slot
to avoid overlap within the hour. (For example, we wanted to separate two programs
on copyright so that one would be going on during each of the two hours slotted for
roundtables.) I learned something about what the "hot topics" are in librarianship;
which proposals were attractive to everybody because they hit a nerve, sparking
conversations we all cared about. We developed a list of guidelines and sent it to all
the program leaders to help everyone understand how to facilitate discussion.

The balance of working with my committee members virtually and then face-to-
face during the ALA conferences helped me get to know their working styles and
personal things about them as well. It has been five years since that project, but I still
remember all of my committee members, and when I see them, we catch up and talk
about our work and our lives. Because of my great experience working on this
committee, I eagerly filled out my volunteer form for ACRL time and time again, and
now, barely four years since I graduated from library school, I have served on several
different committees. For three years, heading into a fourth, I have been a member of
the ACRL Scholarly Communication Committee. For the 2007 ACRL National
Conference, I served on the Executive Committee, the group comprised of heads of
subcommittees and the conference chair, which plans the overall conference. I am
now serving on the 2009 ACRL National Conference Committee as part of the
Keynotes Sub-Committee.

Beyond ACRL, I have held a national appointment on an ALA Committee, the
2006-2007 Committee to Develop a National Agenda for Libraries appointed and led
by Leslie Burger, then-ALA president. Lastly, I have been an active member in the
Progressive Librarians Guild (PLG) since 2003, working on programming projects
with small committees. As always, I am active on my current library's task forces and
committees and at a regional level, but these national level appointments have helped
me develop a big-picture appreciation for libraries, and helped me build
relationships with librarians at all stages of their careers, in all types of libraries.

What can an individual gain? What does the library gain?

Working on a committee within a professional organization is a completely different
experience from treating professional conferences and organizations as a commodity.
Helping put the organization together, helping shape its goals and accomplishments,
is much more valuable and fulfilling than just
being a consumer of its conferences, workshops,
and publications. In terms of ACRL, the
professional organization that I know best, the
ACRL National Conference, the pre-conferences
and sessions during ALA, the virtual conferences

☑ QUICK TIP
Encourage staff to get involved
with the inner workings of the
conference—not just as attendees.

and workshops, and the publications like *College & Research Libraries* and *C&RL News* are all fantastic offerings that add tremendously to the professional development and enrichment of our library lives. Yet, while I do not want to in any way diminish the value of ACRL programming and publishing, I know that making an effort to *work* on these initiatives from the inside of the organization gives one a much different level of understanding and enjoyment. Some concepts and skills gained when librarians offer their time to library professional service are discussed in the following sections.

Professional service: learning how to lead

Even if you're not in charge of a committee, having to jump right in and complete a project in a short time frame with a group of people whom you may have never met forces you to get organized, pitch in, take the initiative for new ideas and improvements, and step up to the plate with the workload. One recent experience brought this truth home for me. Several months ago, I was appointed to work on the Keynotes Sub-Committee for the ACRL National Conference, which will be held in 2009. Our job is to select amazing, magnetic speakers for three time slots during the conference: opening, lunch midway through the conference, and closing. These three speakers should be nationally known, but not overexposed. They should be great speakers and able to talk about issues that academic librarians care about. In addition, since their names will be used to promote the conference early on, they should be recognizable enough to convince academic librarians that the conference will be engaging, exciting, and worth every penny.

Before our meeting at ALA Midwinter, each of us on the committee needed to come up with a wide-ranging list of potential speakers and submit them for our long list of potentials. Then, in a face-to-face meeting, we looked through the large list and started to winnow it down, so that within the space of two to three hours, we would have three speakers and backups in case our first choices turned us down. We had no time to lose. All of us sent lists of names to one another via e-mail before the conference, and our committee co-chairs compiled those into one document for us to peruse. Then, starting at 8:00 a.m. on the Monday of ALA Midwinter, we began debating the pros and cons of our list, bringing other names to the table, and figuring out a winning schedule that would seem balanced to conference attendees.

With a short turnaround time on a project such as this, a committee has no room for dead weight. Each person has to chip in equally and has to make his or her voice known. An early-career librarian such as me cannot feel intimidated by the three library deans at the table and simply nod his or her approval. In fact, I found that my opinions were taken equally and, when I had a different opinion about a speaker because of my age group, people appreciated that perspective.

In short, I had to be a leader within the committee, even though I was not the chair. Each one of us had to be a leader. We had to be able to articulate our opinions and assertively express them in a short period of time. We had to devise a rubric for how to assign speakers to different time slots. And we had to take the initiative to research each of the speakers and then volunteer to write invitations to our final choices. On a small committee with a large task to do, no one can slack off, procrastinate, or be a fifth wheel.

This committee is only one example, but every committee experience I have had within the library professional service community has had similar requirements: be on task, be sharp, be assertive, take initiative, take responsibility. Not only does this help me as an individual to develop my own leadership skills, but I have been able to bring back those skills to the library at which I work. From my experience leading, I am a better participant in library meetings, I know how to

> ☑ QUICK TIP
> Several qualities important to the library can be developed through working on committees. These include responsibility, self-confidence, risk-taking, and leadership.

chair a committee and cut to the chase, and I know how to accomplish big things with a group of dedicated librarians. I credit my experience working with librarians around the country for many of these skills. I've seen how some "pros" do it (deans and department heads and leaders in many capacities) and I have picked up many of their habits and brought them back to my home institution.

For libraries considering whether to encourage their library staff to get involved with professional service (Won't it take time away from their jobs? Won't it be expensive to send them to conferences?), the importance of these experiences in leadership cannot be overstated. Putting together funding and arranging for a few days' time off for staff is rewarded by raising the level of leadership in the library.

Professional service: building bridges to other libraries and librarians on a national level

I will reiterate that building connections to librarians and staff working all around the country is one of the most rewarding activities of working in professional organizations. It is also extremely beneficial to one's home library. A simple example is the creation of this book. Because of the relationships that my co-editor, Miguel Figueroa, and I have, we have been able to ask acquaintances and colleagues from many different types of libraries dispersed around the country to write about their experiences. At first, the task of finding a dozen authors by myself sounded daunting, but after spending some time scratching my head, looking at business cards, and thinking about my experiences within ALA, ACRL, and PLG, I had a long enough list to start calling people—and not have to beg if they said no.

Because I have colleagues who are at all stages in their careers, I am learning about librarianship as a long road, and the possibilities for stops along the way. I hear about the new programs and initiatives of these institutions. I am able to promote my own school, Appalachian State University, and its beautiful campus and new library building. During committee meetings and meals at a conference, we are able to talk about the big issues of the day, hot topics, and controversial news in the library world. Finally, when I was promoted to a new position, Head of Acquisitions, I knew several colleagues who were working in similar positions on whom I could call and ask for advice and words of wisdom.

Again, these connections are personally rewarding and a great benefit to my own growth, but they also profit my home institution. I am a better acquisitions librarian for knowing about acquisitions processes and innovations in other libraries. I am a good spokesperson for my own library, which helps with our recruitment efforts when we have job postings and helps with our national recognition. My ideas are informed by the programs and projects and innovative services and policies happening at other institutions.

Professional service: understanding the big picture for libraries

The USA PATRIOT Act, funding for education versus defense, the landscape of higher education . . . the world is wide open in terms of issues that bear relevance for libraries. However, often it is difficult for library professionals to make a connection between a national issue and their day-to-day job. Through working on national committees, I've been able to see the connection and work on national objectives to move the library profession—and my own library—forward.

One example is my work on the ACRL Scholarly Communication Committee. One of our major initiatives over the past few years has been to shepherd legislation that would make federally funded research available for free on the Internet. Every year, millions of dollars of grants from federal agencies such as the National Science Foundation or the National Institutes of Health are granted to researchers, who then publish their findings in research journals that are prohibitively expensive for libraries to buy. In other words, the taxpayers pay for this research twice: once when they help support the research grants and a second time when they support educational institutions with libraries that buy the research again.

One impetus for libraries to become involved in the beginning was the serials crisis. Inflation of serials has been around 8 to12 percent each year, higher than inflation in the consumer price index or the higher-education price index—higher even than inflation in health care costs. At some point, though, the issue grew larger than just the library's budget. Taxpayers deserve access to federally funded research. Open access to health research leads to faster developments in health care research: More researchers throughout the world can see what is being published. This issue touches on not only the common good and the big picture but also the access to information that our libraries provide and how much that information should cost.

In my own small way, I have helped in this movement, through my work on the ACRL Scholarly Communication Committee. Others on the committee have taken the lead in drafting legislation, calling senators and representatives for cosigning support, and driving public policy and publishing policy. I have written legislators and followed these developments, including the recent bill signed into law that will require open access to research funded by the National Institutes of Health. Success! I have also helped decide on programming at ALA conferences that would highlight our work in this area, written a column for *C&RL News* on this issue and other scholarly communication issues and their relevance to early-career librarians, worked on the applicant and scholarship processes of our committee's Scholarly Communication

Institute. The Institute is one professional development opportunity for librarians, faculty members, and others in higher education to learn about the landscape of scholarly publishing and communication and to understand issues such as legislative advocacy.

The Scholarly Communication Committee is a busy place, with many projects happening simultaneously. However, these projects frequently have a national significance and put the work we do in academic libraries in a different perspective. How are we facilitating the research and publication process on our campus? How are we helping to improve access to information for our faculty members? Perhaps more important, how are we improving research and access to information for researchers beyond our campuses, those working across the country and beyond? These are important issues for which even an early-career librarian such as me can make an impact.

Working on the Scholarly Communication Committee of ACRL is an excellent example of using professional service to understand the big picture for libraries. But other committee assignments have also been fertile educational grounds. In 2006–2007, I worked on ALA President Leslie Burger's task force to create a National Agenda for Libraries. Many nonprofit and business organizations have a national agenda. Like a strategic plan or other organizational documents, a national agenda helps a group articulate its values to stakeholders and helps shape the future of the group's work. Burger invited her task force to meet for a weekend-long think tank that merged library leaders from ALA, IMLS, OCLC, and all types of libraries with leaders of other non-library organizations: the Mellon Foundation, aides of senators and representatives, and the heads of groups such as the Project for Public Spaces and Mobilize.org. We spent the weekend brainstorming the ways in which libraries (academic, public, special, and school) truly transform communities. I worked on a subcommittee dedicated to business and economic growth, dealing with issues such as how libraries help grow the economy of their communities.

Libraries *do* make a measurable and significant impact on positive economic development. Our school and academic libraries prepare people for twenty-first-century careers. Libraries open to the public provide a place for job seekers to do research and develop their skills. They act as a de facto corporate library for small businesses. All libraries enhance the educational process, leading individuals to compete for better job opportunities. We offer outreach programs to learn English, to develop reading skills, to stimulate democracy, and to debate public issues.

> ☑ QUICK TIP
> Building relationships with librarians who work in all types of libraries—academic, public, school, and special—is important and can best be accomplished by working through ALA and other organizations.

Understanding the weight of these issues and how they impact the world around us is part of what I mean when I say that committee work in professional organizations can lead to understanding, and even impacting, the big picture for libraries. Normally in my day-to-day work, I would not have an opportunity to talk about these issues. In fact, even when I do collaborate with other librarians and libraries through the course of my work, it's typically limited to working with other college and university libraries. Only through working in a library professional organization have I had the opportunity to work with public and K–12 librarians, and that experience is crucial to understanding the landscape of education and libraries across the board.

Reinforcing one of my themes, these perspectives benefit my library even as they benefit me as an individual. I have been asked to help draft library responses to the PATRIOT Act and other issues, lead our strategic planning effort, and participate in the university's strategic planning committee. I can make the case for what we do in a macro sense. Even as a relatively new librarian, I see what we're doing and why it impacts the campus and our community.

> ☑ QUICK TIP
> Library service benefits both the individual and the library at which he or she works.

Myriad reasons exist for librarians to participate in professional service beyond the three just highlighted. For example, librarians bring back new project ideas and initiatives to their libraries. And of course, it's important for all of us to contribute to our library organizations to make them the most productive and beneficial they can be. Library service is of significant value to an individual's growth and makes an enormous impact in the libraries in which active participants in professional service work. Sometimes, though, it's difficult for librarians to know how to get started.

Encouraging library staff and professionals to get started

My own involvement in library service was fostered by having a mentor lead me into committee work. That leads me to the first tenet of encouraging others: Get yourself involved. If a library manager or leader is involved in professional service, whether that's through ALA or one of its divisions, or through another organization, her or his experience can be a guide for employees. Looking at yourself in the mirror and realizing that you already can be a mentor (even if you feel more at the "mentee" stage of your career) to others seeking professional experience can be the first step to reaching out to others and making an impact in their careers. The next steps may include the points discussed in the following sections.

> ☑ QUICK TIP
> Whether you realize it or not, you already have a lot to offer as a mentor, even if you are at the beginnings of your career.

Encourage library school students to join student government or library student organizations

My first library service commitment was on the Library Student Organization (LSO) of my library school at the University of Arizona. I served as president of LSO, an ALA student chapter, for two semesters. We started a Webzine so that students could publish their scholarships, held many educational programs and speaker series, helped pay for students to attend the Arizona Library Association meeting, and started many distance-student services. It was an exciting introduction to working on committees with people in a virtual and face-to-face realm. It was also a great place to meet other library school students and get to know them in a professional capacity. My fellow officers from those two semesters are still some of my best friends and roommates when I attend ALA conferences.

Encourage people to start within their region and state

I have focused on experiences at the national level because I believe that those experiences can have a great impact on librarianship. However, state and regional library organizations can also have a major impact on library work and education, and they are a place to connect with librarians doing work in a similar venue. State library conferences and state library organization committee work can bring together K–12 and higher-education partnerships, encourage collaboration between similar organizations, and help forge relationships that will improve library services.

The best way to start: encourage people to simply show up

On the other hand, it's perfectly okay to start with a national committee appointment or volunteer opportunity if that seems fun. I would urge library managers and leaders to talk openly with their employees about their experiences on committees. Don't make it sound more intimidating to join than it is, or seem like a club that only library managers can join. Instead, help people understand that committee work is a task for which anyone willing to work is welcome.

Filling out volunteer forms is the official way to become involved. Another way to gauge one's own interest in a committee and to show interest to current committee members is to attend an open meeting of a committee. Most ALA committee meetings are open to anyone who wants to attend, unless they involve a selection process such as the Caldecott awards or selecting award winners for national library awards. Joining the listserv of a section or division can help librarians learn about the work of that group and be a place to look for opportunities to join or take on a leadership role. For those newly interested in ALA, the New Members Roundtable is a good place to steer people, and a place to meet other members, new and old. New librarians can also find groups that match their interests, whether it's the Social Responsibilities Roundtable, a distance-learning section, or a group of young-adult librarians looking at graphic novels.

Support for professional travel: why it is crucial

While many committees within service organizations can do a great deal of work virtually, members are usually required to travel for face-to-face meetings. I personally find in-person meetings rewarding; it is nice to get to see someone and talk about our personal lives after sometimes months of working only online. Beyond personal rewards, though, traveling to meetings is often a required aspect of accomplishing professional service.

Even at this early point in librarianship, I have had many different levels of support for attending professional meetings. Working as a paraprofessional in three different libraries, pre-MLS degree, the concept of professional service was never even mentioned to me. I've worked in two public libraries and one university library; in each library, some of the professionals likely attended ALA meetings or state association meetings. It was only in my semiprofessional job in the dean's office at the University of Arizona that professional service was first explained and encouraged. I've gone from being able to arrange time off in order to attend meetings (but not receiving any financial support) to my current situation at Appalachian State where librarians and staff are able to attend ALA or other library/education related conferences with registration paid up front and a flat fee (typically in the $500–$600 range) offered to pay for hotel, food, and transportation expenses. This arrangement is excellent for me because, as a new librarian who doesn't mind sharing a hotel room with two or three friends, I can use my stipend to cover almost all if not the whole cost of traveling to professional meetings.

Supporting professional travel is crucial, especially for early-career librarians, for several reasons. Two important reasons are that travel is often prohibitively expensive, especially for new librarians, and second, attending meetings while working on a committee is typically a required aspect of committee service.

Early-career librarians are generally at the bottom of the pay scale, and attending meetings in another city is expensive. In the best-case scenario, a librarian might be able to find a budget motel off the beaten track (and away from the conference hotels and their easy transportation options) for $50 per night, manage to spend $25 per day on food by having a breakfast snack in the room, and spend $200 on a plane ticket or other transportation to the meeting. For a four-day meeting, that's $450 already, and I've detailed the most economical scenario I can envision. Looking back on my own first years working as a librarian, it's clear that finding $450 in an already stretched budget would be impossible, much less finding that amount of money more than once a year. One of the best investments a library can make is to find the money to support staff travel to conferences and professional meetings, particularly when they've taken the initiative to work on professional service through a committee or task force. The benefits to the library far outweigh the costs.

> ☑ **QUICK TIP**
> Supporting staff attendance at conferences, especially when they are doing professional service, is a great investment for the library to make.

Second, for most librarians working on a committee appointment, notably through ALA, attending meetings is required. Someone who misses a meeting or two may be dropped from the committee or be perceived as lazy. Some libraries have a policy to let staff attend only one professional meeting a year. It's impossible to keep up with the work of a busy or high-profile committee with half a commitment.

In addition to supporting library staff financially, library managers and administrators can help in other ways. The traveling professional will need some time off and backup while they're out of the office. If colleagues can understand that service is a value in the library, this break won't be perceived as a vacation but part of the very important work that libraries do. Also, if everyone in the entire library becomes involved in one professional opportunity or another (whether it's attending or participating in the Music or Medical Library Associations, the Society of American Archivists, LOEX, Educause, or a division or section within ALA), the result will be more support for the new librarian trying to establish his or her own niche. For example, a midcareer librarian may want to take his library's new hire along with him as he attends an important meeting or even a social hour during a conference. Active librarians may have a chance to forward "calls for participation" or "calls for volunteers" to everyone in the library. Even having a roundtable discussion in the library before or after a big conference may help give ideas to new librarians about events that would be fun to attend or aspects they'd like to be involved with next time. Last, but just as significant, librarians who have been active in service may want to reach out to their newer colleagues in terms of attending conferences, whether it's for a roommate, a committee appointment, or just to introduce a friend from another part of the country.

The crux of the issue: developing professional strength and confidence through interest and passion for library issues

As I try to bring together my thoughts on why professional service is crucial to staff development, I return to personal stories of my own committee work and the relationships and experiences developed there. It may be humorous to a library dean or director to think of my friends and me in library school as we talked with a sort of hero worship about some of the big names in library land. John Berry, editor of *Library Journal*; Rory Litwin, who edited a progressive library newsletter called *Library Juice*; Kathleen de la Peña McCook and her amazing writing; Jim Neal, dean and CIO at Columbia who has spent his career advocating for a more rational approach to scholarship and publication; Elizabeth Martinez and Pat Tarin and Carla Stoffle, whose efforts in diversity in librarianship have made national impact; Elaine Harger, who as ALA Councilor and in other capacities is one of the most passionate and compassionate speakers I have ever heard. My list goes on to include dozens of others. In library school, these were just names to us, but we knew them; we read their articles and books, listened to their presentations at conferences, and talked about their ideas because we were passionate about librarianship. One may think that 20- and 30-year-old library school students don't know who is in charge of the big library systems in the country, but my friends and I did, and we could rattle off their names and some of their accomplishments as well.

So to me, it was a great surprise that I could not only meet these people, but share a meal and talk about the history and the future of librarianship with them, and come to understand that not only was I interested in them, but that they were often interested in me. They valued young librarians because we brought new ideas to the table and opened the doors of librarianship to new voices. At this point, I have done just that with all of the people I just listed. I've worked on committees with several of them, shared a meal with most of them, and started new projects along the way. I've had a friend take me to dinner with ten library deans during an ALA conference and have heard the talk range from copyright issues and organizational change to family and personal life. I've sat in a committee meeting with directors and department heads and listened to their ideas and gotten to know them as people as well.

Perhaps most important, I have sat in those committees and found my voice. I will admit to being incredibly intimidated during the first committee meeting in which I sat as an equal partner alongside a group of library leaders. Who am I to be suggesting we take a different course? What could I add to this discussion that these brilliant big-wigs don't already know? Yet, somehow, gradually everyone gets over those fears and plunges forward into being an active participant, even if they're debating ideas with the dean of a large ARL library. This confidence—the confidence that can be gained from professional service—is a critical factor in leadership. It is not something that was peculiar to me when I started in the profession, but something that I believe any person can develop from showing up at the table and working on issues with others. It is a skill that is developed, not necessarily a talent that is innate. Through tackling projects with a wide range of people and accomplishing important things, anyone can develop a level of confidence needed to be a leader.

Because I am intensely interested in the issues in our profession, I have a role to play in influencing its future. And I have found that I have a chair waiting for me in those rooms in which the work of our profession is carried on. I believe that is true for anyone willing to step into the work of shaping our profession.

Further reading

Acree, Eric Kofi, Sharon K. Epps, Yolanda Gilmore, and Charmaine Henriques. 2001. "Using Professional Development as a Retention Tool for Underrepresented Academic Librarians." *Journal of Library Administration* 33, no. 1/2 (January): 45–61.

ACRL Professional Development Committee. *ACRL Statement on Professional Development.* Position Statement approved by the ACRL Board of Directors on July 8, 2000. ACRL. Available: www.ala.org/ala/acrl/acrlpubs/whitepapers/acrlstatement.cfm (accessed July 13, 2008).

Davidson, Jeanne R., and Cheryl A. Middleton. 2007. "Networking, Networking, Networking: The Role of Professional Association Memberships in Mentoring and Retention of Science Librarians." *Science and Technology Libraries* 27, no. 1/2 (May 7): 203–224.

Fisher, William. 1997. "The Role of Professional Associations." *Library Trends* 46 (Fall): 320–330.

Flatley, Robert K., and Michael A. Weber. 2004. "Perspectives on . . . Professional Development Opportunities for New Academic Librarians." *The Journal of Academic Librarianship* 30, no. 6 (November): 488–492.

Frank, Donald G. 1997. "Activity in Professional Associations: The Positive Difference in a Librarian's Career." *Library Trends* 46 (Fall): 307–318.

James, Brenda R. "New Wine in Old Bottles: Making Library Associations More Relevant in the 21st Century, with Special Reference to the Library Association of Trinidad and Tobago (LATT)." *66th IFLA Council and General Conference: Conference Proceedings.* 66th IFLA Council and General Conference, Jerusalem, Israel, August 13–18, 2000.

Kam, Sue. 1997. "To Join or Not to Join: How Librarians Make Membership Decisions About Their Associations." *Library Trends* 46 (Fall): 295–306.

Kenney, Donald J., and Gail McMillan. 1992. "State Library Associations: How Well Do They Support Professional Development?" *Reference and User Services Quarterly (RQ)* 31, no. 3 (Spring): 377–386.

Makara, 'M'abafokeng. "Library Associations as Prime Movers of Professional Development in Seven Selected Countries of Southern Africa." Paper presented at the World Library and Information Conference: 72nd IFLA General Conference and Council, Seoul, Korea, August 20–24, 2006.

CHAPTER 15

non-library conferences for development

Joseph Nicholson

Professional library associations provide many excellent opportunities for career development, including networking, programs, and committee work. However, focusing one's efforts solely on library associations limits the possibilities for staff development, especially if your library position involves subject mastery outside library science. Associations outside of libraries, but focused on subjects of interest to staff and the institution, offer significant opportunities to build subject expertise, career opportunities, and leadership skills.

My first job after graduating from library school was working for Touro University–California, a young and growing medical school with several programs. Having never studied medical or health information in my graduate program, this job required that I hit the ground running and learn very quickly about a new and very demanding subject matter. Through my daily work cataloging materials, answering reference questions, and conducting literature searches, I began to grow significantly in my knowledge of the subject. The support and direction of my supervisors also helped build my area expertise. Ultimately, however, it still felt like I was missing something. I was not on equal footing with my users. I couldn't help feeling that I was missing a piece of the puzzle and that I needed to know more in order to perform my job duties at an appropriate level.

Like many people, I find that learning and growth come best through experience. In order to increase my knowledge of the subject, I needed to find experiential opportunities that would put me in contact with the subject matter I was working with and the professionals I was serving. I began by taking the advice of my supervisor and joined the relevant professional organization, the Medical Library Association (MLA). As I became more active in MLA and at my job, I began to notice that I needed additional subject background information that I just was not getting through MLA; I needed to look elsewhere.

Subject specialty

Librarians experienced in managing knowledge and teaching informatics can supply quality information by becoming ongoing members of the health care team. Immersion in the health care environment is necessary for librarians to understand how health care professionals solve problems individually and through consensus. (Institute of Medicine, 2001)

Although this quote is specific to health care, the main concept can be expanded to any field. To truly understand what is needed and provide the best service, immersion with the people you serve is absolutely necessary. Keeping this in mind, it is key that librarians find ways to get out of the library and into the environment of their clientele.

Before getting out of the library, you first need to identify your subject of interest. For me, this was easy: I worked in a medical library that did not yet have a liaison to the public health program. This was an excellent opportunity to jump in headfirst. Initially I expressed interest in serving in the role as liaison and my supervisor was very encouraging. She thought it was great that I wanted to be more involved, and wanted the library to be more involved in a fledgling program at the school. My role within the library would expand to include working more closely with the students on their various projects that required them to use library resources, including supporting research for the school's field work in East Africa.

Throughout this process my supervisor was very encouraging, always willing to help with any difficult questions and happy to add her years of expertise. Encouraging me to take on the additional responsibility of this work, she informed me of the section within the Medical Library Association dedicated to public health. Jumping actively into my new role, I joined the Public Health/Health Administration Section (PH/HA) of MLA to learn from more experienced colleagues out in the field.

> ☑ QUICK TIP
>
> In addition to looking to outside organizations, encourage new professionals to look within library associations for divisions or roundtables that may already be focused on a specific subject or specialization.

Always attentive to several listservs, I noticed an opportunity through the PH/HA list to apply for a stipend to attend the American Public Health Association (APHA) conference with a group of other librarians. The aim of the stipend was to connect librarians to public health professionals and increase librarian identification with the clients they serve. This funding was not only a great opportunity to enhance my library career, but also learn through immersion about the people I served. While I knew of APHA, I did not realize until I saw this announcement that many librarians do participate in organizations that are outside of library science but in their subject specialty.

I knew this was exactly the kind of opportunity I needed to learn more about my subject and to boost my career. However, I had never applied for anything like this before and was quite nervous. I realized, though, that I had to take the chance.

Institutional support

Attending a conference not clearly related to libraries is not something you can do without the support of your institution and your supervisor. Seizing this opportunity, I approached my supervisor and asked for her support. She enthusiastically agreed, encouraging my development in this new realm. Having my supervisor's support enabled me to write a succinct and clear application for the stipend, showing how my attendance at this conference would directly benefit my library, the institution my library served, and me.

Another strong support within the school was the faculty and students in the public health program. They could see the direct and immediate benefit to having one of their librarians learn more about how they worked and what exactly they did. Previously, the library had worked closely with the public health program, supporting its students' information needs when they were preparing to go to Tanzania to do public health work. Since the program leaders already knew how helpful the library could be, they were thrilled that one of the librarians was expressing a keen interest in learning even more about their subject area. Keeping the relevant key players involved was important throughout the process. They were able to provide support in writing the stipend application as well as being able to guide me around their conference.

It is important to have your supervisor and your institution behind you not only so you can get time away from the office, but also so they can help you in gathering relevant information about the conference to determine if it is the right fit for you. In my case, APHA was a perfect fit. It included a dedicated group of librarians, and funding was available for inexperienced library professionals to attend and learn more. This helped everyone involved. It raised the profile of the library in the eyes of the school, showing how involved in the subjects the librarians are. It raised my profile in the eyes of my supervisor, showing how engaged and enthusiastic I was to take on new responsibilities and specializations.

> ☑ QUICK TIP
> Promote your activities within the library and to appropriate interested parties outside the library, such as department heads, student organizations, or administrators. Make specific targets of others from the larger institution who may be attending the same meeting.

Conference attendance

Attending a conference outside libraries can be intimidating. Unlike our library association meetings, where most attendees understand the professional language and structures, attending a conference outside libraries requires adjusting to new issues, terms, jargon, and even social groupings. As with any conference, taking the time to prepare ahead of the event can help to maximize the benefit for both the institution and the new employee.

Navigating a new conference

Having successfully written my application and been awarded one of the stipends, I prepared to attend my first APHA Annual Meeting. Attending the conference on this stipend had several benefits. One of the requirements of the stipend was that you shadow someone who had attended the meeting in the past, attending a scientific session with them and learning on a personal basis how they handle the meeting and how attendance benefits them.

Shadowing, of course, is something that you can do on your own. A great way to find a mentor is to look for someone from your organization who is attending and has attended in the past. Often they will be excited to find someone who is interested in learning more about them and how to help them. Not only will this shadowing relationship help you get a handle on how to navigate a new conference, but it will greatly enhance your relationship with your users.

> ☑ QUICK TIP
> Finding shadowing opportunities with either other librarians attending the conference or with non-librarians from the institution can help to make sense of the new environment.

A second requirement of the stipend was to attend a meeting with all the other stipend recipients and other librarians who also attend the conference. Having a meeting with other librarians in the field who are in attendance may not be easy to arrange, but it is incredibly beneficial. These more experienced librarians who have previously attended and participated in the meetings can really help you navigate. In addition, the networking benefits of meeting with a group of professionals with similar interests are numerous. Ultimately, making connections with likeminded individuals in the group can create a comfort zone in what could otherwise be a foreign environment.

Deciding what sessions to go to is one of the most daunting tasks of going to a new conference, especially one as large as the APHA Annual Meeting. Part of the aim of having a person to shadow is to have someone help you narrow down what sessions may be of interest to you. Also, part of being able to meet with the other librarians in attendance is to see get suggestions regarding what sessions to attend. However, the needs and interests of your user group and your library might not be the same as those of the librarians and professionals with whom you speak. To figure out what sessions might be of interest to your library, review the conference program with your supervisor. In my circumstance, my supervisor and I had picked out several sessions that would be of key interest to our library, and I blocked off those times on my calendar. Because of the variety of sessions to choose from, it is important to keep in mind the needs of your library and users.

> ☑ QUICK TIP
> Take time with the conference program and encourage staff members to consider their own interests, the needs of the institution, and the needs of the library. Plotting out a list of sessions of interest can make sure the new librarian is not overwhelmed and can come back with information to share with all audiences.

Participating in the conference

Once you have figured out your way around the conference, your focus should be on finding ways to participate and interact with the other attendees. You can participate in a conference that is new to you in many ways. This advice applies to attending any conference.

First, you should attend the business meetings and socials of the sections or groups that are of interest to you. If you are outgoing and introduce yourself to people, saying that you are a new member and a librarian, you will surely get some interest. Public health professionals, for example, are always excited to have information professionals interested in helping them. At every meeting I attended, participants seemed to know that a librarian was in the room and could potentially help them with their information needs.

> ☑ **QUICK TIP**
> Get new staff to put their faces in front of the crowd at either receptions or in the exhibit hall at booths for the institution or an interesting section or roundtable.

Second, you should volunteer to work at a booth in the exhibit hall, so you can connect with others at your workplace (if your institution has a booth) or meet other conference members (e.g., of sections you're interested in) and learn more about what they do. Spending an hour or two working a booth will enable you to meet a large cross-section of the conference population. Personally, I found it valuable to spend time in different booths. At my institution's booth, I made connections with and promoted library services to the students, faculty, and other professionals whom I served. At the section booth that I joined, I was able to meet a variety of professionals from around the country and the world who offered me great insights on what they do and how they do it.

Benefits of participation

Attendance at a non-library conference offers many potential benefits to your library. Not only do you benefit directly—the library staff, the library patrons, and the library's reputation also will profit from your participation.

How the new employee benefits

The direct benefits to the new employee are probably the easiest ones to notice. Knowledge, prestige, and experience are three things a new employee can gain from participating in a non-library conference. They are certainly interconnected and all serve well in career development both immediately and in the long run.

Networking with colleagues in and out of the library world increases exposure to new thoughts, ideas, and resources. This exposure increases knowledge of the topic, which is beneficial in the short term for making collection-development decisions, giving presentations, or even answering reference questions. This new knowledge will continue to serve the individual down the road, especially if he or she continues to participate and keep abreast of new developments in the field.

Knowledge and experience gained from conference attendance go hand-in-hand. Typically one can gain knowledge through participation and observation of the conference. By picking up and reading materials, talking to people, attending sessions, presenting at sessions, and even just watching the crowd, new staff can become more in tune with the needs of this select group of users. This all translates to experience. The more sessions you attend, the more people with whom you network, the more papers you present, the more experience you will have under your belt. Experience pays off more in the long term than in the immediate benefits of new knowledge. As one continues to participate and attend the conference each year, he or she will learn more about who to talk to, which sessions will be most beneficial, and how to best apply what has been learned to the specific roles of the library. Naturally, having a lot of good experience is also a great résumé builder.

The continuous buildup of experience eventually leads to prestige. *Prestige* may seem too strong of a word for having merely participated in a conference, but I believe it is an appropriate word, especially after continuing to participate actively. Prestige, in this sense, is the kind of obvious importance associated with successful people. Stepping up to the plate year after year, being able to contribute to the conference and the field on national and international levels, and being able to bring back lessons and apply them to the library and job are the kinds of experiences that lead to prestige. Following continued participation, people begin to recognize names and faces and seek out these familiar faces for special projects. The individual can become an in-demand librarian among the audience with whom he or she mingled at conference. It can, and does, take much experience to build up this prestige, but it is certainly worthwhile for long-term career development.

How your library benefits

Following the conference the benefits are immediate and continuous. Everyone involved in your library gains from participation as the attendees disseminate their knowledge, experience, and prestige gained from the conference. The clear recipients of these benefits are the library patrons. Active participation in their subject or field allows for better service to them. One main benefit of the knowledge and experience gained is that the library will be more adept at answering complicated reference questions. Having the knowledge about new and upcoming hot topics makes it easier to answer those burning-issue types of reference questions, and can also help in discerning patron needs in the reference interview. Not only does all this knowledge help in answering questions, but it will also allow the library to build a better collection through knowing more and different resources. Having a better, stronger, and more focused collection is another great service you can provide to your patrons. Knowing what to buy and when to buy it is key to building a great collection; this kind of information comes largely through experience.

The patrons are not the only people in your library who can benefit from your conference participation. It will take some more work on your part, but spreading your information to the library staff is an excellent way to develop staff knowledge and increase their awareness of hot topics that may be of importance to patrons.

Staff development

Distributing the information and knowledge gained from the attendee's experience is an important step for your library. First, it raises co-workers' awareness of efforts, planting the seed in their minds that the new employee is developing expertise in that subject area. Second, it increases staff awareness of current issues in the field, helping them respond to patron needs more efficiently and thoroughly. This increase in awareness and improved quality of responses to patrons is a boon to any library. When patrons are more than satisfied with their answers, they will come to rely on the knowledge and expertise in your library. It is even more convincing if they are aware that their librarian participates in their association's conference. Being able to show that the library actively participates in the field, and does not just stay within its box and resources, exemplifies the knowledge, connection, and concern your library has for its users and their subjects.

> ☑ QUICK TIP
> Encourage conference attendees to distill their experience into a presentation for all staff. They can create handouts that quickly summarize findings and relevant information for the library.

Asking attendees to present to the library staff can also help new librarians develop valuable presentation skills. Informing the library staff should be a high priority and can take many forms. I have found it effective to give a presentation to the staff as well as distribute some informational brochures and handouts.

In my case, I put together a PowerPoint presentation that covered the sessions I attended, what happened during the time I spent working the booths, and interesting and new connections I made with current and future patrons. This helped the staff in a few different ways.

Knowing about what sessions I attended and what was covered gave them all some insight into the cutting-edge topics in public health at the time. It is critical in public health, as in any field, to be on top of the latest information and to know who is researching it and where. In my case at an academic library, it was very helpful for staff to know what topics students might come in to ask about and some new resources to which they can point them.

Learning about what happened at the booths and your new connections may not be as crucial to answering reference questions, but it does help the staff relate to the experience and understand what was happening at the conference in general. Conferences and meetings may not always include scientific sessions about every topic of interest; many may be low on the radar, so having casual conversations and taking business cards can be helpful. At the very least, if a problem or question related to one of these conversational topics surfaces, the other staff in the library would know that they could ask you for more information.

Following the presentation of this new information, it is very helpful to have something to show co-workers. In my example, I created a handout with the hot topics I discussed along with Web addresses for further information about the session I attended, the speakers, and materials currently in the library that could be of use.

Staying current

Going to one conference outside of librarianship, but in a field of specialty, is beneficial in many ways. Making attendance a tradition and going to the same conference regularly multiplies the benefits many times over. Each time you attend a conference you will become savvier at navigating, you will learn more, you will make more connections, and you will have more to bring home. Conferences happen on a regular basis for a reason, and it isn't just about the networking. Building on your first conference experience by continuing to attend and participate is necessary to reap the continued benefits.

In my case, I managed to get funding again for the second year I attended the APHA Annual Meeting. The second year of attending was definitely much easier and more beneficial than the first. I knew where I was going and which sessions I wanted to attend, and I was familiar with some of the people involved in those sections. Returning from the second conference, I was able to bring back more focused and in-depth information, partly because I had entered it already knowing more about what kind of information I was seeking and where to find it.

Continuing to build on the strength of the first two years of attendance made a very strong case for going a third year. My supervisor was able to see the benefits to me professionally, as well as to our library and our patrons. Having proven the value of my conference attendance in the first two years, I was able to justify time off and receive some funding for my third year of attendance.

Continuing to participate for multiple years in a row has its own unique value. This is true of conferences both in and out of librarianship. Once you begin to know people at the conferences, participate on committees, and present papers, you gain a new level of understanding about the field through continuous and active engagement. Even though the conference may not be specifically about librarianship, it is still contributing to professional development.

Attending the conference multiple years in a row translated directly into increasing professional development for me. In my first year at the conference, I mostly just observed, but I also took some time to staff booths and attend business meetings. Following my successful first conference, at my second one I knew more people and managed to be more involved by reading abstracts, staffing booths, and attending meetings. In my third year, I co-chaired a committee, read abstracts, and helped out at meetings and sessions. For my fourth year, I am working with a group to put together a continuing education proposal, chairing a committee, reading the abstracts, and writing articles. All of these activities translate directly into professional development in the library world. Many committees and groups are often in need of interested people to take over functions. However, the only way to find out about these opportunities is to network with other conference attendees and get your name out there. Keep in mind, in some ways, having experience and interests outside of libraries can make you more well-rounded as a professional.

Final thoughts

Being able to show that I am active and involved has definitely helped my career. By documenting my interest and passion for the subject through conference attendance and participation, I have been able to show prospective employers what I can do and what interests me. Pursuing professional activities outside of your workplace and other libraries demonstrates an extra level of involvement and dedication. The benefits are on not only a professional level but also a personal level—through the experiences had and friends made.

Further reading

Casto, Michael. 1995. "Inter-Professional Work in the USA: Education and Practice." In *Going Inter-Professional: Working Together for Health and Welfare*, edited by Audrey Leathard, 188–205. London: Routledge.

Davidson, Jeanne R., and Cheryl A. Middleton. 2007. "Networking, Networking, Networking: The Role of Professional Association Memberships in Mentoring and Retention of Science Librarians." *Science and Technology Libraries* 27, no. 1/2 (May 7): 203–224.

Fisher, William. 1997. "The Role of Professional Associations." *Library Trends* 46 (Fall): 320–330.

Frank, Donald G. 1997. "Activity in Professional Associations: The Positive Difference in a Librarian's Career." *Library Trends* 46 (Fall): 307–318.

Ritchie, Ann, and Paul Genoni. 1999. "Mentoring in Professional Associations: Continuing Professional Development for Librarians." *Health Libraries Review* 16, no. 4 (December): 216–225.

Virgo, Julie A. 1991. "The Role of Professional Associations." In *Library and Information Science Research: Perspectives and Strategies for Improvement*, edited by Charles R. McClure and Peter Hemon, 189–196. Norwood, NJ: Ablex Publishing.

White, Gary W. 2001. "The Professional Development of Reference Librarians: Implications of Research, Publication, and Service." *The Reference Librarian*, no. 73: 337–350.

Reference

Institute of Medicine. "Crossing the Quality Chasm: A New Health System for the 21st Century." Washington, DC: National Academy Press, 2001. Available: www.nap.edu/books/0309072808/html/.

CHAPTER 16

supporting active conference participation by new staff

Monecia Samuel

In a profession with various avenues for growth, a librarian or information professional has many choices. Most choose opportunities that mirror the path taken by their mentors or academic advisers from graduate programs. Many hold to a prescribed set of steps that must be climbed in order to reach professionalism or true achievement in the library profession. Many others believe that their biggest first step might be joining a committee or designing a poster session. For reasons unknown to me, presenting at a national conference is rarely considered by a new librarian—and this is truly unfortunate. Although the act of presenting at a conference poses many challenges, it also requires many skills and abilities that provide ample opportunity for professional development. Conference preparation, begun early in a career and repeated regularly, will foster skills that will lead to promotion and growth throughout one's career.

In this chapter, I share how I, as a new librarian, discovered conference presentations as a truly liberating experience, and how I believe supervisors can support conference activity to meet not only their organizations' strategic goals but also the ambitions and professional or personal goals of their employees. In addition, I discuss how and why a manager would want to make his or her institution or workplace active or visible, how to find speaking opportunities, how to afford to send employees to local or national conferences, and how to make the opportunity memorable through internal workplace event promotion and after conference workplace wrap-up events.

Why promote conference activity to your staff?

Some institutions or corporations do not promote or encourage conference activity. They may think it a practice reserved only for the most experienced in the profession or that it is not an effective use of the institution's staff or resources. However, getting published and making professional public presentations are two major ways librarians or information professionals can begin to promote, develop, and network themselves to advance their careers. Through each step of the process, from writing the proposal to presenting onstage, there are benefits in store for the presenter and his or her employer. The manager has numerous opportunities to develop a relationship with employees. Supporting conference activity requires helping staff discover skills transferable to a national stage. It can also include planned mentoring and coaching to demonstrate sincere interest in staff.

Marketing conference presenting as a staff development option to your employees

If staff development opportunities are promoted and supported by management, they can be perceived as an institutional benefit and tool for recruitment and retention. Employees may increase their loyalty to an institution that seeks to put them front and center at a conference or that wants them to grow within the profession, not just serve. Conference participation—whether as a presenter or simply as an attendee—is often considered by many employees as a perk or benefit of their job. Conferences stimulate minds and keep employees from feeling isolated or becoming burned out in their roles. When they feel relevant and recognized among their peers in the profession, they are motivated to new levels of productivity and progressiveness. Many librarians return from conferences feeling invigorated with new energy and ideas that will advance their library departments.

Supervisors should take the lead in marketing conference opportunities to their units. New librarians are not always in the know about such opportunities, as their networks consist of mostly new librarians like themselves. If your staff does not have a diversity of well-connected members who publish or network regularly, your library may be circulating a limited flow of information. As a supervisor, you do not have to be an experienced conference presenter to be a champion of this activity. Simply keep your ear to the ground and market opportunities as they come across your desk.

> ☑ QUICK TIP
>
> Market presentation opportunities as they come across your desk using communication channels such as e-mail, bulletin boards, or even mentioning upcoming conference presentations during monthly or weekly staff meetings.

Another way a library may have a limited flow of information is if only one or two well-connected individuals receive information and keep it to themselves. Staff members who do this may be competitive, but more than likely simply don't think that others in their organization would be interested. As a supervisor, you can create a collaborative environment that encourages the sharing of announcements. You may find this an excellent way of overcoming fear by building partnerships and sharing the work of conference presentation. Encourage information sharing and you may eliminate competitiveness in your workplace.

Your audience or market should be considered immediately before choosing an avenue or medium to announce the event. If you think conferences are only for experienced individuals, you may be sending messages only to managers. Filter down to all staff members and utilize conference presentations as a staff development tool instead of just an expertise-sharing tool. The idea is to develop your staff, and with that in mind, think of ways of addressing or catering your message to *all* of the staff members. A salutation that uses the word "everyone" is a start. You can also use a postscript to emphasize that the opportunity should be considered by staff of all levels or rank. Boldface select words in the call for submission that you feel might be appropriate for staff members in your library. Target calls directly to teams with appropriate projects or skills. In other words, no one should wonder, after reading a posted announcement or mass e-mail, whether or not they should attend the conference or meeting.

A calendar of proposal deadlines is another way to communicate your sincere wish for your staff to become more involved in the profession. Too often, we only list the conference dates. Adding deadlines for conference proposals may encourage your staff to think more broadly about their conference attendance. Turn them from attendees into presenters by populating your calendar with dates and deadlines of interest to presenters. Add deadline dates with a reminder five days in advance of the actual due date. This will help your presenters stay on target and let them know that you are encouraging their participation.

Create a sense of possibility by highlighting the achievements of yourself or colleagues. Look in your storage areas at work or home and find programs on which you or other colleagues were listed as a speaker at local or major conferences in years past. You can make these available along with photos showing that it is possible to be a presenter. Your staff may appreciate these photos and programs, especially if they're displayed on a bulletin board with large letters stating, "This Could Be You!"

With each of these strategies, you can help market conference participation and eliminate staff secrecy and competitiveness, and employee perceptions that they are not allowed to take professional initiative and that conferences are only for managers.

Helping staff discover the benefits of conference activity

A supervisor with experience presenting at conferences would obviously be the best one to sell the idea of conference involvement. Experienced presenters will know the details and processes for preparation, organization, submission, and presentation of programs. However, even supervisors who have never presented at conferences can serve as cheerleaders for new staff; even better, they can get involved in the process and learn with the new employee.

Seasoned managers—whether seasoned program presenters or not—can always help new employees discover their strengths and talents. With a mind toward conference presentations, they can also help explain how their skills may be directed toward conference involvement. Finding individuals who are interested can be difficult, depending on staff members' personalities and confidence levels. A manager should begin by stressing that everyone has something to contribute, regardless of job titles, years of experience, or perceived popularity within the institution.

Convince your colleagues that the task of planning, preparing, and delivering a presentation will be quite easy provided it is well-planned and participants are well-chosen. Imparting the importance of discipline will be necessary, as well as encouraging your staff to establish a timeline for accomplishing project goals and cushion deadlines.

> ☑ QUICK TIP
> Seek outwardly social librarians among your staff. These librarians and staff may be best-suited for conference presentation.

The best staff to push in this direction might be those predisposed to social situations. Have any of your staff:

- Performed in a play?
- Performed in a recital as an instrumentalist or vocalist?
- Been a member of Toastmasters?
- Ran for any type of student government or other government office?
- Delivered a speech for the PTA?
- Spoken at any graduation?
- Written a book or grant proposal?
- Planned a wedding?

The key is to identify skills and traits that would transfer well to public presentations and speaking.

The freedom inherent in designing one's own conference session is very satisfying, but can also be a challenge. In addition to being comfortable in social situations, presenters should have a certain degree of self-motivation and independence. Preparing and submitting a presentation can often be a very liberating experience, as the planning and presentation are controlled by the individual. Supervisors must stress discipline and time management.

In addition, the blind review process by which many conference proposals are evaluated can liberate new employees from the preconceptions and judgments often placed on young or inexperienced professionals. In the blind review process it really can be the words on the page that do the talking. The blind review of the proposal can guarantee an equal playing field, especially for new employees who may believe a clique of high-level professionals dominate the conference speakers' circuit.

Making an HR diversity statement real for your employees of color

Employers that promote cultural diversity at their corporation or institution can put their equality statements into action by encouraging minority employees to become active participants in major conferences the organization supports. By encouraging employees of color to present at conferences, managers can re-enforce their institution's commitment to diversity.

Very often, minority employees can assume that their employers hired them for the numbers, and unfortunately other employees can silently agree. This puts new minority employees in an awkward situation from the very beginning, regardless of their résumé or talents.

Encouraging diversified conference participation—ethnically, racially, and intellectually—can demonstrate the institution's pride in every employee. A diversity of backgrounds with unique and often untold perspectives can add real value to the standard conference program. Leading the charge by encouraging diverse participation from your institution can help build a positive reputation. Ultimately, actions speak louder than words, and this type of encouragement solidifies your organizational diversity statement.

How to get your units or departments out of their shells

If your employees are hesitant to write and submit conference proposals, you may want to find out why. If they simply don't know how to write a proposal, then your work will not be so difficult. However, if they have confidence issues, you may have to work with them in creative ways. Convince your staff that they have been ready to present for a while, especially if they have mastered their particular areas or specializations. Mastering an area or skill involves practice, assessment, reassessment, thought, and even more practice. Over the years, one gets feedback and advice from colleagues, the public, students, faculty, family, and peers. Undeniably, your staff has acquired knowledge worth sharing over the years as they've practiced new models, converted library systems and online catalogs, and embraced online technologies. If they had something to think about during all those transitions, they have something to share.

> ☑ QUICK TIP
> Encourage librarians to speak about what they know. Conference presentations often share the experiences all of us have had. Every staff member has an opportunity to share some learning experience without having to be a confirmed expert on a particular topic.

Most people find it exciting to talk about themselves and what they do. Your staff may be delighted to finally express the best practices from *their point of view*, in a non-controversial way or setting. It will be easy for even the shyest person to talk about themselves in the context of their work environment. They could talk about why they changed a system or why they follow strict procedural methods in their department. Needless to say, the message will be passionate and their audiences will think well of the institution with which they are affiliated.

> ☑ QUICK TIP
> Find opportunities for collaboration among staff or between supervisors and new librarians. Collaborations can help share the workload and also help ease fear of presentation.

A group of shy employees may want to design a poster session together. Another group may want to organize a panel of colleagues from a local consortium, while two staff members who typically work together might enjoy organizing a conference roundtable for which they are the co-facilitators. As their manager, remember to start these conversations and remind them of their respective accomplishments outlined in previous performance reviews or end-of-year reports.

Does your organization support conference participation?

If conference participation is important to your organization, at particular times of the year, it likely is understood that work attendance will be low. Some organizations only support conference attendance in the most passive ways. Library conferences are considered by many to be important events at which needed information is disseminated to improve library services. Other institutions perceive conference opportunities as a way to share their institutions' strengths and promote themselves within the profession. If your organization does not support conference attendance, you might want to find out why. You may want to make conference participation a strategic goal to improve your institution's visibility and value.

It is not difficult to support an employee's wish to participate in a conference. If you are a supervisor or director, meet your staff's interest with enthusiasm. Think of their project as a marketing opportunity for your institution. It should always be viewed as a way to advance or introduce your library or organization to the larger community or other organizations like your own, locally and internationally. What is important is the attachment of your institutional name to the proposal. Its date will represent the time you as director, supervisor, or manager led the group, department, or organization. When attendees remember the presentation, they'll remember first what university the individual represented. That is what should count for a manager or director. Good managers recruit good people.

If you find you have really ambitious individuals on your staff, promote them and their project to other important players in the institution. Their excitement should never be questioned. You *want* your employees to be on fire. Just remember to openly give them credit for their work. Never present the idea or the project as your own and never hide their accomplishments. Recognition at work is important to everyone. You want to be cognizant of your retention efforts, and supporting employees in a positive way will keep them loyal and on board, and not shopping around for a job at another library that may show a greater interest in their potential.

Partnering with a new employee on a project or presentation can be a great way to bond with or mentor the employee. However, remember to maintain appropriate measures of responsibility and ownership of the project. You and your protégé may have skills that complement each other. Show support by giving new staff the honor of being the lead presenter or by being *their* co-presenter, especially if the project or paper is their creation. Make sure to ask them if they want to collaborate with you. This is important, as they may already have their own peers in mind and may not want to offend their supervisor.

Entertaining the conference attendance idea as an affordable goal

If budget issues are a concern, you may want to identify local conferences as future attendance targets. Local can mean conferences held in your own city or state that do not pose much of a financial travel issue. For those who work in smaller states on the East Coast, states within a few hours' driving distance could be considered local. In some large cities such as New York City, one does not have to leave the city to find an affordable professional conference. Many librarians living in New York City only attend those meetings that are in town. If you're from a large state such as Texas or California, a drive or bus trip may not be far out of the question.

As for national conferences, the American Library Association, the Public Library Association, and the Institute of Museum and Library Studies offer many scholarship opportunities. An organization could also meet employees halfway by offering to pay for room and airfare or conference registration only. Every little bit will mean a great deal to someone who really wants the opportunity.

Identifying speaking engagements for new and experienced librarians

When I knew I was seriously interested in becoming an active conference presenter, I wondered how one broke into the business. Initially I believed that to qualify, one had to be an administrator. Before I began presenting, all sessions I attended at any conference were led by those who did not look like me. Regardless, I wondered how they knew about the opportunity in advance. With a background in music and performance, I knew a lot of planning, programming, and rehearsing went on behind the scenes before "show time."

I began to pay attention to every mailing that crossed my physical inbox at work and I read the listserv announcements regularly. I eventually found a "call for proposals" postcard in my work mailbox requesting presenters for the Virtual Reference Desk (VRD) Conference in Cincinnati in 2003. I successfully submitted my proposal and presented solo at the VRD conference. Although my session competed with much larger sessions, my crowd of approximately 30 attendees seemed to be satisfied with their selection. It was a rewarding and unforgettable experience for me.

When I look back on that experience, I am indeed happy I had the courage to submit my proposal. My supervisors did not hesitate to fund my travel and registration. They even offered to form a committee that would listen to my presentation in advance. I will never forget how they supported me in traveling to advance my professional development. As I was a library fellow following my VRD 2003 Conference experience, it opened the door for other fellows to submit proposals and travel to conferences as well. It later became a fellowship expectation that wasn't initially written into the fellowship program.

After the 2003 VRD Conference, I began searching Google on a regular basis for additional conference opportunities. This opened up a world of opportunities that included presenting at other conferences. I found it helpful to seek out conferences with themes relevant to my area of expertise. Next, I thought of keywords, key organizations, and key locations I would like to visit. If you plan with care, you will not only be able to identify an opportunity, but you'll also be able to travel to a city you've always wanted to visit.

> ☑ QUICK TIP
> In addition to monitoring the conference opportunities that come across your desk or e-mail, make a conscientious effort to seek out upcoming opportunities through search engines.

You may want to guide your employees through searching online for conference opportunities. Start with a search engine. A number of them are available. Google is the most popular; however, search engines such as Ask.com and Dogpile.com offer variety and unique search features, respectively. Ask.com will present the clean interface most Google users are accustomed to. Dogpile, a metasearch engine, searches many search engines at once: Google, Yahoo! Search, Live Search, Ask.com, About, MIVA and LookSmart.

The illustrations that follow will walk you through finding proposal or paper calls for conferences in 2009, using Google's Advanced Search on the Internet. Figure 16.1 shows an Advanced Search Google screen. As you can see, this screen offers options beyond those offered on a basic Google search screen. Begin by focusing on the shaded area and initially include the language, file format, date, and domain of your choice.

Domain selection is particularly important, as you want to identify the type of organization you wish to find. Most nonprofit organizations are ".org" while

Figure 16.1. Google advanced search screen

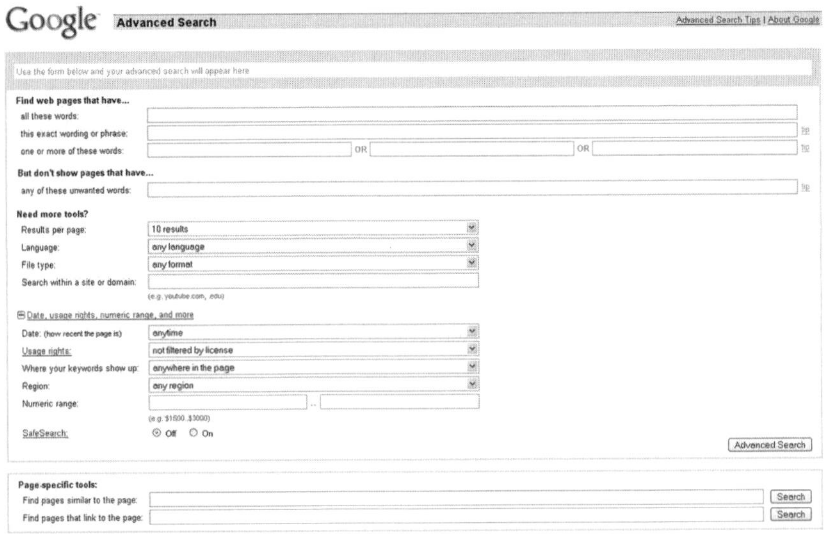

commercial or for-profit companies are designated as ".com." It may be worth it to try changing domains to increase precision throughout your search process. It may also be helpful to change file formats. This way, you can control the language, file type, date, and domain of all pages you receive. To further increase search output, you can include more or less information. Sometimes, adding an additional word or excluding a word is all that is needed for the best results.

In Figure 16.2, I inserted keywords that told the search engine what type of information I wanted to find.

By entering the search term "call for proposals," with the word "library" and for year 2009, I can limit my Google results to what I want and avoid having to filter through conference Web sites to find the actual calls for proposals. I also want the sites that would have first appeared in the past year, in any region, and ones that are in English and in any format. An example of my search results is shown in Figure 16.3.

The search statement in the example in Figure 16.3 found that 2,790 sites in English were posted over the past year. You will have to click through the links to see if the results meet your needs, as all results will not be relevant.

In Figure 16.4, I changed the search statement and the search itself, by using different terms and requesting different information for the same purpose. I simply changed the phrase word "proposals" to "papers." This resulted in different hits. Some of the best sites to seek out are those that list a number of opportunities on one Web

Figure 16.2. Google advanced search screen with terms for searching conferences

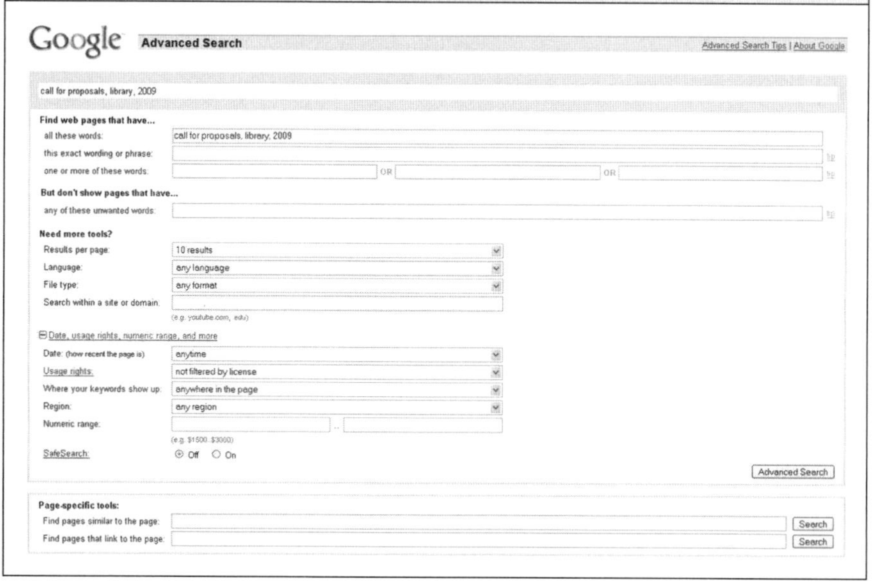

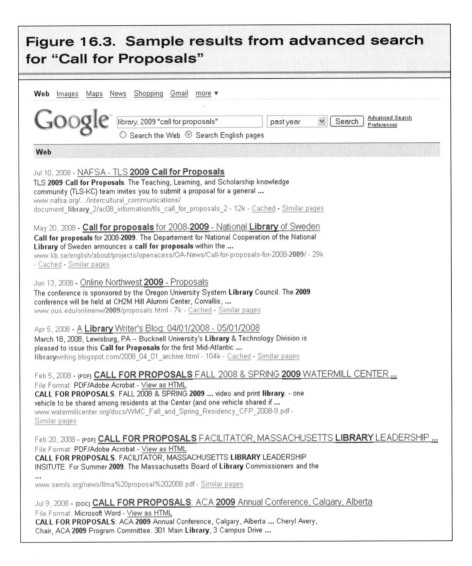

Figure 16.3. Sample results from advanced search for "Call for Proposals"

site or blog dedicated to generating information about paper announcements and conference calls. You can also get more or less specific while you're searching. Do not be afraid to try different search phrases or keywords as if searching an academic database.

One of my results found the announcement for the 2009 Information Online conference in Australia shown in Figure 16.5.

In the next search illustration (Figure 16.6), I change my request slightly to indicate opportunities in the United States only with the words library conference and "call for" as the exact phrase, with 2009 as one of the "words." This search strategy found the 2009 ACRL Conference Call for Proposals as its first hit. It also found an

Figure 16.4. Sample results from advanced search for "Call for Papers"

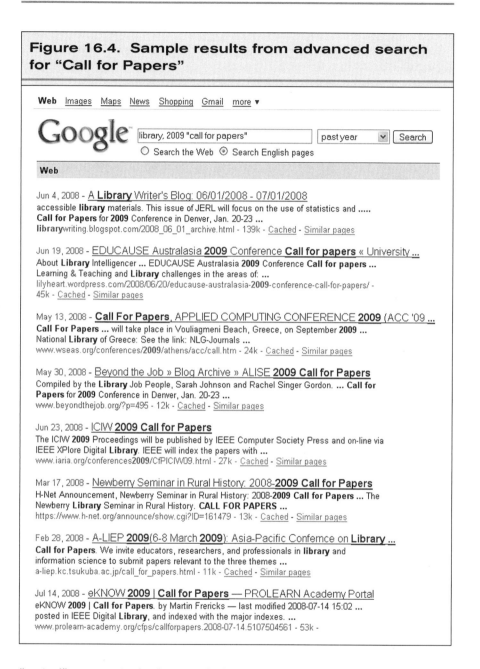

"expired" opportunity for the Special Library Association Conference. It may be best to be cognizant of the "Date" field. In the date field shown in these figures, I indicated I was looking for opportunities made available in the past year. Searchers will want to change their selection to customize the output to meet their needs.

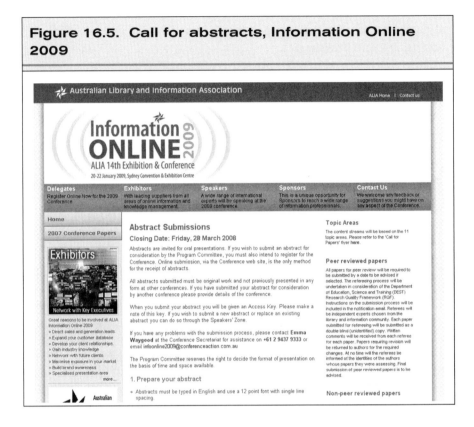

Figure 16.5. Call for abstracts, Information Online 2009

The screen shot in Figure 16.7 represents one of the most prestigious conferences for academic librarians. The previous screen shot of the advanced search was basically a simple search that could be made even more specific. In this example, a domain choice was not indicated. Making a domain choice such as ".edu," ".com," or ".org" tells the search engine from where or what type of site the information is desired. If you seek local opportunities, try searching educational domains; local libraries may have smaller conferences or summits that newer employees may find less intimidating and easier to afford. Commercial sites, ".coms," may lead to events held by large corporations, and ".org" sites will most likely indicate nonprofit endeavors.

File format is another limiter to consider. Many announcements are made available online as a portable document (pdf) or as a Word document. However, the more one limits the more one could possibly exclude, so limiters must be chosen with care. It is important to guide employees through a creative-opportunity search online. This could include recruiting the help of talented library instructors familiar with formulating search strategies.

Regardless, however one approaches the search for professional opportunities, it is best to remember that there is no one right way to find them. Any successful search-and-find endeavor is boosted by creativity. Different terms, phrases, or key words will

Figure 16.6. Google advanced search screen with terms for searching conferences limited to 2009

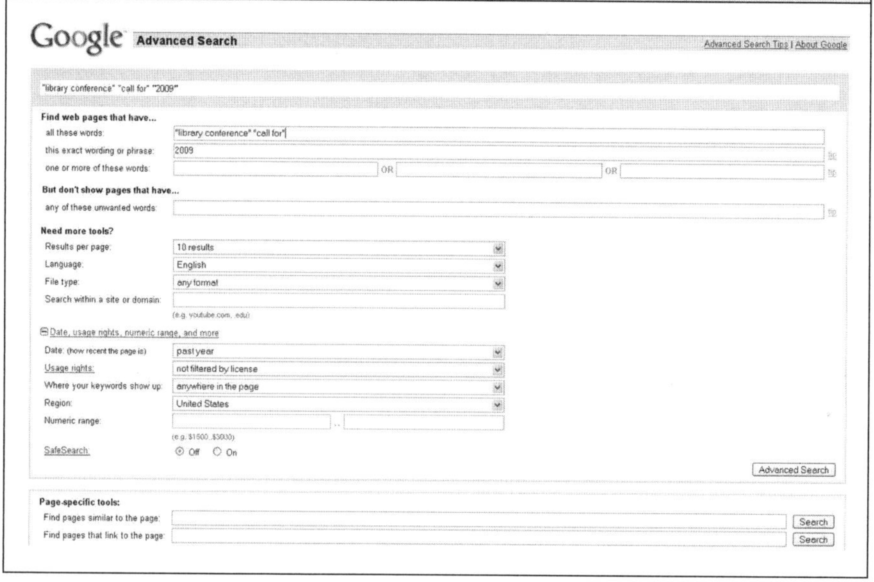

produce a number of varying results. However, this quick method is one that should be used on a regular basis. The best advice is to make sure you are looking for opportunities at least one to two years in the future. It would also be helpful to circulate information about conference opportunities, especially preconference, invitation, or special-ticket events that make available many networking opportunities younger employees normally may not have.

Conference exposure

You may want to decide in advance how you plan to recognize or reward staff for their participation at a conference. Recognition should happen before and after the conference. A supervisor could organize a mock presentation that could generate supportive feedback and improve the overall presentation. As a manager, you could encourage staff to take these opportunities seriously; presenters would be encouraged to dress for the occasion and have slide shows prepared. Technical setbacks as well as instructions on how to deal with these types of issues could be planned into the session.

Some staff who worked toward the good of those attending will likely not participate in the conference. A wrap-up session after the

> ☑ QUICK TIP
> Promote upcoming conference presentations by staff members in order to demonstrate support for those staff members as well as to encourage future presentations from other employees.

Figure 16.7. Call for proposals, ACRL 2009

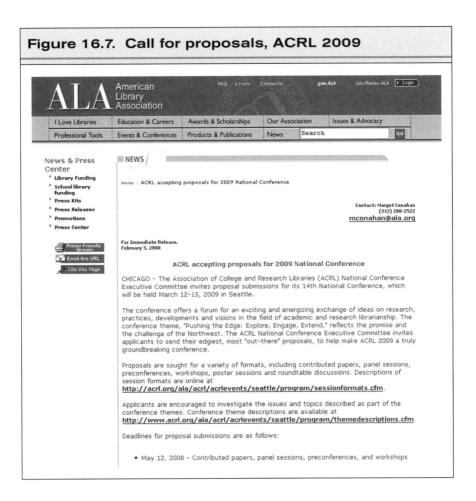

conference may be a nice way to recognize the efforts of these staff members. This session could include refreshments and a "take- away" table filled with conference gifts such as posters, books, and pens collected by the attendees at the conference. Library conference materials are exciting for student workers and librarians alike.

Conference closure

A special meeting between the management and staff presenters might add a nice lead-in to a conversation about what to do and not do the next time around. Attendees might want to avoid certain travel days, hotels, or areas the following year. One might be able to attract a better crowd the next time around with a particular session-marketing strategy. Possible tricks to avoid particular technical difficulties that may arise could be discussed. Collaborating presenters from various institutions might have something to gain from a discussion about timing communication sessions in advance of a group presentation.

Ask your group what they have learned and how they'll approach a conference differently if needed. Finally, send them a personal message about how the institution or library will benefit from their work and the related exposure. An expression of appreciation goes a long way.

Although librarians can find an array of various professional development opportunities throughout their careers, conference presenting may be one of the most rewarding, as it is linked to other benefits that include recognition, collaboration, and networking. An experienced supervisor can be instrumental as a staff mentor and motivator throughout the entire process from proposal to post-presentation. Managers can help staff identify their own skills, acknowledge the need for diverse perspectives through the inclusion of ethnically diverse staff members, and emphasize the importance of participating in the conference to promote the organization and a staff member's individual talents. Becoming involved in the conference arena on a local or national level creates a win-win situation for employees, management, and the institution.

Further reading

Asher, Joey. 2001. *Even a Geek Can Speak: Low-Tech Presentation Skills for High-Tech People.* Marietta, GA: Longstreet Press.

Desberg, Peter. 2007. *Speaking Scared, Sounding Good: Public Speaking for the Private Person.* Garden City Park, NY: Square One Publishers.

Huddle, P. A. 2000. "How to Present a Paper or Poster." *Journal of Chemical Education* 77, no. 9: 1152–1153.

Koegel, Timothy J. 2007. *The Exceptional Presenter: A Proven Formula to Open Up! and Own the Room.* Austin, TX: Greenleaf Book Group Press.

Reynolds, Garr. 2008. *Presentation Zen: Simple Ideas on Presentation Design and Delivery. Voices That Matter.* Berkeley, CA: New Riders Pub.

Wilder, Claudyne. 2008. *Point, Click and Wow! The Techniques and Habits of Successful Presenters.* San Francisco, CA: Pfeiffer.

community engagement and advocacy: skills and knowledge to expand library services

Annabelle Nuñez

I n an ever-changing information environment, libraries must continuously assess and redefine their mission and vision to manage the trends that make them vital institutions for their users. As traditional face-to-face library services decline and the virtual information environment grows, information professionals must find creative and effective ways to connect and deliver services to their clientele based on their information needs and information-seeking behaviors. This chapter outlines the development of the Arizona Hispanic Center of Excellence (AHCOE) Services Librarian position that later evolved into the position of Information Services/College of Public Health (CoPH) Liaison Librarian. It will focus on how my efforts in community engagement and the encouragement of my supervisors made me an important member of the information services team at the Arizona Health Sciences Library (AHSL) and enhanced my development as a new librarian. Upon reading this chapter you will learn how to encourage librarians to:

- identify community stakeholders,
- develop strategies for networking with community,
- develop community-campus collaborations,
- create information resources to support community collaborations, and
- strategize with library administration for custom librarianship.

With each step of the process, as with each step on my path, you will find new ways for librarians to develop their professional skills and increase the value of the library within the community.

Background

In 2003 the University of Arizona's College of Medicine was awarded a substantial grant to develop programs and services of the Arizona Hispanic Center of Excellence (AHCOE). The AHCOE was created to improve the health of all Americans by producing the highest-quality scholarship with regard to Hispanic health by training the next generation of culturally diverse and culturally fluent health care providers. A core AHCOE team worked together to establish partnerships with university departments, state school districts, hospitals, clinics, politicians, and many community-based organizations and agencies, and to connect people and programs that promote recognizing Hispanic health issues and/or serve the Hispanic population.

The Arizona Health Sciences Library's (AHSL) administration had the foresight to request to be a partner on the grant to create a new information services position. Initially, the primary role of this librarian was written to serve AHCOE clientele. The AHCOE position, as it developed, would become the foundation for the development of the liaison librarian position for the College of Public Health.

The AHCOE and the new librarian

As a recent library school graduate, academic librarianship seemed to be a far-fetched reality for me. What gave me pause were my lack of library work experience and my poorly formulated, preconceived notion of academia. Fortunately, a former library school classmate and university library employee urged me to apply. She knew of my strengths as a community leader and advocate and of the work I did with different community organizations. What was encouraging, and ultimately drew me to the position, was how the job description was written (see Exhibit 17.1). It outlined duties and responsibilities I recognized as opportunities for me to parlay my previous work experience as a liaison for community engagement.

In 2004 I was hired as the AHCOE Information Services Librarian. The position required knowledge and practice of working with the Hispanic community. It called for a bilingual, bicultural individual demonstrating a capacity for working collaboratively within the institution, as well as with external targeted partners.

My primary goal in the first two years as the AHCOE Services Librarian was to support the mission and goals of the center of excellence and expand library services to a targeted audience. Unfortunately, the funding source to continue the AHCOE was not reauthorized and the core team disassembled. During my two years as the AHCOE Services Librarian, I had the good fortune to develop a strong network of cross-campus colleagues, particularly in the College of Public Health (CoPH). Library administration valued my work and offered me a continuing eligible appointment. I was no longer on a year-to-year contract and was given the position of liaison librarian to the CoPH, just as AHSL was looking at moving toward a library liaison model for delivering information services. The CoPH embraced the idea of having

---

Exhibit 17.1. Position available: Arizona Hispanic Center of Excellence, Information Services Librarian

---

The Arizona Health Sciences Library (AHSL) is seeking an AHCOE Information Services (reference) Librarian (Assistant Librarian), fluent in Spanish, to develop and deliver informatics services to the Arizona Hispanic Center of Excellence (AHCOE) of the College of Medicine AND to library clientele involved in scholarship, clinical care, or research into Hispanic, border, cross-cultural, bilingual, and culturally sensitive health issues. This position reports to the Head of Information Services and works with other reference librarians committed to delivering sophisticated knowledge-based services in a fast-paced academic health sciences environment.

Duties and responsibilities: Develop and deliver information (and consultative) services and instructional programming in informatics for targeted faculty and students, AND library clientele involved in scholarship, clinical care, or research into Hispanic, border, cross-cultural, bilingual, and culturally sensitive health issues; Working with others, improve the print and electronic collections, develop AHSL's Web site into a bilingual culturally sensitive Web site, and improve access statewide to instruction in Hispanic health informatics skills; Work closely with AHCOE faculty and staff, AHSL faculty and staff, and participate in Information Services department projects and functions.

Minimum qualifications: Master of Library/Information Sciences or other relevant area; Health reference experience, including database searching, computer applications, and finding quality information on the Internet; Fluency in Spanish; Knowledge of Hispanic culture and customs.

Preferred qualifications: Experience in a health sciences, academic, or life sciences setting; Excellent interpersonal and communications skills; Initiative; Flexibility; Ability to manage projects and to work independently; Enthusiasm for teaching; Interest in developing advanced competencies; Understanding of developments in the delivery, management, and use of health information; Ability to work collegially and collaborate with others within and beyond the Library and AHCOE; Record of involvement in professional associations and/or evidence of publications or presentations.

"their own librarian," mainly because a number of the faculty's research agendas focused on health disparities, U.S./Mexico border health issues, and community health education, prevention, and promotion.

The role of the Arizona Hispanic Center of Excellence librarian

As the new AHCOE Services Librarian I had the latitude to develop and define my role as a member of the Information Services team. The most exciting and challenging part of this position had been the element of the unknown. What weighed heavily on my mind was the responsibility and expectation to successfully serve the information needs of a targeted clientele, and the risk of creating an information services model that missed the mark. On the first day of my job I asked myself, "Where do I begin? What will be my approach?"

The core AHCOE team was meeting on a regular basis. Staying on track with the goals and timeline of the AHCOE grant, the team had a year of project planning already outlined and implementation was in progress. I was invited to join the principle investigator, co-investigator, financial manager, and the program director, coordinator, and assistant in their monthly meetings. I immediately began to establish relationships with AHCOE faculty and students through an aggressive e-mail campaign. I introduced myself (via e-mail ahead of our in-person meetings), attended student-faculty mixers, and presented at orientations and special events. I offered information about my services to assist with extensive literature searches, set up individual consultations, conduct information-seeking skill-building workshops, and research support material for grant proposals. I presented at events, professional conferences, and meetings relevant to both librarianship and Hispanic health.

Because the AHCOE only targeted College of Medicine Hispanic faculty and students, I felt marginally successful. It was clear to me I needed to develop a new strategy to reach a broader audience. I enlisted the AHCOE staff to promote my services on their Web site, as well as through their listserv distribution. I attended campus lectures, symposiums, grand rounds, and workshops that were relevant to the AHCOE mission, and where I thought I might have an opportunity to introduce myself and offer my services. I specifically sought out outreach coordinators for some of the departments or programs to expand my targeted audience of university stakeholders. As a result, I saw an increase in requests for customized literature searches from health sciences faculty and office consultations with students. I e-mailed more information about grant opportunities, provided information on Hispanic demographics and statistics, and distributed reports related to Hispanic health issues. My ultimate goal was to increase my visibility within the university as a resource for obtaining access to and training on information resources.

The role of the information services/College of Public Health liaison librarian

Much of the work I had accomplished as the AHCOE librarian served as a strong foundation for my new role as an Information Services/College of Public Health (CoPH) Liaison Librarian. My department head negotiated office space within the CoPH for on-site reference services and consultations. In April 2007 I started working in the CoPH office a few hours per week. I connected with one faculty member and conducted two PubMed and RefWorks workshops. I was not able to connect with other faculty and students since it was well into the spring semester. The fall semester went similarly, although I gave a few more teaching sessions and worked with two additional faculty members on special grant projects. In preparation for the spring semester of 2008, I took cues from my success as the AHCOE Librarian. I increased my presence with more hours at the CoPH office, e-mailed CoPH faculty with a list of my services (see Exhibit 17.2), and presented at the CoPH student-faculty orientation.

Five new faculty members contacted me, and some of them worked me into their course work. They offered extra credit to students for attending the searching workshops and promoted my services on their syllabi. During the spring 2008 semester I taught 11 workshops for six faculty members and averaged three individual consultations with students or college fellows per week. I now spend

---

Exhibit 17.2. Sample e-mail to faculty

Dear College of Public Health Faculty,

I am available to provide the following services for course/class curriculum support for the spring semester:

- Schedule appointments to visit classes during the first few weeks of the semester (or anytime throughout) to introduce myself and briefly present on research, library, and information services.
- Schedule CoPH computer lab time to conduct sessions on general literature searching, reference management (RefWorks), and database navigation.
- Schedule customized searching for resources and/or tools (grants, statistics, databases, etc.) on specific topics for research papers or class projects.

In addition, the Arizona Health Sciences Library (AHSL) Scavenger Hunt (www.ahsl.arizona.edu/scavenger/) was created to give students an opportunity to navigate the library's Web site. It's a good exercise for utilizing library resources and tools to find specific information. In the past some CoPH faculty have offered students extra credit or bonus points for participating in the Scavenger Hunt. I would be responsible for reviewing and providing feedback to the students, then I would forward the results to the professor. In turn, the professor would grade or rank according to his or her scale for credit earned. Students would be better equipped to answer the questions in the Scavenger Hunt after participating in one of my workshops; however, they can still do the Hunt if they're up for the challenge.

If faculty are interested in any of these services please contact me to coordinate any one of the activities. Thanks.

Annabelle Nuñez
Information Services/CoPH Liaison Librarian
Arizona Health Sciences Library

approximately 85 percent of my time in the CoPH office, and my individual consultations and drop-in services have increased dramatically. It is a clear indication that my availability to faculty and students, "on their turf," has been important.

The library administration felt it necessary for me to keep my office at the library. We set up a laptop computer docking station in both offices, and a telephone in each as well. I am able to schedule workshops in the CoPH computer lab for the convenience of the students. I developed the College of Public Health Curriculum Support Web page dedicated to resources for faculty and students (www.ahsl .arizona.edu/curriculum/publichealth/). As I make more contact with other CoPH faculty I believe more teaching opportunities will emerge. I will continue to teach community workshops that serve a broad range of constituencies and I will target both internal and external communities by further developing in-reach and outreach strategies.

Community-campus partnerships

Coming into the university, I had, and continue to have, a strong connection to the community at large. I had served as my neighborhood association president for a number of years. In that capacity I established a strong relationship with my city council representative, my county supervisor, other neighborhood leaders, business owners, and several community-based organizations (CBOs) and agencies. I worked on issues that affected our community and engaged in programs that built community capacity among residents, many of which related to public safety and health. After being hired by the Arizona Health Sciences Library, I found myself in a position that could benefit from collaborative opportunities with these partners from a health perspective. As a representative of the university I am able to give my campus partners an entree to those government officials, CBOs, and agencies for community-campus partnerships.

Prior to becoming a librarian I worked at a nonprofit arts agency funded in part by the City of Tucson. One of the primary functions of my job was to work with cultural arts organizations and neighborhood associations to develop art programs for youth. My job was to identify the stakeholders and plan and implement an art project that would benefit a neighborhood. Very early on I learned that the most successful projects where driven and owned by the community. I knew that it was my responsibility to facilitate a process that would bring together an agency, a community, and its stakeholders to create a product. The premise of this model would be the foundation to my approach in developing the AHCOE position and later the position of Information Services/College of Public Health Liaison Librarian.

Who are the community stakeholders?

As the AHCOE Services Librarian and with the encouragement of my supervisors, I took time to inventory my community contacts with an eye toward community information collaborations. I was mindful of any opportunity to engage community partners on projects that were under development for the AHCOE and the AHSL. I would begin with (1) what organizations or agencies directly serve the Hispanic community, (2) what organizations or agencies have initiatives, as part of their organizational goals, to serve the Hispanic community, and (3) what organizations or agencies could benefit from my services as a librarian.

In addition to my personal contacts, I began by looking at resources such as the *Directory of Community Resources: A Guide to Services in Tucson and Pima County* (in the public library), calling our Information and Referral agency for information on organizations that

> ☑ QUICK TIP
>
> Encourage new librarians to draw connections between their personal lives or interests and the functions of the library. Where do the two overlap? Does opportunity for partnership or development exist?

may be listed as such, and looking for calendars of events in the local news weekly, the newspaper, and on the Internet. I also called the organizations directly once I had a contact name (see, e.g., Exhibit 17.3). If all else failed, I would simply ask colleagues and friends if they had any contacts with said organizations or agencies. The real work was getting on the phone, pounding the pavement, and having a presence whenever and wherever possible.

Through each step in the inventorying process, it is important to speak with supervisors and more experienced librarians. So often when working with community organizations, we find preexisting relationships and previous attempts at collaboration. As the new librarian learns and shares information with his or her supervisor, so too can the supervisor share experience with the new librarian. The inventorying stage is a perfect opportunity to bring new staff up to speed on what the library has done, its collaborative success, and its lessons learned.

After inventorying community contacts and building a few through phone calls and introductions, I began to carry a collaboration hat with me as I lived my life in the community. I kept an ear out for opportunities and viewed once-ordinary experiences with an eye toward collaboration. With the support of my supervisors, I began to seek new opportunities and present possible collaborations to those I met.

Exhibit 17.3. Sample call

"Hello, my name is_____, and I'm calling from the Arizona Health Sciences Library at the University of Arizona. I visited your Web site and saw that you have a healthy-breast initiative targeting Hispanic women. The Arizona Hispanic Center of Excellence [explain further] and I am a resource to you and your organization. Would you like to meet to discuss ways in which I can offer

_____?

Or we can partner on _____."

Working with community stakeholders: education

In my role as a neighborhood leader I was at a community policing event when I ran into an acquaintance and Sunnyside Unified School District (SUSD) board member. During the course of a conversation we were having, I learned that the district was designing a new program for high school students interested in health careers. I immediately saw an opportunity to explore a potential partnership that would serve both entities. The AHCOE was looking at developing an educational pipeline for university student recruitment and workforce development, and SUSD was looking at training the teachers in database searching and information resources for development of the Medical Careers Academy curriculum. The AHCOE team was invited to meet with district instructors and curriculum specialists to look at collaborative planning for searching workshops.

Working with community stakeholders: business and politics

The League of United Latin American Citizens (LULAC) is an example of an organization that promotes political, social, and economic programs for the advancement of Hispanics. The local council hosts an annual youth leadership conference that targets middle and high school students. Every year they have a keynote/motivational speaker who speaks on the theme of the conference, which is generally about education, health, and/or safety. They also have a career fair with exhibitors, and they offer hour-long information workshops on a variety of topics. In 2007 I presented teen health information resources in a presentation titled, "Too Hot for Health Information? What You Should Really Know." I provided MedlinePlus bookmarks and pens, a National Library of Medicine brochure on medical librarianship, and a Webliography of health information resources. At previous LULAC conferences I had teamed up with the university's Office of Minority Affairs and the AHCOE team to exhibit on information about health careers, including medical librarianship.

Working with community stakeholders: government

The county supervisor for my district is a strong advocate for library services and public health education. In 2006 he attended a government agency conference and learned of successful health education programs in public libraries. He was very enthusiastic about the idea that the public library should be a "place for public health education and promotion." He called for a meeting to brainstorm ideas of how this might work. Those in attendance were the director of the county health department, the director of the public library system, public health nurses, members of the university community, and individual and community stakeholders. As a result of this meeting, the Pima County Community Health Task Force (PCCHTF) was formed. In December 2007 a retreat was held to identify the roles of all partners and the overall agenda of the task force. The task force had now gained new members from the University of Arizona's College of Nursing and College of Public Health, and community leaders. The PCCHTF is currently working on developing a public health lectures series hosted by Pima County Public Library, and creating internship and training opportunities for public health and public health nursing students to work with, and in the community. My role will be to train public librarians on finding health information resources, to provide support for curriculum development for the university faculty partners as they design their course work, and to assist students in utilizing information resources for the development of their programs.

Working with community stakeholders: social service agencies

So many social service agencies are ripe for community collaborations with libraries. For example:

- Family and child resource centers
- Churches and faith-based organizations
- Senior services
- Neighborhood organizations
- LGBT organizations or centers

Oftentimes in my experience, collaborations could be as simple as offering workshops on basic searching skills, presenting on information resources for specific health topics, providing patient and consumer health information at health fairs, and providing train-the-trainer instruction. Our contribution strengthened their programs and established the AHCOE and the library as a collaborative partner. It placed the library and the institution on their radar as a possible partner and established me as a go-to contact point.

Support from within the library

Having a list of partners was useful for me to develop new relationships and offer information services promoting the primary goals of the AHCOE, as well as expand the library's outreach goals. In turn, these partners supported the value of the AHCOE, then the College of Public Health, and the Arizona Health Sciences Library. In building these community-campus partnerships, I grew as a leader both in the library and within the community. Ultimately, this involvement created cyclical benefits: The more involved I became with community-campus collaboration, the more community organizations came forward seeking the services of the College of Medicine, College of Public Health, and the library. We were all benefiting from creating a Rolodex of partners and keeping an ear to the ground for collaboration opportunities.

In addition to finding new opportunities for myself to become involved, I also sought

> ☑ QUICK TIP
> Stay connected with staff's community involvement. Find ways to sit in on meetings, contribute additional expertise and knowledge to new staff's communications with community partners, and listen for employees' goals and strategies, as well as the overall goals and strategies for the various colleges.

new opportunities for other library staff and departments. The AHCOE's dean's advisory committee met on a quarterly basis. This group was represented by faculty clinicians and researchers, community physicians, program coordinators, and representatives from the Hispanic community (health professionals, educators, and advocates). I saw an opportunity for my department head to network with these key players. I asked that she be formally invited to join the advisory committee.

Her appointment to the committee had numerous benefits. For my direct benefit, her involvement allowed me to witness leadership in action. For the AHCOE, her experience and knowledge allowed her to think broadly about the library services that could be offered, services of which I, as a new librarian, was still unaware. In turn, she gained firsthand knowledge of the programs I was working on to meet the goals for university-affiliated stakeholders—faculty, students, and staff. Ultimately, this benefited both my supervisor and me by making yearly goal-planning sessions extremely productive. Her approach was to provide me with the parameters of my goals, and then allow me to take the lead on utilizing my past work experience and knowledge to outline the steps in attaining these goals.

As an employee, I believe her "hands-off" management style is one of the best features of my job. She provides guidance where needed and when necessary. She encourages involvement with committees so that the library has a presence both on campus and in the community. I appreciate that I am given a good degree of autonomy to employ my skills and assets all within the mission of the Information Services department.

Information services outcomes

Outreach and community collaborations can become a full-time job, but it wasn't my only job. My supervisors took their cues from my efforts and created new opportunities for me to expand my library experience. They infused projects with my passions and allowed factors to interrelate in ways that were truly innovative.

☑ QUICK TIP

Find new ways to infuse personal interests into more traditional library functions.

Hispanic health web page

One of the most significant goals accomplished within my first year as the AHCOE librarian was the development and launch of the Hispanic Health Web page (www.ahsl.arizona.edu/topics/hispanic). This portal was designed as a "one-stop" shop for online Hispanic health resources. Designed for the needs of health care professionals, students, and community users alike, it features information on border health, consumer health, cultural competency, professional associations and resources, publications, PubMed alerts, statistics, subscription information for related listservs, and daily news.

My supervisors wisely saw this as an essential library resource as well as a logical extension of my own personal interest in community collaborations. With its creation, the institution's commitment to the community and to Hispanic users reached far beyond the limits of geography. Our services were now accessible to anyone in the world via the Internet.

Simultaneously, this Web page provided an instant tool to promote in building future collaborations. It was a tool that could be spoken about and highlighted at both local and national events. It could also encourage other institutions to become involved with the library by having their Web sites added to the page as a resource for Hispanic health.

Finally, this tool provided an excellent opportunity for me to learn essential librarian skills such as information organization and resource evaluation. It also challenged me to utilize technology in the pursuit of community service.

Conference presentations

Over time the demand for information on Hispanic health disparities and cultural competency increased my knowledge of these topics. Although I would not characterize myself as an expert on them, I was certainly seen as one who could address an unmet need for information resources about them.

In 2005 I was invited to speak on Hispanic health disparities at my very first Medical Library Association (MLA) Annual Meeting. Approximately 25 conference participants attended my presentation titled "Bridging the Gap on Health Disparities: A Librarian's Role." Eight months later the Office of Minority Health accepted my paper for a similar presentation at their National Leadership Summit on Eliminating Ethnic and Racial Disparities in Health. At the 2006 MLA Annual Meeting I was invited to present at a continuing-education symposia on cultural competency and diverse populations.

By supporting my unique interests, my supervisors created an area of interest and expertise that I could utilize for library research and presentation. In their own indirect way, they led me to these opportunities for conference presentations. By participating in these professional circles, I gained valuable experience in networking and presenting. I was also able to speak with my peers on this topic and bring back new ideas for our own institution to implement. And throughout

> ☑ **QUICK TIP**
> Create areas of specialization that new staff can mine for possible presentation or publication.

every phase of my conference involvement, I was able to spotlight the great things my library was doing in this unique area of medical librarianship.

The Trejo-Foster Foundation *¡Salud se Puede!* Hispanic health information for Hispanic/Latino populations institute

As the library's and the university's interests and involvement in Hispanic health increased, so too did our commitment to fostering new discourse on the subject. In 2006, the Arizona Health Sciences Library administration agreed to collaborate with the University's School of Information Resources and Library Science (SIRLS), on a conference dedicated to Hispanic health information.

Recognizing my involvement in the library's efforts and my skill in collaborating for programs, the administration gave me the opportunity to take the lead on planning the conference program. The Trejo-Foster Foundation ¡Salud se Puede! Hispanic Health Information for Hispanic/Latino Populations Institute (www.sir .arizona.edu/trejo/) took place in July 2007 and was a success for librarians, health professionals, and the community.

Working with the library administration and several members of the library school staff, the planning committee designed a program that broke free of the library-centric mold. The final program featured a physician researching health issues among Hispanic women, a Mexican-American professor conducting research on HIV/AIDS in Hispanic men, a county health department policymaker, an information services program evaluator, several librarians involved with programs that target the Hispanic/Latino community, a Hispanic community activist, a nationally recognized community health worker/promotora trainer, a nurse practitioner and promotora for diabetes management, a health promotions professor from the College of Public Health, the American Library Association president, and two leaders in outreach for the National Library of Medicine. It was an embodiment of everything I had been working toward—libraries, community leaders, local service organizations, and academics working together to solve issues through information.

In addition to sharing a wealth of information with both the University of Arizona and the Tucson community, the program brought together national figures and librarians from across the country to share their ideas and take away new lessons for changing the state of Hispanic health.

Conclusion

Ultimately, my development as a librarian is a partnership between myself and my supervisors. The risk of looking at this in a negative context, a push-and-pull relationship of blame and fault, is always a possibility. However, from my experience, working with my valued supervisors, I find that this partnership has been a harmonious relationship of my finding my talents and passions and my supervisors finding the best ways to utilize those passions within the context of my job.

I was lucky to find a position that could capitalize on my community involvement. I was luckier to find supervisors who wanted to utilize that involvement and were willing to invest their time and guidance to focus and direct those interests toward appropriate efforts.

I walk away from my early years knowing that community collaborations can be an excellent tool for librarians to develop their skills—essential skills such as assessment, networking, planning, programming, and teaching. Offering new librarians an opportunity to develop a catalog of contacts, discover library services for their community users, and market those services is an excellent way to orient them to the library's services and its role in the community.

This chapter focuses on my efforts as librarian for the Arizona Hispanic Center of Excellence and later as Information Services/College of Public Health Liaison Librarian. It is my hope, however, that the lessons and experiences could be replicated by committed librarians in any area of librarianship with the support of encouraging supervisors who recognize the value of community and are prepared to engage their staff with community organizations.

Further reading

Cataldo, T. T., M. R. Tennant, P. Sherwill-Navarro, and R. Jesano. 2006. "Subject Specialization in a Liaison Librarian Program." *Journal of the Medical Library Association* 94, no. 4 (October): 446–448.

Cogdill, K. W., A. B. Ruffin, and P. Z. Stavri. 2007. "The National Network of Libraries of Medicine's Outreach to the Public Health Workforce: 2001–2006." *Journal of the Medical Library Association* 95, no. 3 (July): 310–315.

Humphreys, B. L. 2007. "Building Better Connections: The National Library of Medicine and Public Health." *Journal of the Medical Library Association* 95, no. 3 (July): 293–300.

Tennant, M. R., L. C. Butson, M. E. Rezeau, P. J. Tucker, M. E. Boyle, and G. Clayton. 2001. "Customizing for Clients: Developing a Library Liaison Program from Need to Plan." *Bulletin of the Medical Library Association* 89, no. 1 (January): 8–20.

Tennant, M. R., T. T. Cataldo, P. Sherwill-Navarro, and R. Jesano. 2006. "Evaluation of a Liaison Librarian Program: Client and Liaison Perspectives." *Journal of the Medical Library Association* 94, no. 4 (October): 402–409, e201–204.

about the editors and contributors

Georgie L. Donovan is Lead Acquisitions Librarian at Appalachian State University in Boone, North Carolina, where she manages a team of five colleagues who handle monograph and serials acquisitions and interlibrary loan. She earned a master's in information resources and library science degree in 2004 from the University of Arizona. She then worked in the university libraries as Special Assistant to the Dean before moving to Appalachian State. Before attending library school, she taught college-level English language and literature at universities in Texas, Tokyo, and Copiapó, Chile, after earning a master's of fine arts degree in creative writing from the University of Texas at El Paso. She also has worked as a paraprofessional in public and university libraries.

Georgie is currently an active member of the American Library Association (ALA), especially the Association of College & Research Libraries (ACRL), working on several committee assignments, and the Progressive Librarians Guild (PLG). Her areas of scholarly interest within librarianship include scholarly communication and leadership studies. In addition to her work in librarianship, she plays piano for contra dances, is an ardent cook and organic gardener, a tremendous film buff, and news junkie.

Miguel A. Figueroa is Network Services Coordinator for the National Network of Libraries of Medicine Middle Atlantic Region at New York University Langone Medical Center's Ehrman Medical Library. In his current role, he trains and supports users of the National Library of Medicine's products in Delaware, New Jersey, New York, and Pennsylvania. Previously, Miguel was Associate Director of Publishing at Neal-Schuman Publishers, where he worked to acquire and market professional materials for librarians and information professionals.

He is a graduate of The University of Arizona School of Information Resource and Library Science and the Knowledge River Program. Miguel is actively involved in the ALA and Special Libraries Association (SLA).

✍

Toni Anaya is Multicultural Studies Librarian at the University of Nebraska-Lincoln, where she is a member of an innovative Multicultural Services Team and serves as

Liaison Librarian to the Institute of Ethnic Studies. Her master's in library science is from the University of Arizona, where she worked as Library Information Analyst for several years before moving to Nebraska. There, she coordinated billing and fee recovery for the libraries. Toni also held a position with the public library system in Tucson, Arizona.

Toni is currently an active member of the Nebraska Library Association (NLA) and ALA, especially ACRL and REFORMA, working on several committee assignments. In addition to her work in libraries, Toni is an avid roller skater who enjoys spending time with her daughter, Analicia, and extended family, and caring for her menagerie of pets, which includes two tortoises, a spoiled Chihuahua, and an equally spoiled hedgehog.

Stephen Brooks is Head of Acquisitions and Gifts for the University Libraries at George Mason University in Fairfax, Virginia. Before coming to Mason, Stephen worked as a library paraprofessional at UNC Asheville, Asheville-Buncombe Technical Community College, and UNC Chapel Hill. He earned his bachelor of arts in English from UNC Chapel Hill and his master's degree in library and information studies from UNC Greensboro. Stephen is a regular attendee of the Charleston Conference on Book and Serial Acquisition; he also has attended Virginia Library Association (VLA), ALA, and ACRL national conferences, and participated in workshops on relationships with library vendors and collection development. Among his research interests is the future of publishing and information dissemination and its implications for library technical services processes.

Stephen, a former certified massage therapist, is an avid Ultimate Frisbee player and bird-watcher, and enjoys occasional games of chess in his spare time. A North Carolina native, he has grown accustomed to the infamous traffic in Northern Virginia, where he lives with his wife and daughter.

Scott Collard is Social Sciences Collections Coordinator and Librarian for Education and Linguistics at New York University in New York City. He is currently working on a number of projects, including an effort to enhance and extend space and service capabilities for NYU's large and diverse graduate student body; chairing the library's virtual reference group; and acting as a mentor to a current dual-degree library school/NYU student. Scott got his MSLIS from the University of Illinois, Champaign-Urbana.

Scott is active in ACRL, and he is currently working for that organization on a number of committees, particularly in the Education and Behavioral Sciences Section. When not being a librarian, he is a sometimes-musician, Italian cheese fanatic, and very happy new dad.

Ida Z. daRoza has always had as a professional goal to work in a place where she could provide Spanish materials and cataloging to serve Latino communities. She has achieved that goal through her work as the system-wide Cataloging Librarian for the San Mateo County Library. Ida received her bachelor's in Italian literature and international business from Santa Clara University and her master's in library and information science from San Jose State University. Before coming to the public library system in San Mateo County, Ida was the Cataloging Librarian at the Academy of Art University in San Francisco.

In 2007, Ida was elected to the statewide position of Vice Chair/Chair Elect of Access, Collections and Technical Services Section of the California Library Association (ACTSS of CLA). That same year she was a presenter at one of the Spectrum tenth-year anniversary programs at the ALA conference in Washington, DC. In DC, she was initiated into Beta Phi Mu, the library and information studies honor society.

Besides cataloging, Ida enjoys the study and practice of foreign languages. She is fluent in Spanish and Italian and is a member of REFORMA, Bibliotecas para la Gente. In addition, in 2007, Ida was one of the 150 librarians awarded by the ALA to attend the Guadalajara International Book Fair to purchase Spanish-language materials.

She is a casual blogger at http://idazlibrarian.blogspot.com and a social software junkie. She encourages other librarians to look her up or write to her via Facebook under the name Ida Zee or via MySpace under idzeee. Other than that, Ida and her husband Ken like to travel to odd locations and collect kitsch, especially floaty pens and snow globes. They hope to have a dog someday and/or learn how to cook.

Mary Evangeliste is the Director of User Services & Outreach at Gettysburg College and co-founder of Fearless Future: Marketing & Design for things that matter. Mary holds a bachelor's in art history from Allegheny College and a MLIS from the University of Pittsburgh.

Mary has been honored with two national library marketing awards: 2001 3M Check-it-Out Yourself Day and ACRL's 2005 Best Practices in Marketing Academic and Research Libraries @your library Award.

Kim Leeder is Reference and Instruction Librarian at Boise State University in Boise, Idaho, where she provides reference services, teaches research skills, and serves as liaison to English, Theatre Arts, Environmental Studies, and Extended Studies. She holds an MA in information resources and library science from the University of Arizona, and spent two years as Special Assistant to the Dean at the University of Arizona Libraries. Before her career in libraries, Kim earned an MA in English from the University of Nevada at Reno's unique Literature and Environment program. She worked for four years as an editor for a variety of publishers, including *Orion* magazine and the University of Arizona's Udall Center for Studies in Public Policy.

Kim is actively involved in ALA, especially ACRL's University Libraries Section and the 2008 Emerging Leaders program. She is particularly interested in using technology to provide reference services and to find new ways to reach out to undergraduates. In her free time, Kim enjoys active pursuits including hiking, backpacking, running, walking her two big dogs, and horseback riding, as well as a few quieter activities such as gardening and reading.

Tamika Barnes McCollough is currently the Library Director at the EPA Library in Research Triangle Park, North Carolina. This is a contracted position through the School of Information and Library Science at the University of North Carolina in Chapel Hill. Before becoming the EPA Library Director, Tamika was the Head of Reference and Information Literacy at North Carolina Agricultural and Technical State University in Greensboro, North Carolina (2005–2007). Tamika began her professional library experience as the Engineering Services Librarian at North Carolina State University in Raleigh from 1999 to 2005. Prior to receiving her MLS, she worked in several positions in the acquisitions department at the NCSU Libraries.

Tamika is active in the profession and serves as a board member for SLA. She is also a member of the ACRL Professional Development Coordinating Committee. She has been very involved with ALA's Spectrum Program, which is an effort to increase the number of minority librarians in the profession. Tamika is also involved on the local level and currently serves as the Secretary/Treasurer for North Carolina Library Association's (NCLA) Roundtable for Ethnic and Minority Concerns. She is the employment relations committee chair for the North Carolina chapter of SLA.

Tamika is currently an adjunct lecturer at both North Carolina Central University School of Library and Information Sciences and the University of North Carolina at Chapel Hill School of Information and Library Science. She received a bachelor's in biology from the University of North Carolina at Chapel Hill and her MLS from North Carolina Central University. Tamika's scholarly interests include mentoring and staff development. In her free time she likes to spend time with her family and friends, volunteer, and watch college basketball.

Cat Saleeby McDowell currently serves as Digital Projects Coordinator for University Libraries at the University of North Carolina at Greensboro. There, she supervises digitization and digital preservation initiatives, directs metadata implementation, manages electronic records, provides support for faculty e-scholarship, and serves as an adjunct lecturer in the library school. Prior to joining the Electronic Resources and Information Technology team at UNCG, she worked in archival departments at Duke, and Wake Forest and Winston-Salem state universities in North Carolina.

A proud Duke University graduate and avid college basketball fan, Cat also holds an MA in public history/archival administration from North Carolina State University. Keeping it all in the ACC, she is married to a UNC grad who currently works at Wake Forest, and they live in the other K-Ville.

Alanna Aiko Moore is the Sociology, Ethnic Studies and Gender Studies Librarian at the University of California at San Diego. As a subject specialist, her duties include library instruction classes and collection management for the Sociology, Ethnic Studies and Gender Studies departments on campus; reference services; and outreach. Alanna has also worked as a librarian at the Illinois Institute of Technology and as a paraprofessional at Roosevelt University.

Alanna received her master's in library and information science from Dominican University in River Forest, Illinois, in December 2004. Prior to graduate school, she worked for eleven years in the nonprofit sector as a community organizer, fund-raiser, training coordinator, researcher, and director on issues of social justice impacting low-income communities and communities of color.

She is an active member of ALA and ACRL and also sits on committees in the Asian Pacific American Librarian Association (APALA) and on the steering committee of the Joint Conference of Librarians of Color II. A 2004 Spectrum Scholar, she is committed to addressing diversity issues in the profession and currently chairs the Spectrum Scholar Interest Group and is a past chair of the Spectrum Leadership Institute. Her areas of scholarly interest within librarianship include mentorship, information literacy, and diversity. In her spare time, Alanna enjoys hiking, camping, gardening, reading, and hanging out with her dog Ozzy.

Joseph Nicholson is a Database Trainer/Online Analyst for the National Library of Medicine's National Training Center and Clearinghouse (NTCC), located at The New York Academy of Medicine in New York.

He has worked with French-speaking African refugee students at the College of North West London, osteopathic medical students at Touro University, California, and public health professionals and graduate students at the Sheldon Margen Public Health Library at the University of California, Berkeley. He now continues his travels by trekking across the United States training librarians how to use National Library of Medicine databases. He earned his BA in linguistics from the University of California, Davis, his MLIS from the University of Pittsburgh, and is currently pursuing an MPH at Columbia University.

Annabelle Nuñez earned an MA in library science in 2003 at the University of Arizona as a School of Information Resources and Library Science (SIRLS) Knowledge River Institute Scholar. In her position as the Information Services/College of Public Health (CoPH) Liaison Librarian at Arizona Health Sciences Library (AHSL), she works to deliver information by providing consultative and instructional programming services for faculty, students, and health professionals involved in scholarship, research, and clinical services.

Her areas of interest include working with community-campus partnerships, to improve access to information resources in the areas of Hispanic, border, cross-cultural, bilingual, and culturally appropriate patient/consumer health issues. She developed and manages the Hispanic Health and CoPH curriculum support portal Web pages, which centralize special information for students, educators, public health workers, and the community.

Annabelle is a member of the Medical Library Association, REFORMA, the League of United Latin American Citizens (LULAC), and sits on many local boards and committees. She enjoys traveling, cultural and artistic activities, and hanging out with her friends. Annabelle was a 2008 *Library Journal* Mover and Shaker.

Antonia Olivas received her master's in library science in 2003 from the School of Information Resources and Library Science at the University of Arizona. She is currently the Education Librarian at California State University San Marcos.

Mark A. Puente is Coordinator of Digital Projects and Special/Gift Collections and Assistant Professor of Library Administration in the Music Library at University of Illinois, Urbana-Champaign (UIUC).

He is a 2004 graduate of the University of Arizona School of Information Resources and Library Science (from the Knowledge River Program) and a 2003 Spectrum Scholar. He began his position at UIUC in October 2007 after having served two years as a Minority Resident and Music Librarian at the University of Tennessee in Knoxville. Previously, he has worked at the University of Arizona Fine Arts Library and the University of North Texas Music Library.

Originally from San Antonio, Texas, Mark was a private voice instructor for 12 years prior to entering the field of librarianship. He holds a bachelor's degree in voice performance from St. Mary's University and a MA in music from Stephen F. Austin State University in Nacogdoches, Texas. Mark has been active in professional organizations on local, regional, and national levels. He has served on panels and maintains research interests in a wide range of topics including diversity in academic libraries, the use of technology in music libraries, LIS education, library leadership, and networking within the profession.

Jennifer Rutner is the Program Coordinator of Marketing and Assessment at the Columbia University Libraries, where she works with 20 of the 25 libraries on campus. A graduate of the University of Rochester (BA) and, later, Pratt Institute's School of Information and Library Science (MLS), Jennifer is involved with several professional organizations, including the American Library Association, the Association of Research Libraries, and the Special Library Association. She is also a contributor to the www.libraryassessment.info blog. Jennifer lives in Brooklyn, New York, with her husband, a musician.

Monecia Samuel directs The College of Westchester Library in White Plains, New York. She was introduced to library work at Howard University Libraries' Technical Services Department while she was an undergraduate student at Howard's School of Music. After working for several years at Howard's Social Work Library, she decided to pursue library science professionally at the University of North Carolina at Chapel Hill.

Her professional career in libraries began immediately at UNC-Chapel Hill's Health Sciences Library after the completion of her graduate work. As a user services librarian, she worked with their educational services and reference departments serving the medical and allied health students in the UNC community. Her experience prepared her for an identical role at Duke University, where she became an inaugural Library fellow in the Duke Libraries Fellowship Program.

In New York, Monecia was the head of public services at Purchase College Library and an adjunct library faculty member for Manhattanville College Library before taking on her current role as director of the Library at The College of Westchester.

Monecia has been an active member of numerous American Library Association award juries, including the prestigious Melvil Dewey Medal Jury. She has presented in sessions, talk tables, and roundtables for the Virtual Reference Desk, the Public Library Association (PLA), ALA, ACRL, and Information Today.

Iyanna Sims is currently Electronic Resources Librarian at North Carolina Agricultural and Technical State University in Greensboro, North Carolina. She received her master's in library science from Clark Atlanta University and a bachelor of arts in English from Elon University. She has experience working in special and academic libraries. Iyanna's professional interests include library technology and a newfound enthusiasm for recruitment in the field of librarianship.

index